D1707096

TAMING THE SERPENT

How Neuroscience Can Revolutionize
Modern Law Enforcement Training

Michael G. Malpass

DISCARDED FROM
GARFIELD COUNTY
LIBRARIES

Garfield County Libraries
Carbondale Branch Library
320 Sopris Avenue
Carbondale, CO 81623
(970) 963-2889 · Fax (970) 963-8573
www.GCPLD.org

Ockham
Publishing

Copyright © 2018 Michael G. Malpass

All rights reserved. No part of this publication may be reproduced, stored in or introduced into a retrieval system or transmitted in any form or by any means, electronic, mechanical, photocopying, recording or otherwise without prior written permission from the publisher.

Published by Ockham Publishing in the United Kingdom in 2019

ISBN 978-1-912701-34-6

Cover by Claire Wood

www.ockham-publishing.com

DEDICATION

To Jack Malpass, my dad, who taught me to always question, to seek the truth, fight for what you believe in, and who taught me how to teach and love doing it. I miss you every day and still can't find the words to express how much you mean to me.

High Flight

Oh! I have slipped the surly bonds of earth,
And danced the skies on laughter-silvered wings;
Sunward I've climbed, and joined the tumbling mirth
Of sun-split clouds, – and done a hundred things
You have not dreamed of – Wheeled and soared and swung
High in the sunlit silence. Hov'ring there
I've chased the shouting wind along, and flung
My eager craft through footless halls of air...

Up, up the long, delirious, burning blue
I've topped the wind-swept heights with easy grace
Where never lark or even eagle flew –
And, while with silent lifting mind I've trod
The high untrespassed sanctity of space,
Put out my hand, and touched the face of God.

– John Gillespie Magee, Jr

TABLE OF CONTENTS

PROLOGUE

Emotion has taught mankind to reason.

– Marquis de Vauvenargues

Emotions exist to map memories of things that lead us away from excessive risk and toward possible rewards. These memories are indexed in the emotional system to create biases and hunches that steer human behavior. For example, I can't stand the smell of a grill at the start of the burn. I used to love it. While on the SWAT team, I responded with other personnel to an active shooter situation at a house. Upon initial entry, I could smell what I thought was the burn from the grill. Our thought was a family cookout gone bad. We were wrong. It was an honor killing. Once we got into the backyard, we found the family had been shot and set on fire. Now that smell of the initial burn from the grill kills my appetite.

Seeing the name Campbell, whether on a can of soup or driving anywhere near Campbell Avenue in Phoenix reminds me of a schizophrenic man, armed with a handgun, who wouldn't stop pointing it at me and another SWAT officer. While that officer was doing an amazing job of trying to negotiate with a man whose brain wasn't processing reality, the man raised his gun toward the officer and I was forced to take that man's life.

A friend of mine had a twin brother that was killed by a drunk driver who crossed the center line striking the vehicle driven by my friend with his twin brother in the passenger seat. After the accident he would experience severe anxiety and would have a hard time breathing while driving. Through some intense psychotherapy, it was found that the Beach Boy's song, "Surfing USA," was the trigger for the anxiety. Why, you ask? They were big fans of the Beach Boys and that song was playing on the car's sound system when the crash occurred. He consciously did not associate the song with the crash but his emotional system indexed it for future reference. Only after some serious therapy was he able to again listen to the song and enjoy it for the much fonder memories before the crash.

Recently, I made repeated trips from my home in Chandler, Arizona to Tucson. The cognitive part of my brain registers it is roughly ninety-two miles with an average posted speed limit of 75 mph. It will take around ninety minutes to make the trip. But you see, the emotional side of my brain had a different way of marking the miles and letting me know I was getting closer to Tucson. Why? Because my father was in the University of Arizona Banner hospital fighting for his life. Instead of marking the miles and assessing the amount of time the trip would take, the emotions associated with the trip indexed reference points along the way that let me "feel" closer to Dad and not have to keep running calculations in my head. My trip to Tucson from Chandler was indexed by a road that runs in a valley between two mountains on the Gila River Indian Reservation. Then, an empty campground with over 1,300 acres for sale marking the entrance to the freeway and the 75-mph speed limit. Looming over the horizon, a mountain called Picacho Peak that looks like the silhouette of Batman with his cape extended to the sides. Rooster Cogburn's Ostrich Farm is off the right side of the freeway. Getting closer. Next, a sign for the Veteran's cemetery. Almost there. The town of Marana passes and on to Tucson. I don't recall consciously thinking about these landmarks, I only recall the "feeling" they gave me as I made repeated trips to see my father at the hospital.

I have been studying the brain and how peak performance is affected by either our ability or inability to control the balance between the cognitive brain and the emotional brain. Emotions exist to map memories of things geared toward reward and away from excessive risk. Many of the skills learned by police officers and military personnel will be ingrained into the emotional system which gives hunches to the thinking brain about risk and reward. Those skills are like the landmarks on the way to Tucson in that the emotional brain, an unconscious system, is always learning and indexing memories for future reference. The emotional side of the brain carries the power to initiate an immediate survival response without involvement from the conscious "you." With an understanding of how the emotional side of the brain indexes information, we are better equipped to teach people in fields that require technical skill under life-threatening stress and pressure. We can then train them how to deal with violence more effectively by making better decisions in compressed time frames and practicing skill sets that are accessible when the decisions matter the most and not only in a sterile training environment.

INTRODUCTION

The devil is a gentleman who never goes where he is not welcome.

– John A. Lincoln

Throughout history, the images of dragons and serpents have been used to represent both man's fight against the forces of evil, as well as his fight against his own overly emotional and sometimes evil self. In the works of Edmund Spenser, the hero Redcrosse battles a dragon representing the hazards of being overconfident and over assessing one's skill set. In *Beowulf*, the Anglo-Saxon poem, our hero battles the dragon Grendel, which scholars say represents greed. Norse mythology, as well as myths and stories from around the world, include images of the dragon or serpents with meanings ranging from representing the devil, the seven deadly sins, evil and on the other end of the spectrum, good luck. From the Bible comes one of the oldest stories known to mankind:

> Now the serpent was more cunning than any beast of the field which the Lord God had made. And he said to the woman, "Has God indeed said, 'You shall not eat of every tree of the garden'?"

> And the woman said to the serpent, "We may eat the fruit of the trees of the garden; but of the fruit of the tree which is in the midst of the garden, God has said, 'You shall not eat it, nor shall you touch it, lest you die.'"

> Then the serpent said to the woman, "You will not surely die. For God knows that in the day you eat of it your eyes will be opened,

and you will be like God, knowing good and evil."[1]

If you are a believer in the Good Book or a fan of Denzel Washington in the movie *The Book of Eli*, we now come to one of my favorite verses discussing the punishment for letting that tricky little serpent fool Adam and Eve:

Cursed is the ground for your sake;

In toil you shall eat of it

All the days of your life.

Both thorns and thistles it shall bring forth for you.

And you shall eat the herb of the field.

In the sweat of your face you shall eat bread.

Till you return to the ground.

For out of it you were taken;

For dust you are,

And to dust you shall return.[2]

Whether you believe the Bible as it reads or think it's a nice old story about the battle between good and evil, these quotes from Genesis highlight problems that have plagued human existence since the dawn of humankind. You may be asking, "What does this have to do with policing in America and current issues involving use of force?" The answer is quite simple: the serpent lives in all of us.

Use of force is a term we'll use throughout the book so for those not directly involved in law enforcement, here is a quick definition:

---

[1] Genesis 3:1-5 (New King James Version)
[2] Genesis 3:17-19 (New King James Version)

Use of force is any attempt by law enforcement to gain control of a resisting suspect through physical actions like control holds, less than lethal instruments like the taser and pepper spray, and lethal force.

Within our brains is a dual processing system: the emotional and the cognitive. The serpent lives in the emotional system. The purpose of this book is to highlight the performance benefits when we tame the serpent to work for us, as police officers. This provides the opportunity for a controlled, educated, legally defensible response to violent situations, instead of an extreme, uncontrolled, fight or flight response. In law enforcement we use terms like, "when you see the dragon," or "when you are facing the dragon," to represent those situations that occur less than one percent of the time. This is when the violence is sudden, real, and must be dealt with effectively.

Because, if the police can't solve the problem then who will?

How Did We Get Here?

In August 2015, the plan was to develop a brand-new defensive tactics program for the Phoenix Police Department. The program included tactical planning, communications, and principle-based concepts for dealing with resistance ranging from passive to extreme violence. Prior to adopting the program, the executive staff of the department requested a presentation on it and why we felt the need to adopt it. During that presentation, the de-escalation strategies included in the program were introduced. The de-escalation strategies were based on the science presented in this book.

De-escalation describes the tactics and strategies used by law enforcement which attempt to make the conclusion of the event safe for all parties involved, including the suspect. With the understanding that the suspect has a say in how the situation is concluded regardless of law enforcement's attempts to conclude the event without a use of force.

By the end of the presentation the executive staff requested an immediate department-wide roll out on de-escalation strategies. With the help of Officer Tyler Winget, we developed a four-hour training on the de-escalation tactics and strategies that every member of the Phoenix Police Department received. The program was reviewed by the US Attorney General's Office when Loretta Lynch came to Phoenix. In a news brief after her visit, she complemented the program and the neuroscience which aided in its development. The Maricopa County Attorney's Office then reviewed it and introduced the training to county attorneys that respond to police officer use of force incidents.

The goal of this book is to present the science behind de-escalation, the de-escalation program itself, biohacks for better performance, and new ideas for using neuroscience to enhance law enforcement training for peak performance under extreme pressure. Long ago, my father told me the goal of a career should be to leave a legacy; to leave the place better than you found it. This book is my attempt to do so.

Of course, when dealing with law enforcement officers and the idea of introducing new ways of doing things, we must address the question, "What's in it for me?" Here are just a few of the benefits I believe come from understanding the brain under stress and how to apply that knowledge:

1. Understanding the brain under stress can help you learn to biohack your own brain to achieve peak performance. (Because in law enforcement, performing under stressful conditions is a job requirement.)

2. Understanding your own brain in conflict will help you understand the brain of the person you are dealing

with, and aid in forming effective strategies for a safe resolution for all parties involved.

3. Understanding the brain and what happens when the balance between emotional and cognitive control is lost can aid officers and supervisors in awareness of anxiety, poor performance, depression, and PTSD issues.

4. Understanding the brain in conflict aids in comprehending how problems can occur, and aid in developing strategies to prevent issues such as: lawful but awful incidents (police incidents that are lawful but look horrible to the public and media), mistake-of-fact shootings (a suspect reaching for an object that the officer believes is a weapon, but it turns out not to be), and excessive force.

5. Understanding the brain's memory systems to develop better training that focuses on the brain and central nervous system for the best possible performance under stressful conditions.

This is not an all-inclusive list, but just some of the easily recognizable benefits of brain research. Keep in mind, in twenty-five years of law enforcement work, I have never attended training that focused on the brain's performance under stress. Instead, the training has always focused on skill work or scenario training. At the time, the belief was that the more skill work and scenario training you do, the better your performance under stress will be. Unfortunately, it's not that easy. In my career, I have been around officers who handle stress well and make good decisions under pressure and many who do not. Our best understanding at the time was that, after enough experience, an officer would learn to manage their stress and make good decisions. What we have seen is that people who start their careers managing it well continue to do so and eventually get even better at performing under stress. Those that do not start their careers with that ability usually don't develop it or get there by accident.

My name is Michael Malpass and I have been in law enforcement for over twenty-four years as a beat cop, a tactical training officer, and a SWAT officer. I am currently an advanced training officer for my department. During my entire career, I have been teaching defensive tactics for law enforcement. For over thirty-five years, I have been studying fighting systems. The law enforcement training programs I have designed include: ground survival, weapon retention, de-escalation, the optimized brain, compassionate restraint, close quarter crisis, and SWAT entry defensive tactics. I am recognized by the Federal Courts as a subject matter expert on police use of force.

Recently, I designed a brand-new defensive tactics system for my agency with the partnership of Kevin Secours of The International Combat Systema Association, Montreal, QC, Canada. This system has been taught in the basic academy setting, in advanced officer training, and now, portions of that program are being adopted into the state of Arizona's basic defensive tactics program. On three occasions, I have been awarded my department's Medal of Valor and have used every element of force available to officers, and on numerous occasions lethal force, which were all legally and morally justified. However, I am most proud of the many people that I helped to bring in safe and sound using some of the strategies mentioned in this book. Does all this make me an expert? Not at all. I am a student of tactics, strategies, brain science, and human behavior. It is my belief that the job description of the average police officer currently coming on to the job is more complex, requires more thought, skill sets, tactical strategies, and personal perseverance than at any other time in the history of law enforcement.

That serpent can be trained to work for us, because the serpent that lives within us does not have to be our enemy. The one within us is designed to steer us toward reward and away from risk. It does so by mapping memories which are indexed to create biases and hunches. Those biases and hunches are best guesses for behavior because the serpent lives in the portions of the brain that do not require conscious thought. Because they are just best guesses, they are sometimes wrong, and for a cop, can lead to tragic consequences. The following is a discussion of how to train and tame that serpent to work for you when facing a battle within yourself or against those serpents driving the behaviors of another.

Professional skydiver, Luke Aikens, in July of 2016, jumped out of a perfectly good airplane at 25,000 feet of altitude. No big deal. But wait, I failed to mention that he jumped out of the airplane with no parachute, only a plan to save his life by landing perfectly in a 100 x 100-foot net waiting for him suspended above the ground. For reference, the net could not be seen by the naked eye from the airplane. He would rely on his free fall skills, and his ability to orientate himself to certain markers while trying not to contemplate smashing into the ground at the speed of gravity. If that wasn't hard enough, at the last minute, to avoid falling straight through the net, Aikens was required to flip over and seek the net traveling backwards. Amazingly enough, he did it! Look it up on the internet, it's fun to watch.

To complete a feat of this magnitude, Aikens was required to maintain the perfect balance between emotions and cognition (reason) to work his way through this event. That could only be accomplished through training the brain for just the right amount of emotions to spur the system on but not enough to deteriorate performance. His cognitive systems would be in standby, waiting for unexpected things to happen and for problems to solve. But too much cognition brings too many choices and without experienced problem solving related to the situation, you risk paralysis by analysis. Too many options and not enough time.

Again, you may be wondering what any of this has to do with law enforcement. The very same processes going on in the brain of a peak performer in any extreme sport, where severe injury or death are at stake, are the very same processes a law enforcement officer needs in the one percent of their overall job. This is where the violence is real and critically important, life-changing decisions must be made under intense pressure.

The precise decisions are different between extreme sports athletes and police officers. The thought processing, emotional control with the cognitive ability to overrule quick decisions made by the unconscious systems, and training of the long-term memory systems and how they are accessed are entirely the same. The key element of comparison is that life and limb are on the line, that they understand and accept this, and are willing to rise to the occasion.

Neuroscientists have been studying the brains of peak performers using advanced technology which upgraded the average EEG (an electroencephalograph which records the electrical activity of the brain). These devices study which portions of the brain are firing when decisions are being made and tasks performed. This has given a clearer understanding of the difference between the beginner, the intermediate, and the peak performers. A lot of the initial work was performed on extreme sports athletes and some of that research accounts for the leaps and bounds advancements in extreme sports such as Luke Aikens's jump.

Neuroscientists who started by studying the brains of extreme sports athletes were later tasked with research for the Defense Advanced Research Projects Agency (DARPA), a governmental agency whose tasks include making better soldiers for the US military. That research compared the peak performance brain states of US Special Forces personnel with the brain states of extreme sports athletes.

Now consider a police officer on their way to a call of an active shooter at a shopping mall. The officer is three blocks away and knows they are going to be the first officer at the scene. Multiple victims are injured, and the suspect is armed with a rifle and a lot of ammunition. Our officer in question has a handgun, three magazines of ammunition, and knows that they are about to get into a gunfight. How do the thought processes of a rookie officer differ from the thought processes of senior officers, officers with prior military experience, or officers with tactical experience? Is there a way to better prepare our young officers by letting them borrow from the experience of more seasoned officers? Is there a way to train the brains of officers to help them find that right balance to the emotional and cognitive brain and could that be the answer to the many issues plaguing modern law enforcement? The answers, I believe are "Yes," and "Yes, we can." All it will take is a paradigm shift in how we look at law enforcement training by applying modern neuroscience. We have learned more about the brain, the memory systems, and how good decisions are made in the last five years than all of history before it. What we have learned can place us on a clear path for better training and performance in the future.

Before becoming a cop, I was a fighter. What I learned from all the instructors in boxing, Bando kickboxing, combat grappling, and mixed martial arts was that you need to manage your stress to perform at a higher level. The problem was, how do you that? How do you teach that? How do you know when you have achieved the nirvana that is peak performance? It's one thing to have achieved some experience and some competency under stress but how do you pass that information on to people new to the game? These are all questions, which in the past, had few answers. With my level of experience, I know what *I* know. What is difficult is teaching what makes the difference between the beginner and the expert in any field of endeavor.

The answers came within the last five years from research in the field of neuroscience, showing that the brains of military Special Forces operators and extreme sports athletes work the same when performing under extremely stressful situations. Is there a comparison with the professional athlete such as an NFL or NBA player? Yes and no. The decision-making process is similar, but professional athletes get paid whether they win or lose and usually their lives are not on the line when they fail. If extreme sports athletes or Special Forces operators make a mistake, someone usually dies or is severely injured. The balance in the brain systems required for extreme sports athletes and special forces operators are the same for law enforcement, or anyone else for that matter, attempting to perform at their best under stressful, life-threatening circumstances.

Until now, this information has been restricted to these environments. The answers are enlightening. To the experienced cops with established track records of performing under stress, the answers provide a framework, an explanation of how you learn to be better at what you do and how to perform consistently under stress. It may be that you already know what to do but you don't know how to express it or teach it to others. This book will aid you in that endeavor. Or it may be that you are new to law enforcement and would like some help "borrowing" experience to quicken your pace on the road to better performance under stress. This book is for you. Maybe you've been in law enforcement for a while but still haven't managed to figure out how to control your emotions under stress. Yes, this book is still for you. You may not be in law enforcement and are wondering how the system works. You may have opinions about how police work is done and how you think it should be done. Maybe you write about or report on police incidents, are a lawyer, a politician, an activist, or just interested by nature. This book is also for you.

We are all guilty of forming biases in our beliefs. As you will see, it is exactly what the emotional brain is designed to do. Some concepts stir the emotions and beliefs more than others, and we need look no further than social media to see the extreme responses to police use of force on both sides of the issue. I am not here to defend either side of the issue. The goal is to explain how the brain systems process information under life-threatening pressure and why training methods from the past are not producing the results under pressure we have been looking for. In the end, you must decide if this information is helpful or relevant.

While reading, attempt to suspend your biases, which I will tell you is not an easy thing to do. But if you disagree with something at an emotional level, pause for a moment and consider the possibility that your emotional system is hijacking your cognitive system. Our cognitive system will tell us that seeking the truth is right, while our emotional system will tell us reinforcing our pre-established beliefs is right. By the time you finish this book you should understand why the systems work this way. With that in mind, let's start this journey together and see if, in the end, we can form the closest thing to a win/win situation for all interested parties.

CHAPTER ONE

AN INTRODUCTION TO THE SCIENCE

Science is nothing but developed perception, integrated intent, common sense rounded out and minutely articulated.

— George Santayana

The Split Processed Brain

Imagine your brain and central nervous system as a split processing system made up of various sections geared toward cognitive thought, to emotions, and the making of emotional memories. In the early days of our human ancestors, the brain favored the emotional system which is geared toward survival. For instance, our early ancestors may have walked for days in search of food and water. Exhausted, suffering from thirst and hunger, they happen upon an oasis of lush trees and plentiful water. Chemicals were released from the emotional components of the brain. Those chemicals gave them feelings of joy and relief because they had found a chance to survive another day. While the emotional system created these chemical changes, the same chemicals gave information to other parts of the emotional system. It told the system to remember not only the location of the water, edible plants, and fruits but also the associated emotions of relief from hunger and starvation to stress the importance to the "system." The same ancestors in their travels may have encountered wild animals, other humans hell bent on taking any goods they had accumulated, or any of the natural hazards found in whatever environment they traveled in.

The emotional system would respond to these incidents by releasing chemicals like adrenaline, to drive survival behavior like fleeing, fighting, freezing in place, posturing or submission. With the release of certain chemicals, the emotional system indexes the memory of the event to aid in future decisions. When the violence was over and immediate survival was not threatened, the emotional system would release chemicals that would drive the mechanism (that's you) to promulgate the species by mating. Each of these incidents would spark the creation of memories all geared toward driving our ancestors away from risk, toward reward, and the balance of the two for survival. This constant state of pure survival mode would make life difficult as every day would be a struggle to find food, shelter, and a means to deal with extreme heat or cold, as well as protecting the group from animals and enemies.

At some point in time, our early ancestors began a heavier engagement of the cognitive portions of the brain, which was probably sparked by the survival systems to make life easier. Somehow, humans found out how to make fire, tools, and weapons, all things that surpassed other animals' development. Cognitive thought, intuitive thinking and problem solving aided our early ancestors and us. Once cognition was brought into the mix, anyone without those abilities would either die or rely heavily on someone who possessed cognitive abilities. Those who survived, passed on the stronger genes.

Each system, whether emotional or cognitive, has a memory system associated with it. On the emotional side there is procedural memory and on the cognitive side is declarative memory and working memory. Declarative memory and working memory aid you in running mental simulations, thinking your way through problems, and troubleshooting. Procedural memories, spurred by the emotional side, are unconscious physical actions geared toward survival. Procedural memory contains responses that are ingrained in the system from birth like the flinch and grasp reflexes. Procedural memory can also be trained with what Laurence Gonzalez, in *Deep Survival*, calls "secondary emotional bookmarks,"[3] as the unconscious system is always learning, regardless of whether we want it to.

Twenty years ago, the training to become a law enforcement officer was very similar to the training twenty years before that. Not a lot has changed between then and now either. Academies and agencies are very good at teaching the "theory" of law enforcement, the idea of the law, what happens when you break it, the need to be civil in your discourse, educating on race and social and economic disparity. In other words, they are very good at filling your declarative memory systems with information. Declarative memory is part of the long-term memory systems and it requires the conscious "you" to access the information contained within. Declarative memory will take you far in your law enforcement career until the violence starts. Declarative memory is filled with facts, ideas, and concepts that you can consciously describe. Procedural memory is an unconscious system that doesn't rely on the conscious "you" to access information in its data bank,

---

[3] Lawrence Gonzales. *Deep Survival: Who Lives, Who Dies, and Why* (New York, NY: W.W. Norton & Company, 2017), 40.

making it faster to access than declarative memory. If the situation calls for a survival response or a heavier emotional response for that matter, your central nervous system favors defaulting to procedural memory which is where survival responses like defensive tactics, movement under fire, and shooting skills need to be ingrained.

Something law enforcement trainers need to understand is that the procedural memory system is always learning whether you want it to or not. Meaning, certain things we do in training may be preparing the procedural system to do the *wrong thing* in a real-life encounter. A prime example of this is if the officer spends most of their range time shooting from a stationary position. In a real life and death encounter the procedural memory system may default to this same response, even though movement is required when acting against the sudden movement of a suspect. Remember, that turning target on the range represents a suspect with a gun already pointed at you. Does it make sense to train an unconscious system to possibly default to standing your ground against a gun already pointed at you?

What modern trainers of law enforcement, investigators of police use of force, or those who report on use of force need to understand is that, in the past, we have trained police officers in the best way we knew how at the time. Those times have changed. Modern neuroscience is giving us a look at how the brain operates under extreme pressure and why brain training is essential.

A Quick Review

I refer to science in my presentations whether in defensive tactics training, training on de-escalation, or training on the tactical brain. Without the science this book is just a story or a best guess. With the science, the reader can use their own experiences or the experiences of others to gain a deeper understanding of the complexities of training for these one percent of incidents like lethal force encounters, active shooter situations, hostage situations, ambushes, multiple opponent fights, and downed officer or civilian rescues.

Earlier, the concept of the brain as a split processing center was introduced. Before delving deeper into this concept, I'll provide you with an analogy from the ancient Greeks on the balance required between reason (cognitive) and emotion. As it turns out, all the great thinkers and warriors throughout history have known that you must balance reason and emotion to be at your best in any field of endeavor. We now have the science to not only back these thoughts but to train and accelerate the process of finding that balance daily.

According to the ancient Greeks, "the conscious you" drives a chariot pulled by two large horses. One horse represents your emotions (to include gut instincts) and is trying to pull the chariot off to one side of the road. The other horse represents reason (the cognitive side of the house) and that horse is trying to pull the chariot off to the other side of the road. Your job as the charioteer is to maintain firm control on the reigns and maintain a straight, balanced path of travel.

Understanding the cognitive and emotional systems, how they work along with the memory systems and how they are accessed, provides the individual with a firm grip on the reigns. This gives control over the chariot that is on your path in life, at any given time, including under stressful, potentially life-changing situations. This concept of how to train by balancing emotion and reason is the foundation of this book. This is crucial in every aspect of planning, communicating, training, and tactical preparation. It is the secret that has been hiding in plain sight.

Michael G. Malpass

The Peak Performance State

Peak performance is possible when our skill levels match the perceived demands of the situation. When skill levels are high, and the perceived demands are low, as in most police training, you get boredom. When the demands of the situation exceed the skill level of the officer, you get anxiety and as the demands increase, panic. Peak performance is possible only when the individual's cognitive system is in balance with emotions. The balance is possible due to the officer's skill set meeting the perceived demands of the situation. This is where mindset is also important. Any situation can be an opportunity for growth (challenge) or an overwhelming obstacle. Mindset is a byproduct of the skill set training, experience with decisions made before the violence starts, and performance under pressure in training and real-life experience. Mindset and true appraisal of the situation gives the officer the opportunity to avoid an over-emotional response or even worse, an amygdala hijack.

The Amygdala Hijack

Using the analogy of the chariot and the horses named Emotion and Reason, the amygdala hijack describes what happens when the horse named Emotion runs the chariot off the road with its deviation from the straight path. The amygdala's primary role is to interpret incoming data, map emotional memories, and drive the mechanism toward reward and away from excessive risk. The amygdala accomplishes this by creating emotional memories which are prioritized for future use. We will discuss the amygdala and the emotional system in more detail in a later chapter.

The term "amygdala hijack" was first used in the book

Emotional Intelligence written by Daniel Goleman in 1996. His terminology was based on research done by Joseph LeDoux. To keep it simple, as I hope to do throughout the book, the amygdala hijack is what happens when your emotional response to a situation is out of context with the situation and you later realize your reasoning skills had been hindered or shut off. If you are driving in a car and are late and under stress, another driver cutting you off can elicit a response out of context with your normal behavior and you may find it hard to calm down after the event. You have experienced an amygdala hijack.

When dealing with the brain and the split processing system, it's important to note that blood flows where the action is. Too much of an emotional reaction eliciting an extreme fight or flight response and you risk the hijack. The hijack can be useful when unthinking brute force is required as in the story of an elderly grandmother lifting a car off her trapped grandson. When you hear the terms fight, flight, freeze, posture, and submit, you are talking about extreme emotional responses. The fastest pathway for sensory input in the brain is to the amygdala, which then allows a secondary pathway of nerve signals to travel to the conscious portions of the brain. When the amygdala is hijacked, extreme levels of cortisol are released in the fight or flight response. It is believed the release of cortisol acts as a barrier to cut off the high road, the road to conscious thought, thinking through consequences, formulation of tactical strategies, and emotional control. The longer the pathway to the conscious response is blocked by the amygdala hijack, the greater the problems for a law enforcement officer. The block delays a conscious response where formulating plans, tactical thinking, and evaluating consequences of actions occurs. The extreme fight or flight response releases a series of chemicals into the system which inhibit fine motor control and cause extreme tunnel vision. When uncontrolled, a negative feedback circuit ensues which will further excite the emotional side while rational thought is effectively shut off.

Some officers who shoot very well during their qualifications, do not perform anywhere near as well in real-life, lethal use-of-force situations. It is my belief that the amygdala hijack (or at least an overwhelming emotional response) affects performance, diminishes cognitive thought, and can cause procedural skills ingrained into the procedural memory system to falter due to the excessive emotional response. An officer who allows the emotional response to get out of control will most likely lose the cognitive observations that aid in decision-making and prevent the emotional systems from becoming overwhelmed.

On the personal side, the amygdala hijack also accounts for why we sometimes say and do things under stress that later don't make sense to us. Remember, the emotional system is designed for survival, but it is the cognitive side of the house that determines the difference between an argument and a real fight. To the emotional side of the house, the two are the same and an emotional response to a verbal argument can be extreme. Have you ever said something vile and nasty to someone you love in the middle of a verbal argument and later regretted it? You experienced the amygdala dump. Have you ever wondered why a 100-mph car chase with the police is more likely to end with an excessive force complaint? The brain in a car pursuit is attempting to take in data at the speed of the car which it is not designed to do. The brain is in pure fight or flight mode. For the officer, that has morphed into prey runs and predator chases. When the suspect crashes, the car fails, runs out of gas, or the suspect just pulls over to give up, officers untrained in the brain sciences are still in fight or flight mode and the amygdala response indicates fight. In no way do I mean to make light of the situation, but it is easy to assume the officers are evil, racist, or uncaring. However, the simple explanation might be that they have lost control of their emotional system. When they may or may not be in immediate danger at that point, their emotional system is screaming at them to fight for their lives.

Imagine a rookie officer who finished his field training process and has been riding solo on the streets of a wealthy suburb outside of Columbus, Ohio for about a month. This officer was dispatched to a traffic obstruction at a major intersection during rush hour traffic. He was hoping for a call with a little more action attached but a call is better than no call. The officer gets out of his patrol car, squares away his uniform making sure he looks sharp and in command. He looks in the intersection and notices a long line of cars in all four directions moving slowly through the four-way stop and moving around ... a large goose, intent on owning the middle of the intersection.

Never having dealt with a goose before, he's trying to think of a way to move the goose from the intersection. The answer seems simple enough; shoo the goose away from the intersection. After all, how hard could that be? The officer approaches the goose and finds the animal is not willing to give ground and, in fact, tries to nip the officer with his beak. The well-trained officer sensed trouble and jumped out of the way before getting nipped. Then, he looks up to see if anyone saw him jump out of the way with a complete lack of coordination. (Google cats and cucumbers and you will get the picture.)

Still looking sharp, the officer is now embarrassed by the number of people laughing in their cars at the spectacle. He realizes this is not something covered in the academy but doesn't want to be one of those guys who can't solve problems and is always calling for other units. Using declarative and working memory, the officer figures this situation to be no different than a non-compliant subject under arrest. The officer pulls his pepper spray from his belt, shakes the canister, and prepares to re-engage. A nearby truck driver rolls down his window to advise the officer (while laughing hysterically) that a goose does not have tear ducts and pepper spray isn't going to work.

Now, the officer is incredibly embarrassed, confused, and running out of ideas. His working memory accesses declarative knowledge and he draws his expandable baton and prepares to solve the problem. As the officer approaches, the goose becomes agitated and goes after him while he is attempting to use his baton to gently move it along. This time, the heavy beak of the goose finds its mark and nips the officer in the ass. Now he realizes there is some power to those beaks and the nip hurt. The emotional system is now fully engaged as the officer looks up and sees numerous people amused at his discomfort. The officer (who looked a lot like me) was in pain and not liking at all how the situation escalated so quickly. The officer's emotional system was now in overdrive and because of the heavier emotional response, the cognitive system was diminished, and clear thinking was out the window.

I confess, it was me. I'm not going to lie, I was angry and embarrassed. I figured this was my best chance at showing that damn goose, and all the people in traffic, that I could handle this situation. As I approached the goose to move it with the expandable baton (now, with way too much emotion involved), the goose, the evil little bastard that it was, attempted to bite me again. At the time, I couldn't tell you what the hell went wrong in any detail, but I can now tell you that the emotional response with the emotional memory of the first nip in the butt, and the pain and embarrassment associated with it caused an extreme fight or flight response.

As I moved out of the path of the pecking beak, I flicked the baton at a downward angle striking the goose just above where the meat of the chest meets the long graceful neck. If the angry goose at first had a head and neck in the shape of a question mark, it now looked ... well, it looked dead. In fact, it was. I looked up and saw an elderly woman in her car and it occurred to me she looked like Aunt Bee from the Andy Griffith show. (Google it, if you are too young to have seen the show.) I expected a little sympathy from old Aunt Bee, but instead I clearly saw her mouthing the words, "You mother-fucker!" The truck driver, who was nice enough to tell me pepper spray wasn't going to work, was laughing as I dragged the carcass off the road and waved traffic through. Ten minutes later, I was meeting with my sergeant for my very first citizen complaint. It seems that Aunt Bee was not in fact Aunt Bee and was instead, a wealthy animal rights activist.

I had experienced what neuroscientists call an amygdala dump, which is what happens when your performance falls apart under stress. Remember, the amygdala is part of the emotional system. It drives risk/reward to make strong emotional memories. An amygdala dump occurs when the response to a stressor is out of measure with the stress itself. In my case, a violent, survival response was initiated out of proportion to the threat. I love animals, and while I can look at this experience and now get a laugh (and I hope you do too), the fact is I lost control of my response and killed a goose. It did however teach me a valuable lesson. With power comes responsibility. It was my job to make sure I was using the powers granted to me, by the law and the city I worked for, responsibly. In that case, I had not.

Why Do We Need A Split Processing System?

Please understand, when I use the term split processing brain, I in no way mean to say the brain is this simple. Instead, I use the term as neuroscientist David Eagleman does, to simplify concepts for easier understanding.

The split processing system that is our brain and central nervous system exists to separate humans from every other form of life on our planet. Without the higher learning cognitive system, each struggle to survive would pit our emotional brain against the emotional brain of things looking to eat us or kill us. With only the emotional brain, it is survival of the fittest. The strongest men kill off the weaker, take their stuff, and then mate with their women. Without the ability to make weapons (a cognitive function), humans would be no better off than a gazelle being hunted by a pack of lions. We are where we are as human beings because of the cognitive system, although the emotional side of the brain plays an extremely important role in our day-to-day lives.

The emotional side drives us away from things that can hurt or kill us and toward things that make us feel good. It does so by using unconscious learning to map emotional memories about risk and reward. The emotional system then provides "gut instincts," hunches or best guesses which are fast but not necessarily accurate. Science shows that the more experience you have relevant to the subject at hand, the more accurate the hunches. The beauty of the system is that as you gather experience, at say law enforcement defensive tactics, the skills become burned into the subconscious procedural memory associated with the emotional parts of the brain. This frees up the mind from consciously thinking about how to fight and allows the cognitive mind to prepare for what neuroscientists call "violations of expectations."

During a fight, the brain prefers to default to the emotional side of the house and procedural memory for the sake of speed and energy efficiency. Let's say during a law enforcement arrest, the suspect violently resists arrest by attempting to strike the officer. An officer well trained in defensive tactics will have procedural memory that allows them to fight on autopilot if there are no violations of expectations. For instance, if the suspect starts by throwing punches at the officer but then suddenly reaches under their shirt and into their waistband, there is a change in conditions which violates expectations. Once the cognitive system recognizes the change, ideally, we are looking for a trained procedural response of moving, drawing our weapon, and directing our eyes to the subject's hands. These responses should be ingrained in the procedural system through training. The cognitive system must stay online to determine whether the object being removed from the waistband is a gun or a cellphone. A balance between the systems is required for rapid, effective, and correct decisions.

The Brain Systems

The following is a quick list detailing the strengths of the systems; these concepts lay the groundwork for the science that will be presented throughout this book.

Cognitive (Reason)	Emotional
• Explicit system—requires conscious thought. • Analytical thinking, conscious judgment, planning. • Sequencing of activity. • Prefrontal Cortex of the brain. • Slow processing when compared to emotional system. • Allows abstract reasoning, impulse control, personality to be expressed, reactivity to surrounding and mood. • Interprets the conscious self, thinking and reasoning through problems.	• Implicit system—unconscious. • Reactive, impulsive, designed to be fast but not necessarily accurate. • Weighs risks and rewards; designed to steer the complex toward rewards and away from excessive risk. • The horny, hungry, angry monkey of the human brain; do I mate with it, eat it, or kill it? • Emotional system through the amygdala helps interpret facial expression of others and emotional cues conveyed by eyes and shifting gaze.

- Executive functions; determines what stimulus is attended to, what decisions need to be made and what the consequences will be.

- If the entire human body is a company, then the cognitive system through the prefrontal cortex is the CEO of the company.

- If developed in combat situations and training, can balance risks and aid in developing courses of action and creating strategies.

- Cognitive self-control acts as the brains braking system as its most important function may be the role it plays in emotional regulation.

- Through the amygdala, compares incoming data with emotional memories and acts if immediate unconscious response is needed.

- If the emotional system is too heavily engaged, fuel is diminished or cut off to the cognitive system thus decreasing or preventing sound reasoning ability.

- You can do math without the emotional system, but you can't order off a menu or prioritize what to do next without the emotional system.

- Emotional networks are absolutely required to rank your possible next activities in any situation.

Mental Models and Emotional Bookmarks

Using the split-brain processing model, we can now address two important functions of the cognitive system (mental models) and the emotional system (emotional bookmarks). Mental models allow you to reflect on your past, observe and act in the present, and project yourself into the future through mental simulations. This amazing ability of the cognitive portion of the brain through the working memory and its access to long-term memory systems accounts for the tactical planning and communication strategies that will be presented in the de-escalation chapter of this book.

I was introduced to the term "emotional bookmarks" while reading *Deep Survival* by Laurence Gonzales. Primary emotional bookmarks are the instincts you are born with like fight, flight, freeze, posture, submit, and the drive to promulgate the species by mating. Secondary emotional bookmarks are trained into the system through repetition with associated emotions, and through the indexing of memories deemed important to survival by a system that does not require conscious thought. These bookmarks can be chosen by us and ingrained into the system or can be trained into the system by default. As you will soon see, the emotional system is always learning. When these emotional bookmarks create an imbalance with the cognitive systems, these secondary emotional bookmarks also hold a link to anxiety and PTSD issues.

Cognitive Appraisal

Cognitive appraisal is a mental process that at any time aids in defining what is happening to the individual, around the individual, and adapting methods for deciding which issues require immediate attention. In their book *Performing Under Pressure*, authors Weisinger and Pawliw-Fry state:

> It is the process by which we make sense of the world around us and the situations we face. It helps us to answer such questions as: Do I have what it takes to handle the demands of the situation? Is the situation important to me? The single most important question that we face when we are under pressure is: Do I see the

situation as a crisis or a challenge? The roots of how we appraise situations lie in the special qualities and circumstances we bring to the table that shape our personalities: family background, role models, psychological traits and health, systems of belief, fears and hopes. Self-esteem is part of the equation, as is our sense of history, pride, legacy, and entitlement, among others. These factors combine to form the basis for the unique way we interpret our surroundings, give meaning to outside events, and appraise the situations we encounter in daily life, especially in the high-pressure moments we encounter.[4]

Cognitive appraisal is an inside-out and outside-in system. Part of any appraisal is how you feel at any given moment and how you are handling the emotions. This is the inside-out appraisal. Another part of the appraisal is responding to what you see and the information you have gathered to attempt to maintain tactical advantage in law enforcement encounters. This is the outside-in appraisal. Cognitive appraisal is done throughout the day and is not inclusive to law enforcement. It's a brain process run continuously as a response to incoming sensory information, along with reactions to emotions. Without an understanding of cognitive appraisal, an individual can be heavily influenced by their emotions. Understanding cognitive appraisal aids in taming the emotional response and improving performance under pressure and in our day-to-day experiences. We will discuss cognitive appraisal and how to train it throughout the book.

---

[4] Hendrie Weisinger, and J. P. Pawliw-Fry, *Performing Under Pressure: The Science of Doing Your Best When It Matters Most* (New York, NY: Crown Publishing Group, 2015), 71.

Michael G. Malpass

Left of Bang

The Left of Bang concept incorporates cognitive appraisal with behavioral profiling to aid in reading behavioral cues which can be pre-violence indicators, or hints that a situation is about to spin out of your control.

I did not come up with the term left of bang but believe the term accurately describes some of the things we can do to either prevent the violence from happening or anticipating it in time to effectively deal with it as safely as possible. A quick explanation of the concept: Left of bang is an idea that is part of the Marine Corps Combat Hunter Program. Left of bang is everything you do before shots are fired, the lethal threat is presented, or a physical assault begins. Bang is the violent act or the event which occurred where control was lost, and right of bang is what happens after. Most law enforcement and military training in the past has been right of bang. Now, left of bang concepts must be discussed and introduced to military and forward-thinking law enforcement personnel.

The Marine Corps Combat Hunter Program is a behavior analysis program and not a profiling program based on race or ethnicity. It is a brilliant program which has launched a book written by Jason Riley and Patrick Van Horne called *Left of Bang*. I highly recommend the book for anyone who wants to see the science behind why good cops and soldiers know what they know and interpret what they see. Our concept of left of bang includes tactical planning, communications skills, and sound observation skills to either prevent the lethal threat or be in the best positions to effectively deal with it. The concept of left of bang also includes the study of neuroscience and the psychology of peak performance under less than desirable circumstances. I believe we will soon show you that if we can control our brains and understand what the

32

suspect or a mentally ill person's brain may be doing, we can use science to help solve some of the problems created by brains in extreme conflict.

To use terminology established in *Left of Bang*, individuals are constantly assessing their environment to establish a "baseline" for their immediate location. Cognitive appraisal allows for establishing the baseline for an area and, more importantly, recognizing deviations from that baseline when they occur. As an example, let's say you are a police officer responding to a domestic violence situation. As you are approaching the residence you can hear loud voices, one of which appears to be angry and the other scared. As you obtain a visual on both parties standing on the front porch of the residence, you observe a male subject who appears to be angry and hostile. You also observe a female seated on the floor of the porch with her hands up in what you believe to be a posture to protect herself from the male subject. The female appears to you to be scared.

The initial assessment of the situation involves an environmental baseline, and a baseline for each of the individuals present in that environment, including bystanders. By establishing a "baseline" for the situation, cognitive appraisal gives the officer, when appropriately trained, the ability to quickly assess where their primary focus should be to prepare and expect deviations from established baselines. In an initial quick scan of the environment, the baseline for the entire neighborhood would be normal, the baseline for the house where the domestic disturbance is occurring is a deviation from that neighborhood baseline.

For the two individuals involved, the apparent victim is scared (heightened emotional) and the male subject is angry and hostile (heightened emotional). The baseline for the inside of the residence and its potential occupants is unknown and therefore an area of extra concern until other officers arrive to help. As we get into the brain science, you will start

33

to understand the many systems of the emotional brain and central nervous system that are working in the background without conscious knowledge of their processing. Those background systems are outside of conscious thought because they are faster, more instinctive, and primed when trained for steering the "mechanism" (that's you) toward things that reward the system and away from things that can hurt or kill it. Together, the background systems with the cognitive appraisal system are looking for those violations of expectations we previously discussed. It is impossible for the brain to focus on everything all at once. The systems working in the background without cognitive thought are continually absorbing data and freeing up the conscious thought process for problem-solving after a violation of the systems' expectations. This could also be called a deviation from baseline, which is a term from the Left of Bang Program.

For example, when the female recognizes the presence of the officer and appears angry and starts yelling at the officer, you have a violation of expectations; you would have expected her to appear relieved. If the angry husband saw the police presence and immediately calmed down and looked relieved, you would have a violation of expectations. These violations don't mean violence is imminent, it only requires a change in focus to quickly establish a new baseline for the situation and each individual. Sound complicated? If the entire system was only run by conscious control, it would be. Fortunately for us, we have what neuroscientist David Eagleman calls "zombie systems"[5] running in the background aiding the systems that can run on autopilot, only requiring

---

[5] David Eagleman. *Incognito: The Secret Lives of the Brain.* (New York, NY: Vintage Books, 2012).

immediate conscious effort when those violation of expectations occur.

When fight or flight emotions are felt, there are physical expressions of the subconscious emotions. The fight or flight response requires energy and those subconscious emotions create physical behaviors that can be detected by the trained eye. This is one of the key teaching aspects of the Left of Bang Program. These physical expressions of subconscious emotions are things like the bouncing of the leg, crossing of the arms, shifting of eyes, clenching and unclenching of the fists, and numerous others too vast to include here.

Included in any part of baseline evaluations are behaviors, gestures, movement of the hands, posture gaze, emotional expressions, and the list goes on and on. Violations of expectations, or these deviations from baseline, can include but are not limited to: new people arriving on scene or coming out of their homes to see what is happening, the arrival of other officers, children showing up in the area, the subjects' refusal to obey a lawful order, and anything else that could possibly occur to change the initial baseline assessment of each scene, circumstance, and individual. The entire process of how you feel, how the subjects you encounter appear to feel, the baselines of the situation and deviations from the baselines, especially violations of expectations, are all part of the cognitive appraisal process.

Action is always going to be faster than reaction unless the action is anticipated. The only way to anticipate actions is the use of cognitive appraisal to make left of bang observations. Again, the emotional system is designed to read and anticipate risk and reward. Using developed cognitive appraisal skills frees up the unconscious system to interpret facial expressions, posture, and quickly assess changes in baselines.

So that's a down and dirty briefing on the neuroscience

of decision-making under stress. As we go along in the presentation of the de-escalation program and in new training concepts, I will delve deeper into the science of emotion, reason, and the memory systems.

CHAPTER TWO

DE-ESCALATION: STRATEGIES TO STAY LEFT OF BANG

In the scale of the destinies, brawn will never weigh as much as brain.

– James Russell Lowell

Let's get started with the most important question pertaining to the concept of de-escalation. Who is the only person at any scene or circumstance who can de-escalate the situation by choice? Here is the cold hard truth. The suspect, the mentally ill person, or the person being lawfully contacted by the police, is the only person or persons able to de-escalate a scene without some form of coercion or force. Law enforcement personnel have tactics, strategies, and ideas for giving an individual the opportunity to de-escalate a scene, but in the end, the subject of the call must make a conscious choice to de-escalate or risk being forced into compliance. Creating time and space, opening dialogue, and using sound tactical placement can give a subject the opportunity to comply. Even the use of less lethal technologies and tactics can't de-escalate the situation, it can only provide the opportunity for the subject to comply. The important thing to remember is that sometimes a situation can only be made safer by force applied by law enforcement. If, in that application of force, there is injury only to the suspect, the scene has still been de-escalated.

What is my definition of de-escalation? I will show you a sound tactical plan and I will communicate with you in a calm professional manner. I will show you that I am mentally, physically, and spiritually prepared to do whatever I have to in lawfully bringing this situation to a conclusion. I will use all available resources to make this safe for both you and me. However, in the end I will ask you, then I will tell you and detail the consequences. I will gather available resources. Then, I will give you another chance to comply by explaining the situation and its consequences. If all of this fails and I have lawful authority and purpose, then the law grants me the ability to make you comply to my demands. In doing so, if you choose to try and kill innocent people, my fellow officers, or me, then by God, I will kill you first.

Yes, when faced with a deadly threat, an officer is taught to shoot to stop the threat against them. Although, if we are being honest and I believe we should be, the fastest most reliable way to do that is to either create a massive fluid loss of blood (usually the chest) or cut off the central nervous system (the head). Of the two, shutting off the central nervous system is the fastest. When presenting this concept to civilians and the media, the question comes up of why we don't shoot to wound suspects? The most relevant answer is twofold. One: shooting center mass is more dependable than trying to shoot moving limbs. Two: if I wound you in the leg and your next shot kills me, I have not successfully planned this event to its conclusion. I have taught this training to over three thousand people to date and every training begins with the idea presented above. I believe this honest and blunt presentation lets the officers know that, while we need to make changes in how we deal with confrontations (especially those dealing with the mentally ill, unarmed subjects, and suspects driving vehicles) we don't have to sacrifice our safety to do so.

Use of Force and Race

Let's define the perceived problem. According to the media, certain activist groups, certain law enforcement groups, and anyone who spends too much time on social media, the police are killing an inordinate number of people and most of the victims are black men. I am a firm believer in fact-checking everything and I suggest you do the same. With that said, let's delve into some facts. Recently Dr. Richard Johnson, (2015) Associate Professor at the University of Toledo in the Criminal Justice Program, published a study on police use of lethal force. The results surprised many within the academic community, the media, and community activists. The study showed no indications of race being a factor in the use of lethal force by police. It also showed that during the studied time frame, any individual in the United States had the same chance of being struck by lightning as being killed by a police officer.[6] A separate study conducted by Harvard University by Roland G. Fryer, Jr. (2016) showed similar results.[7]

However, when looking at use of force, *excluding* lethal force, several studies have found that black male suspects are more likely to have higher levels of force used against them when resisting a lawful arrest. The numbers are significant enough to warrant further investigation. Unfortunately, each

---

[6] Dr. Richard Johnson. "Examining the Prevalence of Deaths from Police Use of Force." *Force Science*, 2015. www.forcescience.org/forcepresentation.ppt
[7] Roland G. Fryer, Jr. "An Empirical Analysis of Racial Differences in Police Use of Force." *Journal of Political Economy*. Forthcoming. 2016. https://scholar.harvard.edu/fryer/publications/empirical-analysis-racial-differences-police-use-force

law enforcement agency has their own method of documenting use of force as well as their own policies and procedures
regarding use of force. Without a national uniform method of
reporting, each of these use of force reports will have to be
read and documented in a consistent manner to see if meaning can be found in the statistics. To date, this research has
not been done. For example, police reports list levels of resistance by the suspect and force used by the officer using a
coded system, but you would have to read the narrative of
each individual report to match up the officer's use of force
with the suspect's level of resistance. These facts matter but
are difficult to analyze without reading the whole story instead of a statistical breakdown of levels of force.

I have chosen not to print the research studies within the
book as these studies are readily available on the internet
and through the corresponding academic institutions. It is
vital we seek facts and not biased opinions, to identify problems and solutions. Please fact check what you read, what is
told to you in the news, on social media, or even by friends
or loved ones. The facts matter if we are going to find solutions to the real and perceived problems. Keep in mind, the
emotional system will seek to reinforce your beliefs through
the biases created by the system. Cognitive control allows us
to seek the truth instead of bias reinforcement. Always keep
in mind, the emotional system wants to believe what rein-
forces the biases it already holds dear. Cognitive, executive
control allows us to seek the truth and overrule the hunch
played by the implicit bias system we call our emotional brain.

Implicit Bias

If you're in law enforcement, then you should recognize the
term implicit bias. When all the studies came out proving no

racist tendencies in police use of lethal force, the term implicit bias started gaining traction in the media. The facts related to the implicit bias study have been used to such extremes that the Harvard website on the study has posted a disclaimer referencing the use and misuse of the research.

What is implicit bias? The emotional system is an implicit system which means it does not require conscious thought. The emotional system, through the amygdala and hippocampus, attempt to steer "the mechanism" (that's you) by providing quick hunches to guide behavior toward reward and away from excessive risk. The amygdala also carries the power to cut off the rational system and initiate an immediate survival response like fight, flight, freeze, posture, or submit. These hunches or quick insights are fast but not necessarily accurate. The more experience you have in making decisions relative to a task, the higher the likelihood your hunches are more accurate. The emotional system is geared toward survival and it's adapted from times long ago when every minute of every day was a struggle for survival. So, if it doesn't look like you, act like you, walk like you, talk like you, or believe like you, the emotional system's quick hunch is that you have a potential enemy in your midst. Race, sexual preferences, political affiliation, gang affiliation, job affiliations, hair color, body type, I could go on and on, but I hope you have the point. At first, the emotional system will say don't trust, be careful, or we might have a problem here. The mistake that some are attempting to portray is that it is racism and it can only be expressed by certain members of society and not others.

So here is the truth about implicit bias. See what neuroscientists and psychologists without political agendas have to say about implicit bias. Once you understand what it is, you're armed with the ability to try and do something about it. Have you ever met someone who you immediately dislike but don't really have a conscious reason that can be verbally expressed? That is the implicit system giving you a hint. *This person is different, they are not like you, don't trust them.* Now, have you ever met someone like this who later turns out to be one of your best friends? Then you have experienced the rational system overruling the hunches provided by the emotional system.

For law enforcement officers assigned to neighborhoods of races or ethnicity other than their own, these implicit hunches can lead to problems. The problem is of course, that most law enforcement agencies are understaffed. Due to this, most of the time on duty is spent going from call to call dealing with people in various states of emotional distress. Without enough of a sample size, the emotional system starts to make guesses geared toward survival and stereotyping is usually the result. For example, if a cop is only dealing with people at their worst and without some cognitive override, the emotional system starts to tell you things like, all Mexicans are illegals, all Native Americans are drunks, all African Americans are violent, etc. Only with cognitive override and a break from the extreme emotions are law enforcement officers able to comprehend the fact they haven't met every single person from every race and ethnicity so their sample size to make an educated guess on these topics is ridiculously small.

My suggestion is to solve the personnel problems with adequate staffing and then teach the old beat-cop mentality instead of the race to answer calls all over the city. The beat cop mentality says, *I am responsible for this beat and what happens in it, for the safety of the people in it, and it's my job to let them know it.* Beat cops get out of their cars and they talk to people. They treat people, even criminals, with respect because today's foe may become tomorrow's ally, and, honestly, at times I have liked the gang members in my beat more than some of the fellow officers I had to work with. These lessons are not my own. I learned the beat-cop mentality from two of the finest cops I have ever seen or heard of, Mike Yatsko and John White. By the time I made it to the SWAT team, Mike and John had moved out of their beat areas and on to different positions. On numerous occasions, years after they left their beats, the SWAT team would be serving warrants in the area, and afterwards people in the area would recognize me as Mike Yatsko's former partner. They would ask about Mike and John and would tell stories of things they had done to help the neighborhood, whether arresting criminals, looking in on the family members of incarcerated criminals, or helping former gang members get into college or trade school. That is a lasting impact, and that is leaving the place better than you found it. Officers need to get out of the car and engage with people. We will all have the chance to learn that the same operating systems running in the same methods are driving us all, and when we understand that, we have found some common ground.

There was a famous implicit bias study done and it did in fact show that white males have an implicit bias against black males within a certain age group. You don't have to think too hard to understand that the unconscious system doesn't trust what it doesn't know, and we ALL have this implicit system. The most fascinating part of the study, to me, was that black males showed an implicit bias toward other black males within certain age groups. Researchers were surprised because they believed implicit bias was more about race, and why would black males be biased against black males? As it turns out, implicit bias is more about the 'in group' and 'out group' and less about race, although race can be a factor. 'In group' can be decided by who looks like you, acts like you, believes like you, or a host of other factors. This led scientists to believe that there is a social aspect to the unconscious learning done by the implicit systems. Reason should tell us that black males should not hold implicit bias against other black males, but with the stereotyping of Hollywood, the violence of rap music and video games, certain life experiences or media coverage, it is not surprising that the unconscious system is gathering information and making guesses that show this form of bias.

Reason should tell us a white male should not hold an implicit bias against another white male. The subconscious system can make the 'in group' about money, beliefs, looks, preferences and the list goes on. A white cop in a majority white neighborhood of lower socio-economic status can still be considered a member of the 'out group' even though they share the same race.

Look at the political discourse in the United States. Far right, far left, liberal, conservative, we are right, you are wrong and if we don't agree we have to hate. What is wrong with us? It's simple science, and the current discourse is spiking the emotional brains of people on all sides of the issues. We all should want to get a handle on implicit bias. Understand the system for what it is: a series of best guesses geared toward survival which are fast but not necessarily accurate. The more experience you acquire in certain tasks and endeavors, the more accurate those hunches will be when in balance with the cognitive system.

The biggest takeaway: we all have implicit bias built into our system and it's there for a good reason. When balanced with the cognitive, those hunches guide quick decision making. Under stress and without the implicit system all decision-making would risk too many options with too many consequences, more commonly known as paralysis by analysis.

Please refer to the Harvard website on the Implicit-Association Test for more information on what their test does and does not measure. The research is fascinating and often mis-understood, so check the facts for yourself from the source![8]

Lawful but Awful

No one is certain where the term "lawful but awful" came from. It has been used by county attorneys and police inter-nal affairs investigators to indicate a police officer-involved use of lethal force that meets the parameters of a lawful use of force but will look awful to the average citizen, activists, and to the media. With the understanding that within certain time frames the top three lawful but awful situations could change, the current top three in the US are: shooting the driv-ers of moving vehicles, the killing of unarmed individuals fighting with the police, and the killing of the mentally ill.

Keep in mind that all use of force should be judged based on the totality of the circumstances known to the officer at the time and not 20/20 hindsight as all the facts become known once the incident has calmed down and there is time for reflection. This precedent is established in the Supreme Court Case *Graham v. Conner* which we will discuss in the next chapter.

It is a bad idea to shoot the driver of a moving vehicle when you cannot account for the safety of innocent people in the area. This is generally the case, but there are several cases out of the Supreme Court where officers were found justified in doing just that. In most cases, the deciding fac-tors were: the danger presented by the suspect to innocent bystanders, video of the suspect's dangerous driving, and the

[8] https://implicit.harvard.edu/

officer's articulation of the threat posed (usually to others but sometimes to the officers themselves).

In the past, officers have stood in front of a vehicle or placed themselves in the path of a moving vehicle as a challenge to stop the vehicle. The science will show this is an action driven by that fast but not necessarily accurate emotional system. Here's my take. Train yourself not to do this. Not everyone will respect your authority, and this isn't worth dying over. The court's perspective used to be that a criminal must submit to the authority of the police. There is a growing trend of the courts looking at the behavior of the officer prior to the use of force and judging those actions. To date, the Supreme Court has not specifically ruled against an officer for actions before the lethal use of force, but make no mistake, sooner or later it will. More importantly, why lose emotional control and risk your life for nothing?

Later we will discuss dealing with the mentally ill and confrontations with "unarmed" individuals which are two of the other current "lawful but awfuls."

Working Memory: The Chalkboard of the Mind

We can now add a new concept to our left of bang concepts and training as it involves the working memory also known as the chalkboard of the mind. The working memory:

> Is a general-purpose work-space, and most of us experience it as attention or conscious thought. In addition, there are specialized systems for verbal and nonverbal information. They have a type of short-term memory that allows perceptions to be compared with one another over the span of a few seconds. The general-purpose area can take in information from the specialized systems (sight, smell, sound, and so on) and can integrate and process that information through what LeDoux calls 'an executive

function.' That area of the brain, located mostly in the frontal lobes, is responsible for making decisions and voluntary movements, as well as, directing what sensory input we're paying attention to. It's why we can still carry on a conversation in a room where many people are talking, and music is playing. It's why we can choose between getting up and putting on a sweater or turning the thermostat up.[9]

Working Memory and the Lawful but Awful

Working memory is vital for problem solving and running mental simulations but its actions can be inhibited by exaggerated emotional responses. The left of bang cognitive appraisal process should include the simple question, "Who is creating the exigency here?" If the answer is that the suspect or the situation itself is creating the exigency, then the officer must now make choices to ensure the safety of innocent people, themselves and fellow officers, and last in line when possible, the suspect. Stepping into the path of a moving vehicle and daring the driver not to run you over is exigency created by the officer. Even if the Supreme Court never holds them liable, agencies already are. Suspensions and terminations are the result, not to mention the risk to the officer's own life. We will continue to discuss working memory and pre-loading its systems with ideas like exigency and who is the proximal cause of said exigency throughout the book.

When discussing the shooting of unarmed individuals by the police, it's important to collect all the facts. In some of

---

[9] Lawrence Gonzales. *Deep Survival: Who Lives, Who Dies, and Why* (New York, NY: W.W. Norton & Company, 2017), 73.

these cases, we have a suspect attempting to disarm the officer or gain the upper hand in a fight with the officer instead of choosing to flee. A subject who is attempting to arm themselves is not "unarmed." An officer in a fist fight with a subject must account for what happens to their service weapon if they are rendered unconscious. The courts, as you will soon see, indicate that officers must infer intent by the conduct of the subjects they confront. What inference can be made when a suspect is on top of a grounded officer and can leave but chooses not to? Keep in mind, the science works both ways. The suspect or mentally ill subject that an officer is contacting may be having an extreme emotional response with decreased cognitive (logical) function.

Which brings us to cases other than attempted disarms and officers who are on the losing end of unarmed altercations that have escalated to lethal force. We talked earlier about the necessary balance between cognition and emotion and what happens when either side carries too much influence over the other. When the emotional side of the brain and central nervous system is too heavily influenced, the conscious self is inhibited by what scientists believe is a release of too many chemicals (one of which is cortisol) from the emotional systems. When the conscious self is diminished or completely cut off, the "mechanism" takes over in a full survival response. The problem is, this response comes from a time in history where blunt force trauma without a lot of cognitive thought or fine motor control was necessary. When the "mechanism" takes over, the emotional system will default to procedural memory where the fight or flight response and skills (good and bad) trained into the unconscious system reside.

The problem for law enforcement officers is that procedural skills can be trained into the system without the associated emotions of fight or flight. These are skills such as standing your ground when a target turns and trying to out-shoot an already presented threat. As we touched on earlier, under stress, the system can default and produce the action you trained for the most instead of the action necessary in that moment. With adequate, realistic training under stress, those skills can be accessed under combat conditions. Without adequate training or experience, the system will default to its lowest common denominator. This is the pure fight or flight emotional response which prefers no cognitive thought and pure blunt force trauma. Because this system is geared for survival and part of that response is to provide quick gut instinct hunches, we end up with a "mistake-of-fact" use of lethal force. A mistake-of-fact shooting is when the facts and circumstances the officer believed to be true at the time of the use of force, like the presence of or movement toward a weapon, turn out to not be true.

It is vital to remember the emotional system will show you what you want to see and tell you what you want to hear when it is too heavily engaged. Any movement can become a movement for a gun, and any object can be misinterpreted as a weapon because the emotional system is in pure survival of the "mechanism" mode and is throwing fast, but not necessarily accurate, survival hunches at you. On that heavier emotional side, you will lose track of what is important to the conscious self. Welfare of others won't matter, doing things right and by the rules won't matter because, to the emotional side under extreme stress, it's all about ending the fight. Are there bad cops out there? Of course, but to assume that the prevalence of police use of force is because of racism or corruption without facts does nothing to aid in the discussion of what I believe is the true problem.

If training doesn't incorporate an understanding of the brain under stress and include thousands of decisions made under stress to engage the cognitive and improve the accuracy of the hints or instincts of the emotional, then all we are going to get is the same as what we've gotten in the past. It's my belief that the majority of mistake-of-fact shootings of unarmed individuals are caused by the officer's inability to manage the emotional response as a subject starts to resist arrest, and that system telling them or showing them what they want to hear or see. Without a change in the training paradigms which are currently used, we can expect more of the same. The brain must be trained so less-experienced officers or officers who have consistently performed poorly under stress, can borrow experience from the peak performers. The peak performers have the emotional/cognitive balance, in some cases without understanding why, and in the past have been unable to teach it to others. By adding training in this balance of the emotional and cognitive, we create an opportunity to not only help those who need it the most, but also the opportunity to make those who are relatively proficient or even experts better.

These lawful but awfuls can be reduced and the answer to all three issues (mentally ill persons, unarmed suspects, and suspects driving cars) is the same. Study the brain science, incorporate it into training, and follow the precepts outlined in the de-escalation section and you have armed yourself by preparing the most important space on any battlefield, the six inches of real estate between your ears. Anger, fear, and hostility don't win fights. People who can manage their emotions under stress win fights by using trained procedural memory with cognitive control available for the violations of expectations. Guns don't win gunfights. People who have trained in decision-making under stress with sound procedural skills and cognitive control capabilities win gunfights. All the skill and techniques in the world won't matter if the person using them cannot control the emotional side of the house. Without emotional control, the individual must rely on luck alone. Look no further than the Olympics to see what happens when highly trained athletes fail to control the emotional system when it counts. After years of preparation and tens of thousands of repetitions, an Olympic athlete allows the excessive emotions associated with the competition, which the emotional brain interprets as life and death, to run out of control. Their performance of skills, that without pressure they perform flawlessly, is now diminished or completely falls apart.

When we talk about controlling the emotional side of the brain, in no way do I mean to imply it is easy. Remember, in any encounter where a subject is resisting arrest, the officer must account for the fact that, until a subject is searched, there is no way to know if they are armed with a weapon. Attempting to control a human being who does not want to be controlled is not easy if you are trying to prevent injury to them. Have you ever tried to control an unruly three-year-old having an emotional tantrum? These lessons need to be taught to the media and to the community, to start the conversations society so desperately needs. Conversations with an understanding of the emotional/cognitive balance as it pertains to police and suspects under stress and to our own search for the truth instead of information to reinforce our emotional beliefs.

In most use-of-force cases, the initial proximal cause of the use of force was the subject resisting arrest. The secondary problem is when the resistance starts; it's easy for the officer's emotional brain to become overexcited with the unknown factors (i.e. the idea of possible weapons or not knowing that the subject you contacted is wanted for murder or some other violent crime).

In some cases we have a reverse mistake of fact where, for example, a suspect in a car is stopped and believes an officer is stopping him for a crime he recently committed. The officer, however, is stopping the suspect for a broken tail light and has no idea the driver has committed a serious crime. The suspect attacks the officer because he doesn't want to go to jail and the officer, if not trained well, could be way behind the curve in his response to the initial violence.

The De-Escalation Program

Communication Strategies

When I became a police officer in 1993, I went through a state-run police academy in Ohio where I was an officer for about four and a half years before moving to Arizona to attend another academy. In Ohio, we were taught the "Verbal Judo" model of communication. That model basically looked like this:

1. Ask: Be polite, professional and show courtesy.

2. Tell: Be polite, professional and show courtesy but give an order and explain the consequences of failure to comply.

3. Caveat: Say, "Sir, is there anything I can say or do at this time to gain your compliance? I would like to believe that there is."

4. Make: The law gives you the right to use force to gain compliance, but the officer's level of force used should be measured and reasonable.

I was taught this model and have used it effectively for my entire career. The only real difference between then and now is back then you were expected to be able to do these things yourself and not use up resources. Here is where our new model comes into play as we are trying to reduce the situations where the police officer's actions create exigent circumstances. Our model adds an additional step which can be considered at any time throughout this communication process. Here is our updated model: This of course assumes the officer has a lawful purpose for the encounter and not just a consensual contact with a citizen.

1. Ask: Be polite, professional and show courtesy.

2. Resources: If it gets to the point where I must make them, do I have the necessary resources to make the arrest in the safest manner for all parties to include, innocent civilians, officers, and the suspect?

3. Tell: Be polite, professional and show courtesy but give an order and explain the consequences of failure to comply.

4. Resources: Has anything changed? Do I need further or different resources?

5. Caveat: The caveat doesn't have to be the exact wording listed above but should encompass the idea of using logic to avoid the fight (every experienced cop has a form of caveat).

6. Resources: Any changes, further needs? Do I need to make a tactical pullback to wait for more resources?

7. Make: Effect the arrest using the amount of measured and reasonable force given the circumstances.

Within this communication process, if at any time the situation is escalated by either the suspect, mentally ill person or by some changing circumstance not initiated by law enforcement, then we move to our emergency plan of action, which will be presented soon. At any time in the process your tactics, strategies, and the situation itself can change. The versatility of this process is that you can spend as much time as needed in each of the communication stages, if the situation allows, and can continually re-evaluate your plans using cognitive appraisal, to more effectively reach positive results.

When looking at the brain science of conflict, planning, communication, and tactics, the most basic premise applicable to this program is the split processing system of the brain.

This consists of the emotional level and the cognitive level (ability to process information) and their inverse relationship. Meaning, if you are suffering from excess emotions, whether anger, fear, panic, jealousy, hatred, etc., the brain's reasoning abilities will suffer exponentially based on the intensity of the emotion. In the communication process, this is extremely important to understand because if we know and understand the relationship between raw emotions and reasoning ability, we can develop strategies for attempting to decrease the intensity of the emotions and hopefully increase the subject's and our own ability to reason through the problem. The same strategies work on controlling our own emotions to increase our cognitive abilities while attempting to control those we contact.

Can you recall a time in your life where built-up stress has increased to a level where you now knew your response to a situation was way out of proportion to the problem at hand? We all can. The quick science is, your emotions are increased to such a high level that your ability to reason is decreased. Due to the level of emotion in a heated argument, the brain itself is in fight or flight mode. The emotional part of the brain does not understand the difference between a true fight, a heated argument or stressful event and—voilà!—the protective measures kick in and a response you later regret is the result. The same science may explain why some individuals are more prone to be violent offenders even to their own family members. It may also be instrumental in understanding mental illness and what the various mental disorders can do to the brain.

The communication strategies are designed to aid in identifying a subject under a strong emotional response and to attempt to engage the rational portions of their brain to reduce the intensity of the response. Again, keep in mind that the brain cannot be at peak reasoning ability while in an extreme emotional response. The goal of our communication process is to bring enough of a balance between reasoning and emotion to allow the subject to "see" their options to reason through a successful outcome. It is vitally important that we all understand that sometimes an officer doesn't get the opportunity to begin the communication process due to the violent nature of the suspect or mentally ill person they are confronting. In that case, the officer must defend themselves and innocent people. Within the communication process, the suspect's ability to reason may become so hindered and their emotional response so excessive that a violent response is almost a protective mechanism for the brain in conflict. Unless the situation allows for law enforcement to give time and some space, violence may be inevitable.

The same balance of emotion and reasoning is also happening in every officer's brain when they are involved in tense, uncertain, and ever-changing situations. Tactically speaking, if we want to be able to function under stress and make sound decisions, we must train to control the levels of emotional response, including the fear response. The good news is, it can be trained. We will devote a chapter to using neuroscience to develop effective training programs based on science and not guesswork. The lack of science-based training is the reason you see officers, who are extremely competent at shooting at paper on the range, miss shots at close distances under real stress in the street.

The old-school verbal judo concept was not originally based on neuroscience but now that more information on the brain has become available, we gain a deeper understanding of the benefits of this approach to include our updated version. By having a tactical communication plan, you are engaging the working memory system which is part of the cognitive process. Using this communications strategy makes it easier to avoid a heated, expletive-laced exchange which only serves to excite the emotional sides of both officer and suspect. If the suspect's emotional side becomes heavily engaged and their communication vile and nasty, the officer has an opportunity to remain calm and professional, which gives them cognitive control capabilities over their hopefully well-trained procedural skills. An added benefit, given the immediate access to social media, the officer is then seen acting in a calm professional manner which makes it harder to get a million hits on YouTube.

As part of the communication strategy and evaluation of necessary resources, it's imperative for the officer to continuously evaluate exigence, who's causing it, and the need to possibly give time and space, when practical, to a heavily emotional suspect or mentally ill person. By understanding their own brains in conflict, the officer can start to develop their plans and strategies for controlling their own emotional response to improve their cognitive reasoning ability. Translation? Manage your fears, control your response to emotional triggers, use planning and communications strategies. If the suspect or object of the call created the exigency of a lethal threat, you, the officer, are in the best possible position to deal with the threat and protect innocents and yourself, both at the scene and later in court if the need should arise. By managing our own emotions, we keep our reasoning abilities sharper and more focused on the problem and not creating exigency based on our own actions or emotions. By helping those that we can help, we are ultimately helping ourselves to be better law enforcement officers and, therefore, we have a true win-win situation.

These communication strategies also provide the opportunity to stay left of bang. Of course, the suspect, the subject of the call, or bystanders, can have a say in the matter but by having an established idea for how you want your communication to go, you free up cognitive abilities to continually evaluate for violations of expectations to include resistance, ambush, reaching for a weapon, etc. If all else fails and violence is imminent, a well-trained officer with sound procedural skills maintains the ability to execute cognitive control for decisions like shoot or no-shoot, shoot but civilians or officers are in the line of fire, or a shoot that quickly changes to a no-shoot or vise-versa.

Another key aspect to both the tactical communications strategies, including the ABC planning we will introduce next, is the ability they provide to reduce the effects of multitasking. We all want to believe in our ability to multi-task, but science does not support this. Communicating with people, watching their hands, establishing baselines and evaluating for violations of expectations while managing emotions, is the ultimate in multitasking. This is the reason we emphasize not trying to handle situations without backup when practical.

Susan Reynolds points out in her book *Fire Up Your Writing Brain*:

> Recent studies have shown that your brain can't do two activities that require cognitive attention simultaneously. (You can eat and read at the same time because eating doesn't require cognitive attention.) When two activities simultaneously engage your prefrontal cortex (thinking brain), it has to shift from one task to the other, even if you think you are doing both at once.

> Basically, when you focus on a cognitive task, the anterior portion of your prefrontal cortex communicates your desire to perform the task to the posterior portion of your prefrontal cortex, and together they execute the task. However, when you add a second cognitive task, the brain has to split or shift from one region to another, assigning either the right or the left side of the brain to the new task, dividing the resources in two. If you add a third cognitive task, studies have shown that you're likely to lose your train of thought and make three times as many errors. These results were discussed in a 2010 French study that also revealed

that the two areas of the brain are, in fact, competing with each other and not working together, which equated to putting yourself at odds with yourself.

Other studies have shown that multitasking on three or more tasks at once (particularly if they are cognitive tasks, such as reading, writing, or responding to emails) can have the equivalent effect of smoking marijuana or staying up all night, and can reduce adult cognitive capacity to that of an eight-year-old.[10]

Now, let's go out on a limb and assume that the public is not looking for the equivalent of a cop who has stayed up all night, smoked marijuana, or has the cognitive abilities of an eight-year-old making life and death decisions. By reducing multitasking, we free up cognitive space for appraisal and problem solving, thus enhancing our ability to maintain control over the emotional side of the brain which can spike when the cognitive overload becomes too great.

The ABCs of Strategy

The A, B, and C planning format is used by tactical teams around the world and is sometimes taught as a primary plan, a backup plan, and an emergency plan (for when our Verbal Judo mentioned earlier fails). Unfortunately, we rarely teach these concepts at the basic academy level. I once had a kickboxing coach named Dale Minor who helped start me down the road to preparing to become a law enforcement officer. Dale used to always say if you run to the center of the ring and just start swinging, you may show you're tough, but you

---

[10] Susan Reynolds. *Fire Up Your Writing Brain: How to Use Proven Neuroscience to Become a More Creative, Productive, and Successful Writer* (Blue Ash, OH: Writer's Digest Books, 2015), 21-22.

are going to take way more hits than you need to. His philosophy was to always begin with the end in mind. What does this fight look like when it's over and how are we going to get there? ABC planning is just that; begin with the end in mind. Have an idea of what the end of the situation in question looks like and have several ideas for how you are going to get there. With that said, let's look at the plans.

The A Plan

The A plan is the easiest plan to develop because, while there are a wide variety of calls an officer goes to, there are many tactical preparation strategies and concepts that work across this spectrum of calls. The A plan is how I want this call to go if everyone at the scene recognizes my lawful authority and is compliant with my directives. I "ask" and they agree to comply with my request. By some estimates, 98.9 percent of police calls for service go according to plan. The most important part of the A plan is to establish your lawful presence and authority to show you're prepared for possible trouble by how you place yourself at the scene, how you manage your emotions, and how you take control of the scene. In the end, that is exactly what police officers are paid to do: take control of whatever situation they are lawfully present for and successfully manage the situation to the most positive conclusion the parties involved will allow. Part of the A plan are the things you and other officers do to hedge your bets in case the situation gets violent. How you look, how you act, how you communicate, are all indicators to a suspect or any other party involved in the call for whether or not you are prepared. This is important because in interviews with suspects who attacked or killed law enforcement officers one of the deciding factors on whether the suspect was going to attack the officer was how prepared the officer looked, how they positioned themselves, and how direct and confident they were with their communications.

The United States Marine Corps, as we previously discussed, use a concept called left of bang to describe the fact
that everything you do, see, comprehend, and act on before
the shots are fired or the violence begins, matters. It matters
a lot as you should see upon completing this book. If everything you do or don't do before the shooting or violence
starts happens left of bang and everything after is right of
bang then, in your tactical planning your A and B plans happen left of bang. The C plan occurs right of bang. There is a
list too long to include all the things that can be done left of
bang to either prevent violence or place yourself in the most
effective position to deal with the violence. But here, at least,
are some thoughts to get the ideas flowing. For those reading
this that are not interested in specific law enforcement training concepts, please feel free to skip to the end of the list as
it gets a little lengthy.

1. If this goes bad, where is my last point of cover (stops
   a bullet) or concealment (hides you)? The brain under
   stress does not perform well unless it is effectively
   trained to do so. By giving yourself an idea of where to
   go if things go bad, you are pre-loading the brain for
   peak performance. We will discuss the brain science
   later, but keep in mind the old axiom, "failure to plan is
   planning to fail." The idea of last point of cover works
   in every law enforcement contact including traffic
   stops.

2. Parking away from the scene to avoid being ambushed
   while getting out of the car and give yourself time to
   evaluate the scene gives time and space to establish
   your left of bang baselines. Time and distance are your
   friend.

3. Bullets are less likely to deflect through a medium at a
   90-degree angle and more likely to deflect at other angles due to a variety of factors. Don't approach win-

dows and doors head on and don't maintain a perimeter on a location while standing directly in the line of sight of doors and windows. As a quick test, look out the front window of your home while standing about five to ten feet back from the window with all interior lights turned off. What can you see? Now stand outside of your house about ten feet back from the window looking into your house and see what you can see. All advantage goes to the person in the house, so plan accordingly. If you were a criminal standing inside your house with a scoped rifle, how easy would it be to shoot anyone directly in front of and across the street from your home? Why would you, as a police officer, want to place yourself in those positions?

4. Don't answer priority calls by yourself. We previously discussed the hazards of multitasking. You cannot track and control multiple people by yourself and every year officers from around the country are killed or seriously hurt trying to do so. If no one is dying, what is the rush and why go in alone?

5. When working with other officers, position yourselves so that you can see each other. If you can't see each other, you can't help each other.

6. Constantly evaluate the resources you need as you are constantly evaluating your plans to bring the call to its conclusion.

7. Use light to your advantage and understand when it's to your disadvantage. The principle of light control is to put more light in front of you and be careful of backlighting. Backlighting is when there is a greater amount of light behind you than in front of you making it easier for someone looking to hurt you to do so.

8. Evaluate what kind of call you are going to and what this call looks like when it's done.

9. Is this a criminal matter or a civil matter?

10. Practice, practice and practice some more. Train in defensive tactics, tactical shooting and decision making, keep up on the laws in your jurisdiction and case law on use of force and dealing with the mentally ill.

11. Constantly assess the surrounding area and make sure you are aware of innocent civilians and work to keep them out of potential harm.

12. Assess your less than lethal options and have them available and positioned tactically.

13. You choose the location of the traffic stop or contact. Always tilt the odds in your favor.

14. Constantly practice building searches and suspect searches so you are learning to tactically cover the angles. It's all about the angles and who uses them to their advantage.

15. Remember the lawful but awfuls and recognize when your call or contact may be headed down that road.

16. Learn to read people and recognize pre-flight or pre-fight indicators.

17. Always explain your lawful authority and purpose. You would be amazed how many officers forget to establish this baseline from the start of the interaction.

18. If you can't see the suspect's hands or are unsure of what is in them, move to assess and identify. Action is faster than reaction so the only way to change the suspect's focus is to not be where they expect you to be.

Again, this is not an all-inclusive list, just ideas for some of the things you can do left of bang to try and take control of the situation. Each of these examples can and should be ingrained into your cognitive appraisal process and mental models (ABC planning).

So, let's say you are going to a domestic violence call at a home and the information is that three adults are in the house but only two of them, a man and woman are having a physical altercation. You are riding with a partner and the A plan should be developed on the way to the call. Your A plan for this call may include parking three to five houses down and getting a feel for the neighborhood and the house you are going to. You can discuss separating the involved parties as soon as possible while keeping track of each other and the involved parties. Realizing you are two people trying to control three, you may call for another unit. If someone has committed a crime and an arrest is going to be made, take control as soon as practical. These are just some of the preparations that can be part of the A plan.

Always keep in mind what the end of this call looks like. Is someone under arrest or are we just giving out civil information? Always understand that 99 percent of your calls and contacts will end the way you want them to, but your planning and preparation puts you in the best position to deal with the one percent that don't go exactly as planned. Using the tactical communications strategies is also part of your A and B plans, when feasible. They engage the working memory which helps in controlling the emotional response, as well as acting as a "bridge" to declarative and procedural memory systems for faster acquisitions.

The B Plan

The B plan is for what happens when things are not quite going as planned but there is no violence directed at officers yet. The B plan is for your normal contingencies: the suspect resists by passive or defensive resistance, the facts as given turn out to be incorrect, control is slipping but not lost, or more or different resources are required and your ideas of how to work the call to a conclusion have changed. The B plan is also for situations that have de-escalated from lethal or situations where within the A plan we are at the "make" stage and are prepared for and can defend our decision to use less lethal options to control the situation. This brings up an important concept. De-escalation is not a guarantee that everyone will come home safe, just the best hedge we can produce at the time. If a violent suspect attempts to kill an officer or innocent person, the officer must stop the threat, and if the suspect is killed, that situation was de-escalated by force. If the A plan isn't working, and at the "make" stage we use less lethal technologies to gain control successfully, the situation has been de-escalated by less than lethal force. In a perfect world, all our plans would work and everyone, including the suspect, would be brought in safely, which is certainly part of our plan, but it is not reality in all cases.

Say you and several other officers have been dispatched to a busy parking lot at a strip mall where a mentally disturbed man is walking around with a bat in one hand and a machete in the other. The caller states the man appears to be extremely agitated and their concern is that he is going to hurt someone. You have several officers responding and are already formulating a plan to contain the subject and begin communicating while evacuating innocent people. You have already established who will communicate and you understand that multiple officers all yelling at the same time will create a chaotic environment thus potentially over-stimulating the suspect's emotional brain, so one person will do the talking. Officers have been given assignments to include Taser and stun-bag (designated shotgun used for less than lethal force which fires a bean bag inducing pain on impact), both with an officer covering them with a lethal force option if needed.

As you put your small teams together at the scene, the subject in question retreats to a grassy area with a couple of trees off to one side of the large parking lot. The A plan is to keep him on the grass island, clear the fields of fire of civilians, and attempt to open lines of communication. You announce your authority and purpose, and try to start communications, but the subject does not appear to recognize who you are or understand what you are asking him to do. After several minutes and only one-way communication, the subject becomes agitated and starts waving the knife and bat as if fighting off an imaginary beast. As your teams talk to each other you decide this subject is not leaving the grass island and sooner or later he is going to attempt to do so. There are still plenty of civilians in the parking lot and more and more of them are watching you instead of leaving. Your A plan is containing the subject for now, but the major concern is if he can circle around your teams or move between them thus creating a crossfire (officers pointing their guns at one another).

For the safety of all parties involved you move to plan B before the situation can escalate. Part of the B plan is recognizing the potential crossfire if the suspect moves directly between the teams. Understanding the brain science also helps the officers to understand that in a heightened emotional state, they may lose cognitive function and not recognize the crossfire due to an amygdala dump. The teams remind each other to be prepared to move if a crossfire occurs. That reminder reengages working memory and aids in quick decision-making. Team one begins deploying less lethal stunbag rounds with no major effect other than to distract the subject from team two's movement. Team two deploys a Taser which drops the subject to the ground. The teams use shields to approach and clear the weapons away from the subject and he is taken into custody. He is then transported to a mental health facility after he is found to have an outstanding pickup order for a mental health evaluation. This is an example of a transition from plan A to plan B with a successful conclusion all left of bang.

It is important to continuously evaluate the A plan and decide when the B plan is your best viable option. In the past, supervisors have sometimes taken the option of *not* deciding and waiting to see what happens even after indicators are showing your personnel that things are not going your way. Sometimes de-escalation means using force to accomplish the mission thus making it safer for all parties involved, including your suspect/mentally ill subject. Keep in mind the difference between dealing with people who have committed a crime and those who are mentally ill. The decision to use less lethal force on a mentally ill subject who has not committed a crime should be based on the level of threat they pose to themselves or others as in the example listed above. Cognitive appraisal of the situation with the working memory engaged will aid not only in the development of plans but help assess when the A plan must be adapted or switched over to a B plan.

You may be questioning how a less than lethal use of force deployment can be considered left of bang. If you think about it, there was in fact a bang episode. Law enforcement is attempting to prevent the suspect from creating "bang" thus forcing officers to be reactive. When the decision to use less than lethal technology is made, officers are attempting to stay left of bang in their brain processing while putting the suspect, right of bang, in his mental processing. Unless the less than lethal technology can fully incapacitate the subject, the subject must make a conscious choice to submit to law enforcement.

The C Plan

The C plan is your immediate emergency action plan for the sudden act of violence, the ambush, the active shooter, or the hostage situation. Prior ideas for immediate action drills should already be established and trained under stressors, because performance under stress without pre-planning and training under stress can be compromised. This is probably the most under-trained, and under-planned event that most police officers face. In the training section we will explain in more detail how I think this training needs to be accomplished in the future.

It is important to pre-plan for what to do in situations like an ambush while you are in your car. If possible, accelerating through and out of the ambush area is a sound choice. If it's not feasible to move the car, get out and move to cover. Every year officers are killed in ambush situations in a variety of circumstances and we can learn from each of them. In your A plan, if you identified the last point of cover (something that stops a bullet), then your movement to that point is part of your C plan. It is important to explain to anyone you train in the concepts of de-escalation that once we hit the C plan, de-escalation is probably only going to occur after force has been applied, either lethal or less lethal depending on the circumstances. In an active shooter situation, prior planning will aid in decision-making, such as understanding that it is usually beneficial to move immediately to contact with the suspect to get "pressure" on him instead of waiting for a team. Part of C planning is also understanding in what situations it may be more beneficial to wait for other assistance.

C planning includes ground-fighting, weapon retention, shooting on the move and training to differentiate between weapons and objects. As part of the C planning preparation, an officer should stay on top of current brain science and understand that a suspect may be in such a heavy emotional state that they have lost cognitive control. This may account for why suspects reach into the waistband area for objects other than weapons, like cell phones and wallets, when confronted by police. The suspect may believe that the officer will move to cover instead of pursuing if they make a move for an object in their waistband. A well-trained cop should move to cover, but the brain may default under stress to stand still like most officers do during range training.

No matter how good your plans are and how well your personnel are positioned, the suspect or mentally disturbed individual still has a say in how this matter is resolved. Sometimes, despite the fact they see overwhelming odds and no chance to win, or because they are mentally ill and not processing information correctly, they present a lethal threat that must be dealt with. Know the law, understand the rights given to you as an officer of the law, and deal with the situation effectively and expediently.

Teaching law enforcement officers can be challenging and incredibly frustrating at times. Normally when teaching this model to experienced officers we end up with the question, "Are you telling me that if I get out of my patrol car and a guy attacks me, I am expected to run through all this dialogue and plans?" This leads to the most repeated words in any city policy book as it relates to police procedures, "...when practical."

Police officers do not like change, they like to know what they know and stay set in their ways. This is an implicit bias of the emotional system called the Dunning-Kruger effect. The most popular phrase you will hear in relation to law enforcement training is, "Well, that's the way we have always done it and I don't see any reason why we need to change." When practical, use the communications "Verbal Judo" model. When it's not practical, then your ABC planning and preparation will give you the best chance to effectively deal with the ever-changing circumstances of potentially violent encounters.

With the prevalence of cameras available to the average citizen, as well as the cameras worn by the officers themselves in an increasing number of cases, it is vital that we are seen acting in a calm, professional manner. The intent to act in a calm, professional manner has the added benefit of aiding the officer in controlling the emotional response by engaging the cognitive system. We all win.

It is important for all parties to realize that once you point a gun at a police officer, de-escalation strategies default to the C planning and preparation. To expect an officer to begin negotiation strategies with a gun pointed at their head is ridiculous and is an unreasonable expectation. It is vital that police create time and distance opportunities when practical to place themselves in the best position to effectively deal with the circumstances and bring the situation to the safest possible conclusion. When practical, the goal is to show the suspect or the mentally ill individual that we have a sound tactical plan; that our goal is to bring them in unhurt, if possible, and to give them the opportunity to realize the odds are not in their favor. When dealing with suspects, this is usually an effective strategy for a safe conclusion for all parties involved.

When dealing with the mentally ill, it is important to recognize the moments where they are not engaging the higher cognitive brain functions and are stuck in an emotional, survival, extreme fight or flight response. The easiest way to tell if they are in an extreme emotional response is to ask them a question. Answering a question requires higher brain (cognitive) function and that is where our ability to reason lies. Without that ability to reason, the answer from a suspect or mentally ill subject will necessarily be a violent one. In the case of mentally ill subjects, it is important to note that being in a low brain survival response requires a lot of physical and emotional energy.

When practical, we can give them time and distance to burn off energy and hopefully have an opportunity to engage the higher brain and find a reasonable conclusion. This is the strategy the SWAT team has successfully used time and time again to safely bring in mentally ill subjects. This is not a guarantee because in all situations both criminals and the mentally ill have a say in how the situation is concluded. We can't stop them from pushing a violent situation, we can only give them the room to make a sound decision reference their own safety when practical. Time and distance can be used to give opportunities to engage the reasoning portions of the brain instead of a brain caught in an extreme fight or flight response.

CHAPTER THREE

GRAHAM V. *CONNOR*; THE OBJECTIVE REASONABLENESS STANDARD

The law is reason free from passion.

– Aristotle

Now let's look at what the Supreme Court and several of the lower courts have written on police use of force. Police training programs that are not based on the current case law and pertinent issues involving police use of force are not training our officers to respond according to the law and in some cases, can be detrimental to officers' performance under stress.

Knowledge of case law and the laws of your jurisdiction aid in your ABC planning and how to articulate moving from one plan to another according to the situation. Knowing the law aids in the report writing phase, and helps officers present their testimony in court. In other words, knowledge of the law increases declarative knowledge of the subject matter which will aid in developing your ABC plans and preparing for violations of expectations. While individual situations are different, there are enough commonalities that we should be constantly evaluating cases from other jurisdictions and your own agency to improve the decision-making processes for your officers.

In the landmark case of *Graham* v. *Connor*, the court established clear guidelines for how police use of force should be viewed, in this case, and in all future cases. The Supreme Court, in their decision, cleared up some of the past issues with lower courts' judgments of police use of force. The court made it clear that police officers sometimes must make quick decisions based on incomplete information. The court reasoned it is not fair to judge officers based on what you think they should have done once all the facts and circumstances are known to you and from the comfort of an easy chair. The judges also knew that Aristotle had it right in the quote that starts this chapter. Reason and not emotions (passion) must guide the law and how it is judged. The science in this book explains why.

Graham v. *Connor*, 490 U.S. 386 (1989)

Graham was a diabetic and suffering from low blood sugar. A friend dropped him off at a convenience store to get a quick sugar snack. The store was crowded. Graham, not thinking clearly due to a blood sugar crash, immediately exited, ran to the car and the car sped away to find another store. A police officer parked across the street witnessed Graham's behavior and became suspicious, thinking a robbery or grab-and-go shoplifting may have occurred. The officer stopped the car and called for backup. The backup officers stayed with the car and its occupants while the originating officer contacted the clerk of the store. Graham, now with his blood sugar crashing, began to have a medical episode which included what the officers concluded to be bizarre behavior involving drugs or alcohol. Graham exited the vehicle, ran around the vehicle twice and then fell to the pavement. A use of force incident then occurred with Graham's friend trying to tell the officers that Graham needed immediate medical care while the officers believed they needed to establish control of a potential robbery suspect. Graham's injuries included a broken foot, an injured shoulder, and the claim he suffered from ringing in his ears from officers slamming his head into the hood of a patrol car. This is not all the details, but it reflects some of the key components of the case. Was Graham a criminal? No, he was not. Did the backup officers know that? No, they did not. The question may arise, should the officers have taken the medical claims of the need for sugar into account? The answer is, according to the court, it all depends on the articulation of the officers and the objective reasonableness of their actions. Graham sued the city of Charlotte, North Carolina and all the officers involved in this incident for excessive force, failure of the city to train personnel on medical emergencies, and discrimination based on handicap (diabetes). His complaint included false imprisonment by the officers and intentional infliction of emotional distress.

In the initial case in the federal court holding jurisdiction over North Carolina, the judges decided not to send the case to a jury trial and denied Graham's case. Their judgements were based on findings from *Johnson v. Glick*, a 1973 case out of the 2nd circuit court. In the Johnson case, an arrested man detained for trial, accused a detention officer of excessive force. Here, the subjective mental state of the offending officer was relevant as a factor to help determine actionable injury. The question asked by this decision was, "Is the officer's conduct shocking to the conscience?" The problem of the "shocking to the conscience" measurement is whose conscience are we talking about? To the average person, any police use of force looks horrible. Violence is not pretty and only Hollywood can make it seem sexy and cool. Movies are choreographed and can make a physical altercation look easy when they are much more complex in real life.

The judges in that case used a four-pronged approach to

establish precedent in this case.

1. The need for the application of force.
2. The relationship between the need and amount of force used.
3. The extent of injury.
4. Whether force applied was in a good-faith effort to maintain or restore discipline or maliciously and sadistically for the very purpose of causing harm.

These findings were based on the due process clause of the Fourteenth Amendment, which deals with the administration of justice and acts as a safeguard from denial of life, liberty, or property by the government outside the sanctions of law.

Graham appealed the decision based on the belief that the evidence presented was enough to warrant a jury trial to question whether the officers use of force and refusal to provide medical care was constitutionally unreasonable. Graham further argued in his appeal that the court used an incorrect legal standard when it examined the evidence related to the excessive force claim. The case was then taken up by the Supreme Court of the United States. The supreme court ruled in Graham's favor based on the fact they also believed the incorrect legal standard was used in judgement.

The key elements of the *Graham* v. *Connor* standard for looking at police use of force are based on a Fourth Amendment seizure and are established in three key points by the supreme court:

1. What is the severity of the crime? Based on the officers articulated beliefs at the time and not in hindsight after all the facts are known.
2. Did the subject pose an immediate threat to the safety of officers or others? Based on the officer's articulated beliefs at the time of the incident.

3. Was the subject actively resisting arrest or attempting to evade arrest by flight?

So, when we are looking at a police officer use of force the first thing we should look at are the facts as they are relevant to the three points listed above. After that, we look at the "objective reasonableness" of the use of force. In the *Graham* decision the court stated, "The calculus of reasonableness must embody allowance for the fact that police officers are often forced to make split-second judgments—in circumstances that are tense, uncertain, and rapidly evolving—about the amount of force that is necessary in a particular situation." The court went on to say that "reasonableness" is to be judged from the perspective of a reasonable officer at the scene, with similar training and experience, rather than after the fact with 20/20 hindsight. Notice it states, "...judged from the perspective of a reasonable officer at the scene," and not a reasonable citizen.

Prior to 1989, the various courts' viewing of police use of force was ambiguous at best and the courts used a decision established in the 1973 *Johnson v. Glick* case that we mentioned earlier.

In numerous use-of-force cases, judges have advised that police officers must infer the intent of a suspect based on the suspect's behaviors. Unfortunately, sometimes the person confronted is mistaken for a criminal based on behavior or description. Mistakes of fact also happen when the subject of a call or stop is intoxicated or under the influence of drugs or their reasoning is affected by mental illness or a medical condition (like in Graham's case). Inferences are made, and in some cases, mistakes are made. The *Graham* decision gave a method for judging a use-of-force case. Considering what the officer believed and can articulate at the time of the use of force matters. Providing a Fourth Amendment seizure using the objective reasonableness standard as a guideline, the Supreme Court sent the case back to the district court for a finding. Using the Supreme Court guidelines, the district court again ruled against Graham. Graham's own testimony, the testimony of his expert medical witness, and the driver of the car, William Berry, were factors in the final decision. Graham testified the officers slammed him face first into the hood of a patrol car causing ringing in his ears which never went away. William Berry testified they pushed his head down when he resisted handcuffing but did not forcefully slam it into the hood of the car. William Berry testified that Graham's behavior was so erratic due to the diabetes that he asked the officers for assistance in restraining him. Graham's own expert medical witness said it was appropriate to restrain him given the circumstances. Graham's injuries, including the broken foot, were consistent with him resisting restraint while being placed into a police car and not consistent with physical assault. This case was a tragic mistake-of-fact episode that turned into a court case that sets the precedent for the way all future police use-of-force cases would be judged. Could the police have acted better? Yes. Did what they do amount to a crime, or gross misconduct, given the facts and circumstances known to them at the time? According to the court, no it did not.

I can tell you from twenty-five years of law enforcement experience that no altercation is easy because the subject involved in the altercation with police also has a say in the matter. The officer must account for the fact that a physical altercation can quickly escalate to a situation where weapons are presented (including attempts to disarm the officer) and deadly force decisions must be made. The officers in most cases are going out of their way not to hurt the individuals who are resisting arrest but not attempting to hurt the officer.

The *Graham* decision articulated that the Supreme Court did not believe the Fourteenth Amendment standard should be used in judging police use of force. Instead, they deemed the use of force by a police officer should be evaluated as a Fourth Amendment seizure using the "objective reasonableness" standard. The *Graham* decision also established that the underlying intent of an officer should not be a consideration. For example, the argument that an officer is racist and therefore used force because of his racist tendencies. The Supreme Court dismissed underlying intent because a racist cop could still have a good use of force, and a police officer that everyone considers a "saint" could have a bad use of force. The case established that judgments should be based on facts and the totality of circumstances known to the officer at the time without regards to underlying intent. Based on those facts and circumstances, would a reasonable officer of similar training and experience make the same decisions? It is obvious by reading the case and judgments that the court carefully considered how difficult it is to make decisions under "tense, uncertain, and ever-changing circumstances." The court understood that mistakes-of-fact use of force, where the officer believes one thing, but it turns out not to be true, have happened and would happen again. It was important to establish a way of looking carefully at the cases while accounting for how difficult it must be to make life-changing decisions based on limited information and in compressed time frames.

The Supreme Court also understood there is no way to make any police use of force look good to the average person. It's important to note that when this decision was made, the prevalence of security cameras, phone cameras, and body cameras did not exist. It's one thing to hear about an incident to consider the different sides of the story and another to witness the situation on video. When looking at police incidents on video, it is easy to make quick judgments based on your own limited experience. The same mistake is made when you watch professional sports and your team is not performing well; you comment on what you would do if you were on the field. This is using declarative knowledge to create a mental simulation/fantasy that includes your procedural skills evaluated at the same level of a professional athlete.

If you really want to see a prime example of how carried away individuals can get with their opinions, go to a public venue to watch a combative sport like boxing or mixed martial arts and listen to the crowd and their "advice" to the fighters. Most of the people watching these events are not in the mental or physical condition of a professional fighter and, in fact, have never fought competitively in front of a crowd. Yet, these individuals, with no experience at dealing with close-quarter conflict, have strong opinions of how the professionals should fight. To me there is nothing worse than someone who says, "If it were me, I would have done it differently." My answer, based on science, is you have no idea what you would do until the stress and pressure is real and the pending violence is close and personal. Everything else is pure fantasy. I don't say this to be harsh, only to provide information based on experience and science.

The audience gets the big picture from a distance with no threat to themselves while the fighters get a smaller picture under a fight or flight brain response. Time and distance are perceived differently under stress and at variable distances. It is important to understand that the supreme court understood the average individual's proclivity to judge incidents in 20/20 hindsight from the comfort of a chair. Their decision established a way to fairly judge an incident knowing that after the fact, all the details are known, but at the time the officers were working without the benefit of 20/20 hindsight.

Graham v. *Connor* established the "objective reasonableness" standard for judging police use-of-force cases. This "reasonableness" is based on the following factors:

1. The totality of the circumstances.

2. From the perspective of a reasonable officer.

3. Perspective based on an officer at the scene with similar training and experience.

4. Judgment based on the moment force was used.

5. Judgment cannot come from 20/20 hindsight.

6. Must understand decisions were made in circumstances that are tense, uncertain, and rapidly evolving.

The court listed three factors which, along with the above listed measures, could be used to determine the reasonableness of a police officer use of force.

1. The severity of the crime.

2. Whether the suspect was an immediate threat to the officers or others.

3. How the subject was actively resisting arrest or attempting to evade arrest by flight.

Also, it's important to remember that the articulated facts of the case are more important than even a video of the event because the video evidence is judged from hindsight at a distance. I would stress to any law enforcement officer reading this to develop their report writing strategies to ensure all the relevant facts are included by writing the report to the *Graham* v. *Connor* standard while it is the law of the land.

The other relevant facts include but are not limited to:

1. Number of suspects compared to number of officers.

2. Size and apparent abilities of suspect.

3. Known alcohol or drug involvement or perceived by experience.

4. Known mental illness of suspect.

5. Is suspect armed and proximity of weapons.

6. Known violent history of suspect.

7. Environmental factors: day, night, hot, cold, wet, heights or terrain factors.

8. Injuries to officer.

9. Did the suspect exhibit pre-assault indicators like clenching of the fists, shifting of weight, fixed gaze on officer's weapon etc., which are all Left of Bang indicators?

10. From experience does the officer perceive the subject to be armed based on indicators like bulge in clothing or touching the waistband area to ensure the weapon is there and concealed?

This is not an all-inclusive list, of course, just some things to consider. To bring it into perspective, here is an example of how the same call taken by two different officers can be viewed in different ways.

Let's say a young female police officer (approximately five foot four and a hundred and ten pounds) is responding to a domestic violence call involving a known suspect husband who is six foot four and two hundred and fifty pounds of steroid-induced glory. The husband has been arrested numerous times for domestic violence and always resists arrest. The officer, knowing the suspect is dangerous, arrives on scene but is waiting to make contact until her backup arrives. Backup is three minutes out but now she hears the woman inside the house screaming in, what the officer believes to be, life-threatening terror. She decides to try to help the woman and advises her backup to step it up (get there quicker) as she knocks on the door to the residence. There is no answer and the woman is still screaming.

Due to the nature of the screams for help, she decides to enter. In the living room she sees the husband standing over the wife punching her in the face. The officer moves toward the suspect and orders him to move away and submit to arrest. The husband pushes the officer away and moves back toward his wife to strike her. The officer moves between the husband and wife and kicks the male in the groin and then knees him in the face while he is bent over. She is then able to place him in handcuffs. Does this use of force seem reasonable based on the totality of the circumstances?

Here are just some of the facts needed in the officer's use-of-force report: Her size relative to his. His past resistance when arrested. The need for medical attention for the wife and evaluation of how long she goes untreated while the officer fights with the suspect. The suspect's ability to arm himself if he renders the officer unconscious before backup arrives, and her ability to control the subject without striking given the size differences.

Now, say that the husband gets a lawyer and files an excessive force complaint against the officer and her department. Given the listed facts and placing these facts into a *Graham* v. *Connor* context, we arrive at the following:

1. What is the severity of the crime? Aggravated assault on the wife and aggravated assault on the officer.

2. Was the suspect an immediate threat to the officer or others? Yes, the officer perceived the immediate threat to the wife and had already recognized the threat of the husband to her safety by conduct and previous actions.

3. Was the suspect actively resisting arrest or attempting to evade arrest by flight? Yes, by failure to obey initial commands and by pushing the officer away.

Looking at the totality of the circumstances, do you think the Supreme Court would rule in the officer's favor if this case were to work its way to their court?

Now flip the script a little. Say the officer in the example is male and is six foot four and two hundred and forty pounds and the suspect is five foot five and one hundred and fifty pounds. The officer makes the same decision to go into the house due to exigent circumstances and when he tries to intervene the suspect tries to push him away, but it is unsuccessful. The officer then kicks the suspect in the groin and knees him in the head knocking him unconscious. Will this be looked at differently at the Supreme Court level if an excessive force complaint makes its way to the highest court? Differently, yes, but that doesn't mean in the end the officer will be found guilty. In this case the size difference between the two could make a difference because the officer must be able to articulate the threat to himself or another. For instance, if the wife appears to be badly hurt, the longer it takes to take the husband into custody, the longer she must wait for medical treatment. Just because the suspect is smaller doesn't mean the outcome is inevitable. The totality of the circumstances matter. The court may have issues with the choice of force by the officer against a suspect they outweigh by one hundred pounds. The next decision to make is to look at how the force was applied and decide whether the court believes the use of force was attributed to "extralegal violence" or "unnecessary violence."

Extralegal violence is a willful or wrongful use of force by officers who knowingly exceed the bounds of office. Unnecessary violence is by well-meaning officers who prove incapable of dealing with the situation they encountered without a needless or hasty resort to force. I can't say for sure what the court would decide if presented with this case but the problem for the officer could be the reasonableness argument of an officer with similar training and experience. This would be where the officer's initial articulation in the report could make all the difference. The court is looking at three decision-making issues measured against two critical threat issues.

The decisions evaluated are usually:

1. How did the officer determine a threat existed?

2. How did the officer determine the grievousness of the threat?

3. How did the officer choose to control or remove the threat?

The two critical threats evaluated are:

1. Was the suspect attempting to escape?

2. What was the degree of physical threat to the officer or another?

In the findings of the *Graham* decision, you find the context for contributing factors listed above where it states, "in order for an officer's use of force to be deemed 'objectively reasonable,' his/her force response (the 'what' and 'how') must be reasonably balanced with the governmental interests at stake (the 'why')."

The courts understand that when a law is broken, and the police are making an arrest it is against the law to resist that arrest. Each suspect can choose to comply, and in most of the cases involving accusations of excessive use of force by police, the use of force begins after the suspect's verbal or behavioral non-compliance. Read the case laws involving use of force by police and you will repeatedly see a variation in wording indicating that, if the suspect had followed the law and complied, the use of force may have been prevented. The suspect or mentally ill subject has a say in how the encounter will end. This is not blanket coverage for the police to use excessive force, just an understanding of the complexities that come with enforcing the law.

When teaching our de-escalation program, we do a review of the three points of the *Graham* v. *Connor* case mentioned earlier and some of the opinions listed within. On numerous occasions I have had officers tell me they have never heard of the decision and didn't know there were guidelines in place for how use of force is judged. If that sounds crazy, a former chief of police of a major Arizona law enforcement agency was asked about the *Graham* v. *Connor* decision and he indicated he had no knowledge of the case. If you understand this case, it makes your decision-making process more streamlined and your ability to articulate your use of force that much easier. An added benefit of having a thorough working knowledge of this case is that it gives you everything you need to write a good use-of-force report and prepare your testimony for court. If you are not in law enforcement, an understanding of this case makes it easier to understand why social perceptions and legal perceptions are completely different. Remember Aristotle, reason free from passion.

The lower courts have also written briefs involving police use of force that convey their understanding of the complexities involved with judging a police officer's actions. Remember, the courts understand and want everyone else to understand that the law gives police officers the ability to use force to gain compliance. When judging a police officer's use of force, the fact that force was used is usually not the issue. The question is, "Was the use of force reasonable and necessary given the circumstances?" The following review of some briefs written for lower court rulings involving police use of force may aid in understanding.

Martinez v. County of Los Angeles, 47 Cal. App 4th

The officers in this case believed Martinez was high on PCP. Martinez approached the officers shouting, "Kill me, shoot me!" while holding a 12-inch kitchen knife with an 8-inch blade. Officers fired their weapons killing Martinez. The family of Martinez sued for excessive force.

The judge wrote, "We must never allow the theoretical sanitized world of our imagination to replace the dangerous and complex world that policemen face every day. What constitutes 'reasonable' action, may seem quite different to someone facing a possible assailant than someone analyzing the question at leisure." In the same brief the judge quoted a first circuit ruling from another case when he wrote, "It makes sense to surround the police who make these on the spot choices in dangerous situations with a fairly wide zone of protection in close cases."

Thompson v. Hubbard 257 F, 3d 896 (2001)

The police are at a call for gunshots fired. Thompson sees the police and starts to run. He matches the description of the shooter given by the caller, and the police start to chase. The suspect makes a movement, while running, to his waistband in what the officer believed to be the movement to a gun. The officer fired his service weapon killing Thompson.

A lower court indicated the officer should have considered the fact that Thompson's pants were so loose, they could not hold a weapon. The Eight Circuit Court of Appeals found the following: "We disagree with the plaintiffs' contention that if, as Hubbard maintains, Thompson turned and looked at him while the two were in close proximity and moved as though reaching for a weapon, a jury could conclude that Hubbard's use of deadly force was objectively unreasonable because Hubbard should have considered the fact the waistband of Thompson's sweatpants may not have been strong enough to hold a gun. An officer is not constitutionally required to wait until he sets eyes upon the weapon before employing deadly force to protect himself against a fleeing suspect who turns and moves as though to draw a gun."

The key element here is there was no video evidence to support or deny the officer's claims. With video more prevalent since this 2001 case, these mistakes of fact are becoming more of a potential issue. Adjusting training according to science, could address this issue from the police perspective before the judges do.

This again emphasizes the officer's belief based on what they were experiencing at the time and is vital when judging these cases. Why? Because there must be some leeway given to police officers who are in these tense, ever-changing moments. Keep in mind, it is not a free pass for misconduct, just an objective way of looking at these cases knowing the difficulties involved with controlling, fighting, and pursuing individuals who are willing to resist arrest or attempt to kill a cop.

We will discuss the science of the brain as well as the science behind action versus reaction and who has the advantage in later chapters, but the courts take these things into account in their findings.

Mistakes of facts happen, but it is important to remember that police officers often act on limited information in compressed time frames. They also sometimes act on incomplete information before all the facts and circumstances can be gathered. The courts wanted to give officers the ability to investigate suspicious circumstances while understanding the fact that sometimes the suspicious circumstance would result in a mistake of fact. Several cases in the past provide examples where a subject with a legitimate reason for having a firearm in his hand is confronted by a police officer. The officer has no idea that the subject is deaf and the victim of a crime. The officer becomes concerned when the subject does not drop the weapon and the deaf subject has no idea the officer is there. Unfortunately, tragedy is sometimes the result when the subject senses movement and moves his eyes and the gun toward what he believes to be a threat. The officer who has been giving commands now sees a gun turning his way and makes a quick decision. Does it make the officer wrong? No, based on the science and a hunch played by the emotional system, it makes him completely human.

I recommend to anyone I train, and my department has made the recommendation, that all use-of-force reports begin with the key components of the *Graham* v. *Connor* standard. This immediately establishes the most important aspects of the use of force and makes it easier for officers to ensure they don't miss key details in their report.

Allow me to make a quick digression: The day I started writing this section of the book was November 4, 2016. A year later, media outlets are reporting that lethal ambushes of police officers are up 167 percent. On November 4, 2017, two NYPD officers were responding to an armed robbery call which resulted in a shootout with the suspect leaving two officers shot, one of them fatally. Two Missouri officers were shot in the face on the same day going to a possible active shooter situation. Fortunately, in this case, the suspect's shotgun was loaded with birdshot and it looks like both are going to recover. Within the same week, two Iowa officers were killed in an ambush and three Oklahoma officers were ambushed with two officers killed. The year 2017 was a violent one for law enforcement. My heart breaks for the families and friends of the many law enforcement officers who have died and the future deaths that are sure to come. Meanwhile, many activist organizations, media outlets, politicians, and even one law enforcement organization have railed about police use of force and have repeatedly refused to acknowledge facts. Those facts are that in less than one percent of law enforcement contacts an officer is accused of excessive force or misconduct. And this data is available to anyone seeking to find the truth. Video and media reports of police use of force inspire emotional responses. This is understandable. Emotions, however, as we have discussed, and will discuss some more, can hijack reasoning skills. Facts and the truth matter and each use-of-force case must be evaluated on its own merits with emotions suspended. Easier said than done.

When I designed this program, it was with the idea that tactical planning and good communication strategies could make it safer for officers with the added benefit of practical applications for reducing the "lawful but awfuls." When *Graham* v. *Connor* was written, the judges understood how difficult for officers the decision-making process could be and some of the dangers associated with being a cop. Our programs were designed to improve critical-thinking skills by easing the cognitive load and keeping executive control over emotions.

Being resource driven and understanding the science of the human brain in conflict can, I feel, help officers better train, plan, and deal with potentially violent encounters and hopefully drastically reduce the number of police officers killed in the line of duty. As I said before though, in the process of making things safer for our officers we can also make things safer for all parties involved in an incident, particularly those involved in the potential "lawful but awful" incidents.

The following are a few more cases taken up by federal circuit courts related to police use of force. These cases provide insight into the decision-making process of the judges involved and give a deeper understanding into the complexities of interpreting the law based on the *Graham* standards.

Plakas v. *Drinski, 19 F .3D 1143 (7ᵗʰ Cir. 1994)*

Facts: Plakas was shot once and killed by deputy sheriff Drinski. Plakas approached Drinski in a menacing manner with a fireplace poker in his hands. Plakas told Drinski, "Either you're going to die here or I'm going to die here." A relative of Plakas sued for excessive force.

If the actions of the suspect justify the use of deadly force, the officer is not required to use less than lethal force before employing deadly force. The court noted that, "Where deadly force is otherwise justified under the Constitution, there is no constitutional duty to use non-deadly alternatives first."

Does this seem harsh? The courts understand that if you make the job so hard and ask the police to perform in a way that isn't supported by science, then you risk having no one willing to step up and do the job. When presented with an immediate lethal threat, an officer must respond to that threat or risk death or serious physical injury. For example, say an officer is at a scene with a subject with a gun who has known mental health issues. The subject is waving the gun at the officer and at civilians walking in the area. The officer decides to deploy his Taser to attempt to disarm the subject who is repeatedly pointing his gun at the officer. The Taser is deployed but the subject's movements alter the proper probe spread of the Tasers projectiles. The mentally ill subject then raises the gun and shoots the officer. What has the officer accomplished? Nothing at all.

Here is the balance that I believe our model provides. In this case the first question is, does the officer need to make the original contact without backup? If exigency exists, then make the contact because the officer is not the one creating the exigency. The exigency should be caused by the suspect/subject of the call or by the situation itself, but not by the officer. If there is no need for immediate contact then wait, attempt to contain, and use resources to solve the problem (including an officer ready to deploy lethal force providing cover for the officers ready to deploy less lethal force).

The courts are starting to look at the issue of who at the scene created the exigency of the situation. I believe sometime soon we will see a finding where the courts start judging officers who create exigent circumstances differently than cases where the situation, the subject of the call, or a suspect creates the exigency. But remember, in any case where a lethal threat is presented to an officer, the fastest way to eliminate that threat is to completely incapacitate it. The only true way to incapacitate a threat posing immediate lethal force is to kill, render unconscious, or incapacitate the physiology (massive blood loss, or brain systems) of the subject. Harsh? Maybe, but the courts understand that only a select few members of society will take on the responsibility of becoming a police officer, and they can only assume how hard these decisions are to make unless they have worn the belt and badge and walked the beat. In the Plakas case, all exigency was created by Plakas.

Glenn v. Washington County, 661 F. 3d 460 (9th Cir. 2011)

Facts: Lukus Glenn was drunk and armed with a pocket knife. He held the knife to his throat and threatened to commit suicide. The police shot him six times with a bean bag shotgun. As he moved away from the shots, other officers shot him multiple times with their pistols, killing him.

The Court held that police are justified in using deadly force to stop someone from being a threat to the police or others. It does not include the subject themselves. The court further stated "...officers could have used some reasonable level of force to prevent Lukus from taking a suicidal act. But we are not aware of published cases holding it reasonable to use a significant amount of force to try to stop someone from attempting suicide. Indeed, it would be odd to permit officers to use force capable of causing serious injury or death in an effort to prevent the possibility that an individual might attempt to harm only himself. We do not rule out that in some circumstances some force might be warranted to prevent suicide, but in cases like this one the 'solution' could be worse than the problem. Based on the facts presented here, viewed favorably to the plaintiff, the officer's use of force was not indisputably reasonable."

The deciding factors here were what the officers did to put themselves in the best position to ensure the safety of all parties involved. In this case, a group of officers closed in on the suspect. It was apparent that the bean bag rounds were influencing the suspect causing him to move to avoid them. The officers responded to the suspect's movements by mis-interpreting a threat because they had all moved too close to the suspect. Looking at it from our Tactical Decision Model, who created the exigency here? The court ruled the use of force was excessive and from our new perspectives provided by our decision-making models, we can see the officers cre-ated the exigency by placing themselves in a position to re-spond to less lethal force with lethal force without a signifi-cant threat presented.

This and many other cases make several points clear:

- Being a cop is not easy.
- Use of force cannot be judged by the 20/20 hindsight standard.
- Most use of force can be avoided by compliance of the suspect.

The officer who is dealing with a subject who is resisting arrest must infer the intent of the suspect by the conduct of the suspect.

This last point is extremely important in many of the un-armed-suspect-killed-by-police cases. If an unarmed man is throwing punches, which are landing on an officer's head and face, and the officer feels he is about to lose his ability to adequately defend himself, he must infer the intent of the suspect by his conduct. For example, once the suspect ob-tained the upper hand in the fight, did he attempt to escape from the situation or did he continue to assault? What should the officer assume is going to happen to his duty weapon if he becomes incapacitated? Police officers are given a lot of leeway in use-of-force cases because the courts understand these issues.

Brooks v. City of Seattle, (9ᵗʰ Cir. 2011)

This is an interesting case because here a Taser was used in "drive stun" mode as opposed to a full deployment with probes. A drive stun is when the officer presses the Taser into the suspect instead of deploying probes from a distance.

Facts: This case began with a traffic stop on Brooks, a pregnant female, who refused to sign the issued traffic citation which is an arrestable offense in that particular jurisdiction. She refused to exit the vehicle and resisted attempts to be extracted from the vehicle.

She was then touch-stunned with the Taser on the thigh, on her arm, and finally in the side of the neck where the officers were then able to remove her from the vehicle. She had no lasting injuries and the baby was born healthy several months later. Brooks sued for excessive force and the case ended up at the ninth circuit court. The court found the officer's actions unreasonable and excessive although the brief mentions that Brooks bears some of the responsibility for the escalation of the situation. The court noted that using the *Graham* standard, Brooks' resistance did not involve violence towards the officers and she was not attempting to flee.

Two judges disagreed with portions of the findings. The first judge said Brooks was completely at fault and the officers did an outstanding job showing restraint. The second judge dissented from an excessive force finding saying, "There are only so many ways that a person can be extracted from a vehicle against her will, and none of them is pretty." The court determined the officers were still entitled to Qualified Immunity because the law in this area was not clearly established at the time of the incident.

When looking at Qualified Immunity, the courts usually take a two-pronged approach. The first question is, "Did the officers' conduct violate the United States Constitution?" The second question is, "Should the officers have known that their conduct violated the Constitution or court findings related to the Constitution?" If the answer to both questions is yes, then the officer may find themselves in a separate lawsuit from their jurisdiction. This means that instead of the jurisdiction getting sued with the officer as a witness, the officer is being sued and all of their personal assets are now subject to loss.

These last two cases involve police training in preparation for these "tense, uncertain," and rapidly evolving situations.

City of Canton v. Harris, 489 U.S. 378 (1989)

Facts: In this case, Harris was injured in police custody and in need of medical attention which was never provided. City of Canton policies gave discretion over medical attention to shift commanders who had no medical training.

This case is important because many police agencies train using a lot of classroom time and not a lot of practical procedural training. In this case, the court rejected the notion that "a municipality may shield itself from liability for failure to train its police officers in a given area simply by offering a course nominally covering the subject, regardless of how substandard the content and quality of that training." The quality of the training matters and the end user, the officers, are the ones to decide whether the training covers the subject adequately. It also drives home the importance that when your officers are asking for training they need, and a department refuses to provide it, eventually the decision not to provide the training or nominally covering the topic can come back to haunt the city, county, or state jurisdiction in court.

Zuchel v. *City of Denver, 997 F. 2d 730 (10th Cir. 1993)*

Facts: Officers approached Zuchel who was involved in a previous disturbance at a restaurant. Zuchel was now in a verbal altercation with several teenagers on bikes. As police approached the group, Zuchel had his back to the officers. One of the teenagers yelled to officers that Zuchel had a knife and when Zuchel turned toward officers he was shot and killed. A pair of finger nail clippers was found next to Zuchel. His family sued the city for failure to properly train.

Here, the tenth circuit court upheld a jury verdict that the city of Denver was deliberately indifferent to the rights of its citizens because of inadequate deadly force training provided to its officers. Part of the findings in this case was the fact that the city of Denver's only decision-making training on lethal force was a lecture and a movie. Training is important but only in context. You can train the wrong things well, barely train important concepts without context, or you can train based on the science of human performance under stress. Not hard to guess which one I recommend.

The list of all pertinent cases and findings could fill a library, this is just a small sample. The idea is to provide information on how the courts look at training, the elements of force, the tools of force and use-of-force decisions. Officers need to have a thorough understanding of use-of-force case law. The decision to use force on an individual is a serious one. It's important for officers to know that sometimes hesitancy itself escalates a situation leading to too much "time under tension." This can lead to sudden, in-custody death (excited delirium), mistakes of fact, injury to innocents, and possibly a lethal force situation that may have been avoided had other options been used earlier. All that to say that sometimes force is necessary and should be applied judiciously.

Chapter Four

The Elements of A Use–of–Force Incident

The degree of one's emotion varies inversely with one's knowledge of the facts—the less you know the hotter you get.

– Bertrand Russell

The "elements" of force are listed in almost every old-school use of force continuum, not to mention, most of the current use-of-force policies of major police agencies. They are normally not described or explained well and because of that, the officers miss out on learning how to write an efficient, court proof report. I have been asked on numerous occasions to consult for my agency on use-of-force issues. Most of these cases involve a poorly written report by the officer which fails to include the elements of the crime itself, as well as the elements of the use of force. When I interview the officer, they do a better job of articulating "what" happened and "why" it happened. The art of writing good reports has taken a back seat to "good enough" or at least it contains enough information to get themselves back on the street. The reasons for sloppy, expedient reports are probably numerous but include: laziness, under staffing, calls for service holding, poor training from field training officers, or poor training in their basic academy setting.

So, here is the world according to Mike. I tell any officer I train whether it's tactical training, defensive tactics training or de-escalation concepts, that good report writing will save your career and the most important reports are those involving any use of force. The problem is some people are quite good at writing, some muddle their way through, and some are incompetent at detailing the events of an incident involving use of force. Within our de-escalation training we introduced a new concept for how we wanted our use of force reports to be written. The reasoning was simple, if most of the reports don't include the elements of the crime or the elements of the use of force, then we will provide a framework to ensure the proper details make their way into the report.

The elements of force are usually listed as ability, opportunity, and jeopardy. Some agencies include preclusion and I will explain that in a moment. The problem with the way the elements are usually taught is for the sake of expediency or, due to a lack of understanding, these elements are explained in a manner which does not aid the officer in explaining and documenting a use of force. Let's break it down in two different ways.

First, I will explain the traditional method of teaching the elements and then I will provide you with an expanded version that we use in our de-escalation program. The expanded version is based on information provided by city and county attorneys, including input from subject matter experts on police use of force.

I have attended two police academies in my career, one in the state of Ohio and one in Arizona. In both academies, the elements of force were discussed, for the most part, in the following manner.

1. Ability: Did the suspect have the ability to attack you?

2. Opportunity: Did the suspect have a reasonable opportunity to attack you?

3. Jeopardy: Did the suspect place you or another in fear of your life or serious injury?

4. Preclusion: Did you consider all lesser means of gaining compliance prior to the use of force?

That's it. That is usually how I have seen it explained and while it may cover the absolute basics of a use of force, they fail to provide protection for the officers themselves and for the agencies they represent. Now, look at our enhanced version which will include some details previously listed in the *Graham* v. *Connor* section.

Ability

1. Suspect's apparent ability: height, weight, physical build, age, apparent level of fitness, apparent level of skill in combatives, armed or potential for being armed, known mental illness, known violence potential, prior history for resisting arrest, how is he dressed? (heavy jackets can prevent Taser probes from penetrating into skin and very little clothing or naked makes it hard to obtain control), etc.

2. Officer's ability to protect him/herself: officer's height, weight, physical build, level of fitness, skill in unarmed combatives, level of training, experience, other officers present and availability of backup, injuries prior to the encounter, injuries caused by the encounter hindering ability, etc.

The important thing for all officers, administrators, the media, and the public at large to understand is that ability is not only based on the physical aspects of an encounter. The mental aspects are just as important, and unfortunately, we cannot read a person's mind to decide if they are going to attack us, we can only infer their conduct based on their behavior.

Because we can't read minds, we must remember that ability is enhanced with weapons and with opportunities to attack with the element of surprise. A five foot, ninety-pound woman may not be able to physically handle a one hundred and ninety-pound male officer, but if the officer turns his back on her to deal with someone else and she can acquire a weapon or deadly instrument, she has used her ability to negate size advantages by using the element of surprise and a weapon.

Opportunity

A suspect can have the physical and mental ability to attack you, but if he doesn't have the opportunity to hurt you or another and you use force against them, then you might have a problem. For example, a six foot eight-inch, three hundred and fifty-pound steroid controversy can cause some physical damage, but if he is already in handcuffs and leg restraints, how dangerous is he? The answer is, it depends. The officer must be able to describe what opportunity was created for the suspect to attack given the previous listed abilities and the opportunities provided for either the officer to gain control or for the suspect to attack or attempt to escape. Obviously, the more opportunities the officer has to diminish the abilities of the suspect, the better off they are going to be. We teach our officers to remember that while they are looking for opportunities to control the suspect, the suspect may be looking for opportunities to attack or escape from the officer. Part of "reading" a scene is for the officers to make the most of their abilities and opportunities and do everything they can to diminish the suspect's abilities and opportunities.

An example of suspects creating opportunities are situations where officers are escorting a suspect in or out of handcuffs through a doorway or threshold. Suspects who have spent time in mental institutions and prisons or jails, know that the doorway or threshold itself creates an opportunity to launch an attack. If two officers are escorting a suspect, all three of them cannot go through at once. The mistake is to have the suspect go through and follow closely behind as you move them through the door. In this confined enclosure, the side frames can be used to create opportunities to turn or drive the escorting officer sideways into the frame or backwards. We teach two officers to let one officer pass through the threshold, then the other officer passes the suspect through to the first officer and then follows the suspect. I have seen or heard of officers receiving injuries by suspects using the base of the door or a threshold plate to brace themselves and violently send their head backwards to drive the back of their head into the front of an officer's face. I have also seen and heard of cases where the suspect will intentionally bounce themselves off the frame to attempt to free their arms to attempt an assault.

Keep in mind when you read headlines or hear of an officer using force on a handcuffed prisoner that all the details may not be included in the news report. Handcuffs and any type of restraint system can hinder a suspect's ability to assault a police officer but does not make it impossible. In the last twenty-five years, I have known officers who have been shot at by people in handcuffs, received injuries fighting with suspects with no legs, been kicked hard enough to miss a significant amount of time off work, had opportunities created for the suspect by accomplices, and sometimes by random acts committed by strangers having nothing to do with the arrest. It is important to note the opportunity can be created by the situation itself or new events that occur within the situation, by the suspect's actions, by the officer's actions or lack of action, by the actions of a third party, or any other factor that Murphy's Law can contribute.

In Arizona several years ago, an officer was confronting a suspect who was passing a forged check. An important factor in this incident was the fact the suspect's girlfriend was with him in the store. The officer made the decision to make the original approach without backup present on an extremely busy night for officers in that precinct. The girlfriend of the suspect can be viewed on video from the store, drawing the officer's attention away from the suspect and towards herself. In retrospect we know the suspect was armed and the video shows the gun came from a concealed position in the waistband under his shirt. At this point, the officer can see that the suspect is shorter and smaller in stature. The officer probably felt he could physically handle the suspect, so the next concern would be to physically control him, get him in handcuffs and quickly get him searched for weapons. This is exactly what the officer attempts to do and the officer is successful in getting one handcuff on when the suspect's girlfriend steps forward moving toward the officer and drawing his attention to her. While the officer is distracted, the suspect with his free hand, draws a handgun from a concealed position and shoots the officer in the head killing him.

I responded to this call with my squad of SWAT officers and after a night of searching we finally barricaded the suspect and his girlfriend in a house and took them into custody after several hours of negotiations and a limited entry with multiple gas deployments.

Some have criticized me in the past for using real information when I teach instead of just making incidents up or choosing events from other agencies. I believe we do a tremendous disservice to our officers by not thoroughly debriefing these incidents, learning what we can from them, and passing that information on to help other officers in their decision-making process. In no way do I mean to disparage a good cop by listing mistakes they made or by trying to say what I would have done in that situation. Instead, I offer you what-ifs that can help in future decisions of officers in similar circumstances. In this way, I hope that, even in a small way, but hopefully in a much larger way, their memory and their legacy can live on. Because regardless of the learning points or the outcome, these brave souls showed up for the dance and fought the good fight.

With all that said, as it relates to ability and opportunity what can be learned from this? Because, I believe, and I teach that when you write your use-of-force reports, you should also be reviewing the aspects of your plan and thinking about ways, in retrospect, you may have been able to establish control before it went to a use-of-force situation. It's never going to be perfect, but a constant evaluation and critique of each of these incidents that occur to an officer or to officers they know are hard wiring the brain for better future performance.

Before we move on to the next two elements let's do a comprehensive review of how ability and opportunity played into the tragic event we mentioned earlier in this section. When we look at abilities, it is obvious to begin with the abilities of the officer and the suspect. In this case, the officer had a distinct size and weight advantage. The physical confrontation was probably not going to be a problem. Keep in mind though, things are not always as they seem. With the preponderance of mixed martial arts training and martial arts teaching combat systems from other countries, a smaller in stature human being who is trained can surprise a larger individual who is not. All things being equal, size matters. Rarely are all things equal. So, in this incident the officer is feeling confident enough in his ability to handle the suspect and moves in to establish control.

Weapons can overcome size advantages and a suspect's initial action will always be faster than the officer's reaction.

For this reason, the idea of establishing physical control of the suspect as soon as possible makes sense. But what about the abilities of the girlfriend in this incident? If she knows her boyfriend is armed and is probably going to jail, and she does not want this to happen, what can she do to complicate the officer's attempts at control? Physically, she was small in stature with a very thin build but that does not mean she was not a threat. It's not just the abilities of the primary suspect that need to be considered. Instead, the abilities of all persons at the scene related to that individual need to be considered when establishing initial baselines during the cognitive appraisal. The girlfriend in this incident had the ability to distract the officer while he was placing the first handcuff on the suspect. The suspect, probably knowing a physical confrontation wasn't going to go his way still had a free hand, access to a weapon, and a distracted officer dealing with two people at once.

This leads us to opportunity. In the planning stages, opportunity must be considered from multiple perspectives. The responding officers are looking to establish control and are looking for opportunities to do so as quickly as possible. In the planning stages, we would like to see officers recognize that one set of eyes cannot track two people. Ideally, as soon as we recognize that there are several people to control, we would like to have as many sets of eyes on our side tracking the environment, the suspects, innocent civilians, and each other. As soon as this officer arrived on scene, his opportunities for control were diminished by the female repeatedly drawing his attention away. In the end, both the male and female were suspects. The officer was attempting to control the male subject's opportunities to attack or escape. The female, by drawing the officer's attention, created an opportunity for the male to draw a weapon and shoot the officer. Sound complicated? It is, even without the stressors of a potential confrontation.

When I have discussed our program with smaller law enforcement agencies, there is usually a discussion of their limited resources and availability of immediate backup. This goes right back to the idea of exigency. If life-threatening, exigent circumstances are not present, why not ask for and wait for available resources? Mutual aid agreements exist so smaller agencies can get help from their neighboring agencies. Given the fact we should be looking to make things safer for all parties involved, the idea of an agency only having one officer available to work a shift is negligent at best and downright criminal at worst. If no one's dying or at risk of dying, wait for your resources knowing that if exigency is created by a suspect or the situation, the officer can now act knowing the law is on their side.

Jeopardy

That brings us to jeopardy. Given the suspect's abilities, the officer's abilities, along with how an opportunity was created for the suspect to attack or resist, the next question to ask is, what actions of the suspect lead you to believe that either your life or the life of another was at significant risk of death or serious physical injury? Then, clearly explain the actions as well as the threats. Unfortunately, in the case listed above, the report was not written by the officer himself but instead by a homicide detective. In the charges filed against the male and female suspect, the report would include that the female intentionally disrupted the handcuffing of the male suspect providing him the opportunity to draw a weapon from concealment and shoot the officer. The jeopardy was created here, with the distraction and then with the drawing of the handgun.

Now, you can look at the elements of force when formulating a use-of-force report as a review aid to see if there are

things we can learn from the incident to improve future training. To do this we go through the abilities of the people involved, the opportunities created by each person involved,
or the opportunities taken away by each person involved. We
can then look at the jeopardy created and possible preventative measures that may have avoided the created jeopardy.
Again, this is not a slam on the performance of any officer
involved unless the officer's performance does not meet the
objective reasonableness standard. If an officer has paid the
ultimate sacrifice in the line of duty, I feel we disparage their
sacrifice by not learning from these horrible tragedies and
refusing to pass on the lessons that can be learned because
we fear we are tainting their memory. Let's look at the elements again and see what we can learn from them.

In the above case, the officer had several years of experience in one of the busiest precincts in the city. Physically,
he was tall and athletic. In physical ability, the advantage was
to the officer. Remember the officer's actions are almost always *reactive* in nature. An unrestrained suspect can access a
weapon, if they have one, from concealment in under one
second. When officers move for control of a subject, the first
goal should be to prevent the suspect's access to weapons.
Weapons can equalize an encounter, especially when they are
drawn quickly by surprise.

In this incident, we have an officer with plenty of ability,
but the officer's abilities were diminished by the presence of
the female and her ability to work with the male suspect to
keep the officer from taking control. This provided the opportunity to access the handgun. What can be learned from
this? First, was any life on the line prior to the officer's arrival?
The answer is no. Did the officer need to handle the call by
himself knowing a female subject was also listed on the call?
It was a crazy night in the city with multiple calls for service
holding. The officer was trying to handle the calls quickly and

efficiently, but given the known facts at the time, the decision to wait for backup before making contact seems prudent. Backup was on its way but was delayed. Why not wait? Harsh? I don't think so. I would bet his family and friends wish he had and, in the end, what exactly did he die for? And again, this is not said to disparage his service, I knew and liked the man and wish we still had him around.

I know this sounds harsh. I also know that every day officers with good intentions are trying to aid jurisdictions that are asking them to do more with less. It's about response times and how many calls for service are holding which makes politicians and police administrators look bad. This can place officers in situations where they are forced to attempt to fight out of a situation that proper resources could have prevented. If we are going to look at liability, then we must look at it from all angles not just the politically correct ones. I am tired of police funerals. I am tired of accusations of police misconduct with no evidence to support it, and I am also tired of an extremely small percentage of law enforcement officers who tarnish the rest of us because they are either immoral, refuse to train, incompetent, or plain ignorant.

A second officer could provide another set of eyes positioned to watch their partner and both suspects. Now, the suspects must figure out a way to distract both officers and create enough of an opportunity to engage both in a violent encounter. Is that a guarantee the officers will survive the call? No, but why not use resources and tilt the odds in their favor? If the presence of two officers provides enough of an opportunity to quickly establish control of the situation, the weapon may only be introduced to the situation during the search of an already handcuffed prisoner. To put it simply, the job of law enforcement is to use their abilities to hinder the suspect's abilities and to create opportunities for themselves that hinder the opportunities of potential suspects to create jeopardy.

Preclusion

So, the overall goal of our de-escalation training can be summarized as follows: Our officers will bring good tactical plans to each incident consisting of an A plan, a B plan, and an emergency plan (Preclusion). The officers will train hard, know the law, work on their communication skills, and bring a calm, professional, competent demeanor to each situation (Ability). The officers will assess the abilities of the persons involved and constantly evaluate the need for additional resources to hinder the abilities of suspects. Officers should attempt to create opportunities to lawfully and effectively establish control as soon as practical to limit the opportunities for the suspect to create a situation where they can cause death or serious physical injury to the officer or another (Jeopardy).

About ten years ago, several agencies in Arizona removed preclusion from the elements of force. The reasoning at the time was that having preclusion gave the impression there is always a lesser means of solving a violent problem and unless all lesser means are eliminated, lethal force cannot and should not be authorized. In fact, using that definition of preclusion they were correct. However, we recommended and were successful in convincing our agency to put preclusion back into the elements of force. We changed the definition and clearly established guidelines for how to interpret the difference between "lesser means" and showing up with a plan, a backup plan, an emergency plan, constantly evaluating the plan and resources, and using effective communication skills to attempt to de-escalate situations before they turn violent. All of these things contribute to preclusion.

To me, preclusion is written into a report because it is the chance for the officer to provide, in detail, an explanation of the A plan, the B plan, and the emergency plan. It's an opportunity to explain your tactical communication, the Ask, Tell, Resources, Caveat, and Make phases of the encounter. In effect, it provides the framework for the report to ensure the officer does not leave out pertinent facts related to the arrest and use of force. In my opinion, it also shows that the officer is a professional, a tactical thinker, and an effective communicator who is explaining every opportunity given to a suspect to comply and submit to arrest as the law demands.

Keep in mind, preclusion shows you are prepared with a plan and ready to constantly evaluate that plan but does not guarantee the result. We can look at the incident and see where we could have done better, but just because an incident turns violent, it does not mean the officer made a mistake. The suspect or object of a call has a say and always will have a say and that is why we will never be able to eliminate the risk of violence unless we are willing to send massive resources to every police encounter. This is, of course, not feasible.

Let me reiterate, when an officer authors a report, especially those involving use of force, it is imperative they accurately document the events in a clear and concise manner directed toward a legal standard. The benefits are numerous. First, from arrest to trial can be a lengthy time. In the brain science section, we will discuss the memory systems, but let's start with the idea that memory in humans is not good. The brain focuses on making memories for future risk/reward biases, not for exact details. Get the report right as soon as possible after the incident with the facts pertinent to the arrest and use of force and you have the best memory tool available to you for court: a document written and worded by you as soon as practical after the event.

Second, when you are drafting the report and reviewing the abilities and opportunities of all parties involved, you are conducting a tactical debrief on the incident with yourself.

This debrief gives ideas for what you can do better in similar situations in the future. Experience is the best teacher, but are you listening? These critical debriefs with yourself can hardwire the brain for better future performance. In the heat of violent situations, we can't expect to be perfect, but we should expect to learn from our experience and the experience of others.

Third, if an officer is worried about getting sued and possibly losing their implied immunity, what better way to help defend themselves than to write the use-of-force report in the same manner a legal brief would be written. It shows that the officer understands the law as it pertains to arrest, search and seizure, and use of force and it makes it clear the case you will present on your behalf on the witness stand.

Fourth, the officer is not the only individual who needs a clear, concise report. Supervisors need to document and justify an officer's use of force to higher command. Prosecutors need to understand the applicable elements for charging the suspect because there is nothing worse for a law enforcement agency than to have charges dropped on a suspect who had force used against them. The defense attorneys under our legal standard also have an expectation that a detailed report will provide all pertinent facts of the case and their job is to question an officer's competency when all facts are not provided.

The communications strategies (Ask, Tell, Resources, Caveat, and Make), the ABC planning, and an understanding of the elements of force, form the foundation of the de-escalation program we presented to the officers of my department. Even without the science of the brain, if you follow the guidelines of the communication strategies, use ABC planning, and understand the elements of force, and the law, you still have an extremely good shot at a successful non-violent conclusion. If the situation becomes violent, you can articulate the things you did to try to prevent a violent conclusion. But by understanding the science of law enforcement, the science of the brain under duress, and the science of how the memory systems in the brain work, you add the most effective tool available to any human being at any given time; an optimized brain with the right balance of the emotional response and the highest possible cognitive function given the circumstances. With correct training, you can optimize how the brain performs in situations that are anything but normal.

CHAPTER FIVE

EXCITED DELIRIUM, THE MENTALLY ILL, AND EXIGENCY

Any science, we should insist, better than any other discipline, can hold up its students and followers an ideal of patient devotion to the search for objective truth, with vision unclouded by personal or political motive.

– Sir Henry Hallett Dalt

In certain cases, throughout the country, a subject will resist a lawful arrest, be taken into custody, and then suddenly die in police custody. The common belief by the media, certain activist groups, and some police organizations, is the subject was beaten to death by the police and the police are attempting to cover up the details to protect themselves. In-custody deaths became prevalent enough probably through increasing media attention, that certain doctors around North America began studying the problem and developing theories of what may be occurring in many of these cases.

Police are sometimes called to a scene to deal with a person who is exhibiting signs of abnormal behavior. In the process of attempting to control the subject, the subject suddenly dies. The autopsy findings as to cause of death can result in inconclusive evidence. According to some medical examiners 'excited delirium' is a diagnosis of exclusion that you are left with when no certain cause of death can be found, and a certain set of parameters are met. Those parameters would be but are not limited to: died during conflict with police, exhibited signs of bizarre behavior, and subject was violent not necessarily to people but to objects and things like cars and windows. The entire medical community is not ready to accept excited delirium as an official diagnosis of cause of death, but the syndrome is recognized by the National Association of Medical Examiners and the American College of Emergency Physicians. The International Association of Chiefs of Police has also recognized excited delirium as a legitimate concern for law enforcement and the medical community. What is not known about excited delirium far outweighs what is known, but there are certain indicators that can aid law enforcement when dealing with subjects showing certain signs and symptoms of an excited delirium episode.

Dr. Christine Hall is a doctor of Emergency Medicine in Canada and has conducted research into excited delirium, including being an expert witness on the condition. Dr. Hall lectures for the Force Science Institute and her portion of their program exists to educate law enforcement on excited delirium, its signs, and possible preventative post-conflict aftercare. According to her research, excited delirium episodes are rare with an average of one death in every 4,868 police uses of force. Her research also indicates that in the United States, accounting for all known police use-of-force incidents, that in 98.9 percent of police contacts, no force is used. Stay with me on this. Science and excessive facts and figures may not be exciting, but the truths that can be found in their study can lead to solutions to problems we can attempt to control. Dr. Hall's research shows causes which can attribute to an excited delirium episode. The following information on signs and symptoms is from Dr. Hall's lecture presentation.[11]

- acute psychosis
- psychiatric illness
- acute manic crisis (bipolar)
- associated personality disorders

Drug Intoxication

- Street drugs, coke, meth, bath salts, PCP, alcohol, ecstasy and mushrooms.
- Cocaine intoxication is excited delirium.
- Prescription drugs like antidepressants.
- Certain over-the-counter drugs like Benadryl and Gravol.
- Combination of psychiatric illness and drug intoxication.
- Certain medical illnesses.

The signs of an excited delirium episode that law enforcement should consider in their planning stages of dealing with an individual are:

- If picking up a known suspect/subject, do they have a known or suspected mental illness (especially mania or schizophrenia)?
- Is the suspect/subject extremely agitated or showing signs of bizarre, irrational or destructive behavior?

---

[11] Dr. Christine Hall. "Excited Delirium: What It Is, What It Isn't and How We Know." Lecture at the Force Science Institute Certification Course: Principles of Force Science. Phoenix, AZ, September 2016.

- Suspect/subject constantly yelling, screaming, or repeating incomprehensible vocal sounds.
- Suspect/subject showing an attraction to glass.
- Suspect/subject naked or semi-clothed.
- Does not respond appropriately to police presence.
- Insensitivity to pain.
- May have very hot skin.
- May or may not sweat profusely.
- May seem profoundly dry.

If the officers can restrain an individual, they may exhibit the following signs after being taken into custody:

- Struggling violently against restraints used (handcuffs, hobble devices, etc.).
- Facial smashing in the back of the police vehicle.
- Kicking windows of the police vehicle.

Dr. Hall's presentation lists the following features of the death itself:

- Usually occurs once the suspect/subject is successfully restrained.
- Usually occurs within five minutes of subject becoming quiet.
- First symptom of impending death is the death itself.
- Virtually never successfully resuscitated.
- Occurs in police cars, cells, ambulances, and hospitals.

In the past, excited delirium cases have been attributed to the carotid control technique, positional asphyxia, pepper spray, and to the Taser. To date there is no known causality in the proper use of these applications to an excited delirium episode other than as a contributing factor in the time under tension. So, what we know is the subject's/suspect's core body temperature becomes elevated to an unsustainable level along with the previously listed behaviors and indicators. Law enforcement must deal with the behaviors first and foremost for the safety of all present including the subject/suspect. As law enforcement, what we can do is try to control the "time under tension." For the purposes of this discussion the time under tension is the time between when we recognize the need to establish control to the time it takes to get the suspect/subject in custody and under review of advanced life support.

When we recognize the indicators, we also need to recognize the sooner we can establish control, the better off all parties will be. The good news for law enforcement is that this is a sound strategy for any police encounter that involves taking a subject into custody. This is where an honest evaluation of the required resources is imperative in the officer's decision-making process.

An example I give when I teach de-escalation strategies is to look up on YouTube twenty to thirty police encounters and look at windows of opportunity for the police to control a suspect. Usually when police get control of a subject within approximately ten seconds, there are no injuries to anyone. Between ten and thirty seconds, there are usually bumps and bruises but no significant injury to any party. The longer the situation goes past thirty seconds, the higher the probability of an excited delirium episode, a mistake-of-fact shooting, accusations of excessive force, and more severe injury to anyone involved.

When we are discussing the lawful but awfuls and the

things that law enforcement agencies can do to reduce in-conflict and in-custody deaths, the time under tension, planning strategies, and the use of proper resources can all aid in bringing some of these conflicts to a successful conclusion for all parties involved. Part of the resources necessary for the incidents with excited delirium indicators, is the presence of advanced life support.

Advanced life support, whether provided by the fire department or the local emergency room, gives medical personnel the ability to sedate and lessen the extreme effects of the episode on the subject's brain and body which are both under the effects of an extreme fight or flight response. The current theory is that sedatives like Ketamine reduce the fight or flight response and allow the body's core to cool down. Of course, only qualified medical personnel can make the call to sedate and advanced life support must be available. Experts also indicate that these measures are not guaranteed as everyone has different tolerances to the tension created under conflict with one or more indicators present.

Dr. Hall's research indicates that if the first sign of an episode of excited delirium is death itself, then it is vitally important to get the subject under control and contained as quickly as it is safe to do so and then provide advanced life support as soon as possible when the pre-indicators are present.

One of the first things police officers and supervisors must consider when they have information leading them to believe the subject they are about to encounter is a candidate for an excited delirium episode is to reduce the time under tension. If the goal is to reduce tension time, then it is vital we have all necessary resources available before we initiate contact when practical. Of course, if the subject's behavior is placing innocent people in harm's way, the officers must act and are now covered under the law because the subject created the exigency and not the officer. When practical,

have the necessary resources including advanced life support on stand-by, contain and isolate the subject, attempt to
communicate and talk the subject down from the extreme
fight or flight response. If the A plan isn't working and communication is not working, evaluate changing to a B plan. The
B plan would include small team tactics with less lethal
measures available and a plan that accounts for the need to
gain control as soon as practical once the decision to close
distance on the subject is made.

As part of our tactical planning and strategies, we talk
about the need to avoid a police officer creating exigency
unless it is part of a sound tactical plan with the proper resources available to effectively handle the situation. As an
example, say two officers arrive on scene of a pregnant mentally ill female armed with a knife standing in the front yard
of her home. The officers have a mental health order requiring the female to be delivered to the mental hospital to be
evaluated. In our example, the female has committed no
crime other than to have a mental condition requiring treatment. In the past, officers were taught to deal with this situation as they would with any armed criminal: demand she
drop the knife and if she takes a step forward then deadly
force is required. The problem is, what crime has she committed, and would she be less of a danger if you back off, set up
tactically and begin communicating? While the *Graham* v.
Connor standards have not changed, the issue of who created
the exigency has become a front and center issue in examining law enforcement's ability to decrease some of the lawful
but awful deaths. In this case, if the officers approached
within the distance to allow a lesser weapon (the knife) to
come into play against a standoff weapon (the guns), it could
be viewed as the officers choosing to create exigency
thereby creating a deadly force situation. Are the legal rami-
fications a guarantee the officers will be indicted? No, of

course not, but who wants to take the chance? More important, killing is a horrible thing. Officers should understand this as a job hazard but should also do everything in their power to avoid it when practical. Does it make sense to walk up to a person armed with a knife in the hope they will just give up?

Law enforcement must have different options for dealing with the mentally ill unless they are committing a violent crime. The legal aspects of this issue play a secondary role to just doing the right things for the right reason at the right time. Mentally ill people need help and unfortunately in some cases the only help they are going to get is by law enforcement intervention. Do I agree with the police being used as mental health-care providers? No, I do not. Police receive nowhere near the training required to deal effectively with subjects having an extreme mental episode. But my opinion and three dollars will get you a coffee at Starbucks and not much else.

Remember earlier when we talked about emotion and reasoning having an inverse relationship? In the case of the mentally ill or subjects whose mental capacity is affected by drugs or alcohol, an officer most likely will be dealing with a highly emotional individual whose reasoning abilities are in question due to an excess of emotion from a fight or flight response in the central nervous system. By understanding the human central nervous system under stress, you double your opportunities to bring incidents to a non-violent resolution. Why? Because the subject's/suspect's central nervous system is not the only central nervous system involved in the potential conflict. When an officer understands their own brain, they can properly train to control their emotional response and increase cognitive ability. By understanding what a suspect or mentally ill person's brain may be experiencing, when practical, an officer can use appropriate distance and communication skills to attempt to engage more of the rational brain and less of the emotional brain.

Over the course of my career, especially while assigned to the SWAT team, I have dealt with severely mentally ill individuals. I am proud to say we dealt with them in a professional, compassionate manner and were able to bring most of them into custody safely. Unfortunately, I have been faced with mentally ill subjects who were trying to kill me or another (officer or civilian) and I used lethal force to stop the threat. Keep in mind that the set up and plans were based on the information contained in this book. In every case where I used lethal force, the exigency was created by the suspect/mentally ill subject and not by myself or other officers. It is a horrible feeling to take the life of a human being and even more horrible to take the life of a person whose mind was not working right, either by being off medications or having a serious psychotic episode. I can live with the fact that I was left with no choice and did what had to be done at the time, but it has left me with a profound belief that our society is failing our mentally ill citizens and setting them up for failure.

Criminal Behavior Versus Mental Illness

If we understand that mental illness is different than criminal activity and we train to bring a sound tactical plan and effective communication strategy to these situations, maybe we can reduce the number of confrontations that end in lethal force. It must always be kept in mind that even with perfect planning and preparations, the subject of the calls for service has a say in the matter and can still push the situation to a violent conclusion.

An important case from the ninth circuit court outlines

some of the considerations when dealing with mentally ill subjects. In *Deorle* v. *Rutherford* the ninth circuit's findings stated:

The problems posed by, and thus the tactics to be employed against, an emotionally distraught individual who is creating a disturbance or resisting arrest are, and must be, differentiated from those involved in efforts to subdue an armed and dangerous criminal who has recently committed a serious offense. In the former instance, increasing the use of force may, in a number of circumstances, exacerbate the situation; in the latter instance, a heightened use of less than lethal force will ordinarily be helpful in bringing a dangerous situation to a swift end. In the case of mentally unbalanced persons, the use of officers and others trained in the art of counseling is ordinarily advisable and may provide the best means of ending the crisis. Even when an emotionally disturbed individual is 'acting out' and inviting officers to use deadly force to subdue him, the governmental interest in using such force is diminished by the fact that the officers are confronted, not with a criminal, but with a mentally ill person.[12]

The argument in this case was that the officers employed tactics that "needlessly or unreasonably creates a dangerous situation necessitating an escalation in use of force." Deorle was mentally ill but following commands when an officer fired a less lethal bean bag round which struck Deorle in the eye causing the loss of the eye and other injuries.

Now when dealing with criminal behavior, will the same ideas place officers in safer positions to effectively deal with the situation or hinder their safety? This is one of the questions asked usually before the de-escalation program begins and we let them know it will be addressed throughout our

---

[12] www.caselaw4cops.net/

course of instruction.

Let's look at the facts. Say you are a police officer on routine patrol in your beat and you notice a subject you recognize as having a felony warrant for armed robbery and he has noticed you. You bail out of your car as he starts running and the foot pursuit begins. You are confident you are going to catch him quickly, so you hold off on getting on the radio to ask for more help. Your thought process being that taking the time to clear on the radio and give descriptions and locations will reduce your speed and thought processing.

Unfortunately, your initial assessment of your abilities was slightly off, and you now realize you have taken several twists and turns in the neighborhood. You take a corner quickly and walk right into ... a gunshot which strikes you in the chest. This affects your balance, and you fall to the ground as the suspect, lucky for you, decides to escape quickly. Sounds horrible, right? You would never make that mistake, would you? But as we earlier learned, when emotions are high, cognition can be decreased and cognitive appraisal, the means to evaluate the violations of expectations, is hindered or cut off. In the above listed scenario, what has the officer accomplished other than being shot? What was his initial goal and was he able to accomplish it? If he is fortunate enough to be wearing his vest and the bullet strikes his vest, he has a good chance of living to learn from the experience, but the sad fact is many cops are killed each year in foot pursuits. In this example, what if the officer needs medical attention but no longer has any idea where he is? The suspect will probably believe the officer has called for help and will now assume he's in more trouble making it extremely dangerous for anyone he contacts.

Now, let's go back to the idea of being resource driven and having a primary plan, a backup plan, and an emergency plan for situations such as this. If the officer keeps the suspect in sight but communicates with fellow officers and asks for additional resources, such as the air unit and canine units (if available), the officer may find that help is close. The suspect is probably now in an extreme form of fight or flight and is probably not going to be making good decisions. Part of any emergency plan for foot pursuits is the principle of cornering. The principle of cornering is, whoever takes the corner first, owns the corner and if you charge around a corner without clearing the angle first, you could walk right into a bullet.

Going back to our previous example, the officer has cleared on the radio, has help on the way, and is loading his working memory with tactical planning. He sees the suspect take the corner of a building at speed, but our officer has already pre-loaded his working memory with the idea that all corners will be taken tactically. The officer slows at the corner and uses a tactical "limited push" using one eye behind his gun and nothing else exposed to clear the space around the corner. The officer sees a portion of the suspect's foot without exposing any portion of himself and gives commands for the suspect to show his hands and step away from the wall. If the suspect complies, they can be taken into custody safely with the help of responding officers. If the suspect fails to comply and presents a lethal threat, the officer can deal with the threat using cover and cornering to tilt the odds in their favor.

When I teach and use examples such as these to explain my point, the question usually asked is, "What if the suspect gets away while you're being tactical?" My answer, "So what?" So, the suspect gets away. You know who he is, and you now have one more idea where he hangs out. Is the thrill of the chase worth dying for? Many times in my career I have transferred to a new squad or detail and they have mentioned the game that if you lose a foot pursuit you must buy dinner for everyone. My answer is colorful, expletive-filled, and includes an explanation of the ignorance of the concept. I will handle foot pursuits as they come and not chase a suspect like a brain-dumped dog going after a rabbit. The fact is, in the past we have all done some incredibly dangerous things for the sake of expediency, including myself. We are short staffed, so we do more with less. We are over budget, so we forego training. We have created exigency for the sake of keeping resources and overtime down. All these things need to change and why? Because it's safer for all parties involved. It gives us a better chance to bring everyone in safely, but not a guarantee.

There will probably never be a time where the world is crime free and the job of a police officer doesn't have elements of danger to it. What we can do is make the commitment to train hard, take personal responsibility, use tactical planning and effective communications skills, and be resource driven. This gives us, our agency, innocent civilians, and the suspect or mentally disturbed persons themselves the best opportunity to come in safely. If you choose not to do so and happen into a mistake-of-fact shooting, the above listed case laws or many others could be used to judge your conduct leading up to the shooting. Now, if the solution provided by the courts put the officers in more danger I would be the first to complain and do all within my power to fix the problem, but I do not believe that is the case.

I have testified in federal court as an expert witness on police use of force and defensive tactics and this is certainly one venue where an opinion could be made known. But I think we have sufficiently explained that what they are asking for is what we as officers should have been asking for all along. Also, let me add, if I mention a mistake or an unsafe action, then chances are at some time in my early career I committed that mistake. With that said, if you are on your way to a call and no one is dying, and backup is not available, what is wrong with waiting for backup? Again, I have done it and can think of numerous occasions in the past where I have overextended myself for no other reason than resources were short, and calls were holding.

Some officers have complained that they feel pressure from either their supervisors or from dispatch to get calls holding cleared. Maybe that is the case, but if you go it alone and overextend yourself and have a mistake-of-fact shooting, a bad shoot, a controversial encounter, etc., the dispatchers or your supervisor are not going to go to court on your behalf and say, "That's our bad, we put a hell of a lot of pressure on that poor officer." Ultimately, you bear the responsibility for your conduct and that is exactly what you should explain to a supervisor who pressures you to clear calls or as a supervisor feeling pressured by your superiors. The law is on your side and the judges are making it clear the events leading up to a use-of-force incident matter.

CHAPTER SIX

THE SCIENCE OF THE FIGHT OR FLIGHT RESPONSE

Courage is grace under pressure.

– Ernest Hemingway

The previous chapters of the book are the outline for how to achieve better performance by proper planning, communication skills, and a basic understanding of what happens if we don't control our emotional reactions under stress. These points are emphasized in our de-escalation program as a good starting point with the idea we would then add relevant neuroscience and brain hacks to aid in the development of a well-rounded law enforcement officer. Some of the information to follow is a review of previously discussed material as we delve deeper into the brain and memory systems.

The Brain Science

Emotion and cognition are not enemies unless one is over stimulated. Too much emotion and your response will be primal, unmeasured, and probably inappropriate for the situation. Too much cognition and you risk paralysis by analysis caused by overthinking a situation that requires faster decisions than your brain can process at that time. The whole point of understanding the balance between the emotional and cognitive systems is to learn how to develop training programs supporting this balance. As an added benefit, when you learn to train for a balanced brain for on-duty activities, you get the added benefit of learning the pros of having a balanced brain system off duty and the cons of allowing work to affect emotional levels off duty. One of the things we learned by looking at recent research on the brain, was the overall benefits that the balance between the cognitive and emotional systems provides. This pertains to anyone who finds work or life stressors building up, not just police officers.

It is easy to read or hear about an officer-involved shooting or data from numerous shootings and question why officers miss their targets so much when involved in real-life encounters. Many of the officers involved regularly shoot at an expert level on their qualifications and the age-old question is why doesn't that translate to a real lethal force situation? The science is relatively simple. Shooting on paper is a cognitive skill until the skill set is burned into the circuitry of the brain. As skills are repeated, the myelin sheath, which covers the nerves, thickens for faster stimulus transmission. The connections from the nerves involved to the muscles required for performance are enhanced. For pure stimulus response work, that is the most efficient way to get it done. The brain loves efficiency. The problem is that paper doesn't shoot back and criminals sometimes do. Add the emotional components of real-life violence (not present when shooting paper) and the brain will start to heavily favor the emotional side of the brain. Without effective training under stress, where the officer's skills are balanced with the demands of the situation, the burned-in skill of a marksman shooter becomes the uncoordinated movements caused by an extreme fight or flight reaction run by the overtaxed emotional system. The same concept when the emotional response is not regulated, relates to effective communication, defensive tactics, tactical judgment, and personal judgment. Remember, professional athletes get paid for consistency, not perfection. Why? Because of the skill set required and the fact that the other person or team has a say in the matter. The elite performers are consistent, not perfect. They expect the unexpected (violations of expectations) and they train themselves to adjust. But even professional athletes, extreme sports athletes, military personnel, and cops can have a performance choke under pressure. The purpose of training is not for perfection, but consistency.

Implicit and Explicit Systems

To understand the division we have made between the emotional and cognitive brain, you need to understand the subdivision of implicit and explicit systems. For our discussion, implicit systems fall under the control of the emotional brain which leans heavily toward survival and mapping of memories. The explicit systems fall under control of the cognitive brain and require conscious thought to access. The implicit and explicit systems are important to note due to their connection to the memory systems of the human brain and at what speed the information stored by the memory systems is accessible. When we talk about training and proper behavioral responses under stress we are looking for a balance between the faster implicit systems and the slower executive control of the cognitive systems.

In the 1943 Disney cartoon *Reason and Emotion* we see a businessman and a caveman sat inside a human head (where the brain would be). The businessman sits at the front, crammed into a small space, holding a steering wheel. It appears he does not have any leg room. The rest of the brain space is occupied by the caveman, lounging in a comfortable recliner with plenty of room. To use this analogy, the businessman is the conscious you and is the pilot of the ship. The caveman is the autopilot, the subconscious you. Police officers can't afford to have a caveman in that seat. That caveman needs to be trained and dressed up like a calm quiet professional cop. We must always keep in mind though, that under that calm, professional exterior is a caveman. The caveman will always come out when the emotional load is too high. The goal is to have an executive in the pilot seat deciding what the ship, that is you, is going to attend to next. Under pressure and requiring specific skills, the calm quiet professional autopilot takes over with just enough direction and control from the pilot to keep the caveman from showing himself.

When we discuss performance in officer-involved shootings and then introduce the implicit and explicit systems, we can now quickly address a concept we will cover in more depth in the training section. Most law enforcement shooting skills emphasized in training are simply an exercise in operant conditioning. The target turns, or the buzzer sounds, and you draw and shoot at the designated target area within the given time frame. If you have practiced the skill enough, the stimulus response-style training will burn your responses to the target turn or buzzer into the neural circuitry. You will see improvements and you will find yourself having to think less about how to perform those functions. Another easy example is the act of riding a bicycle or driving a car. When first learning, constant thought (cognitive) is required until the proper actions are burned into the neural circuitry. Once you learn how to drive a car or ride a bike, it requires less cognitive control to perform the actions that have been burned into the procedural memory system. In other words, in your normal driving habits, your brain has established a baseline for how much cognitive control is required. Here is where it gets interesting. The implicit system is running the task of driving the car in the day-to-day operations. You don't have to consciously think about the pedal on the right accelerating the car and the one on the left stopping the car. Steering inputs, using the turn signals, observing traffic signals can all be done without a lot of conscious thought. The problem with driving a car, riding a bike, or shooting a gun is what happens when the emotional stress is increased such as being chased on your bike by an angry dog, or the car starting to spin out of control on ice, or a target that shoots back.

Implicit systems are fast because we don't have to think about them and the brain shows its amazing capacity to save energy by burning things into the circuitry to free up the conscious thought process which requires higher energy expenditure. So, here is the balance. When driving and using the implicit systems and an established baseline for the environment, the cognitive system is in a standby mode waiting for a deviation from the baseline (violation of expectations). As you are driving along and are approaching a bend in the roadway, you continue to navigate the bend which you cannot see around. As you navigate through the bend on the two-lane road you discover, much to your surprise, a herd of goats blocking both lanes of the road and the shoulders off both sides of the roadway. You have experienced a violation of your expectations and the cognitive (explicit) system is now evaluating the situation and the choice is made to slam on the brakes, hopefully before any impact can occur. Sometimes there isn't enough time for the cognitive system to override the implicit systems and an accident occurs. If you have extensive experience or training in violations of expectations while driving, the braking could occur by pure instinct driven by the "trained" emotional system. Remember, the cognitive system is slower because it delivers choices and a choice must be made. How fast you can choose the proper choice depends on your experience at making these choices relevant to the task at hand. A novice driver with a couple of weeks driving experience may panic and make no choice or the wrong choice and an accident occurs. A more experienced driver has dealt with violations of expectations while driving and easily navigates the same situation. The novice driver will have a heavier emotional response due to lack of experience and this will show in their performance.

When dealing with the brain and central nervous system it has been discovered that blood flow goes where the action is. If the novice driver's response is heavier on the emotional side, blood flow will be reduced for cognitive function. For the more experienced driver the violation of expectation has an emotional component to it, but experience provides balance to the systems and enough blood flow is available to the cognitive system to quickly make a choice and then default back to the implicit system for a faster trained procedural response.

Now we can relate the implicit and explicit systems back to law enforcement. In a previous example, we talked about establishing baselines at a domestic violence call on the front porch of a house involving an angry male subject standing over a seated female who appears to be frightened. Establishing your initial baselines and the initial communication process is a cognitive function requiring a certain amount of multi-tasking. Within the communication and observation processes, the brain should be primed for violations of expectations which may require conscious decision-making or an immediate procedural response (driven by the emotional system). If, suddenly, the male subject starts to lift his shirt with his right hand there should be a violation of your expectations. The implicit unconscious system should recognize the movement as a potential threat and appropriate counter measures should follow. In order to accurately assess the situation, cognition must be online to identify the movement after the emotional systems hint of danger, or we risk the mistake-of-fact use of force. The emotional system's hint will probably be that it's a weapon. Cognitive control will say move yourself, give commands, and properly identify what he is reaching for. If at the time this occurs the officer commands the male subject to move his hands away from his waistband while establishing a positive grip on his holstered firearm, you have a response to a violation of expectation occurring left of bang. If the suspect was hoping to get the drop on you, with your commands, state of readiness and composure, you have shown the male suspect you are ready for action and fully prepared if necessary to deal with his potentially violent actions. If he follows your commands, you take him into custody and find a concealed firearm in his waistband, you have successfully solved this encounter left of bang.

Now rewind and say that the male subject is making the same movement to his waistband, but you did not anticipate or see the initial movement. The subject removes the handgun from his waistband and is now pointing a gun at you before you realize what has happened. He fires the first shot as you are responding by drawing your firearm and moving between the suspect and the female. Your reactions to the suspect's actions are all right of bang and will necessarily involve a heavier emotional fight or flight response.

If we go back to the idea of most range training provided by law enforcement agencies being operant conditioning training, pure stimulus/response, then we can now recognize the problem. If stimulus is bang, then response is right of bang since action is always going to be faster than reaction unless the action was anticipated. Anticipation of the action can only happen left of bang, but most of training only covers what happens after the threat is already displayed.

Great cops learn how to be keen observers of baseline and recognizing key behavioral indicators foreshadowing potential violence. They develop these skills through experience including good decisions, bad decisions, or no decisions made by themselves, their peers, or the suspects they are dealing with throughout their career. But what if there was a way to train the brain to read these left of bang indicators to be better prepared with a balance between the emotional and cognitive, giving the officers their best chance at solving these complex and uncertain situations? I believe there is, and we will discuss ways of incorporating neuroscience into training to create programs that train the brain for reality instead of a return to the business as usual training. The results speak for themselves. If the training we are currently conducting in firearms is so effective, then why do officers miss so much in real confrontations? I am not picking on firearms training here. The training in defensive tactics, tactical response, and decision-making usually only cover what to do after the threat is already presented. These concepts are usually trained once or twice a year which is inadequate for dealing with emotional stressors. This can also lead to poor responses leading up to and during conflict. For the sake of trying to simplify these concepts I am presenting them separately, but I promise I will tie all these concepts together before we are done.

The Cognitive System

We have already established that the cognitive system is an explicit system meaning it requires conscious thought, the thinking part of you, to aid in problem solving and direction. The main component of the cognitive system is the prefrontal cortex which aids in such activities as thinking and reasoning through problems and interpreting the conscious self. In stressful situations, when the brain is in balance between the emotional and the cognitive, the prefrontal cortex controls executive functioning of the brain. This aids in determining what stimuli to focus on, prioritizing what decisions need to be made, evaluating the potential consequences of those decisions, and choosing immediate actions. In his book, *The Rise of Superman*, author Stephen Kotler describes the prefrontal cortex and its abilities in the following manner: "The PFC is the heart of our higher cognitive abilities. It's the place we collect data, problem solve, plan ahead, assess risk, evaluate rewards, analyze thoughts, suppress urges, learn from experience, make moral decisions, and give rise to our normal sense of self."[13] In other words, if the entire human body is a business, the prefrontal cortex is the CEO of the company.

In research done by Diamond et al. (2007), important effects of stress on the functioning of the prefrontal cortex were documented. In their findings it states, "Stress inhibits function of the prefrontal cortex which is revealed behaviorally as a narrowing of attention and impaired multi-tasking, or more globally as an impairment of complex learning." The research shows, "during stress the brain prioritizes the making of emotional memories and sacrifices the cortical process of determining the most appropriate response to the situation. The prefrontal cortex's ability to regain proper function depends on the intensity of the stressor and how effectively the individual copes with the situation."[14]

Research done by Lieberman et al. (2007) shows "neuroscience researchers have revealed the right ventrolateral prefrontal cortex is activated in almost every form of self-control

---

[13] Steven Kotler. *The Rise of Superman: Decoding the Science of Ultimate Human Performance* (New York, NY: Houghton Mifflin Harcourt Publishing Company, 2014), 49.

[14] D. M. Diamond, A. M. Campbell, C. R. Park, J. Halonen, and P. R. Zoladz. *The temporal dynamics model of emotional memory processing: A synthesis on the neurobiological basis of stress-induced amnesia, flashbulb and traumatic memories, and the Yerkes-Dodson Law. Neural Plasticity*, vol. 2007, Article ID 60803, doi:10.1155/2007/60803

and causally linked to motor self-control." [15] This correlates to the complex decisions in a lethal force situation where the brain understands the lethal threat but must decide not to fire because a civilian is in the way or another officer is in a crossfire situation. As we have discussed, the blood flow goes where the action is, and if more blood flow is going to the emotional side of the house, there will be diminished blood flow to the portions of the prefrontal cortex that aid in decision-making in events that are "tense, uncertain and ever-changing."

Further studies have linked the same area of the brain to cognitive self-control which allows you to suppress inaccurate information or actively avoid thinking of an image. If you are responding to an active shooter situation, your number one priority is to stop the shooter. First aid begins when the gunfight is over. This means you must have the ability under extreme stress to close off images of the severely wounded or your downed partner and focus on the task at hand. Again, too heavy an emotional response without some cognitive balance can drastically hinder this ability. It is balance in the systems we are looking for and should be training for. Emotions are not the enemy, and neither is cognition unless there is an excessive imbalance. Remember, with an excessive emotional response, you risk a pure fight or flight unthinking, disproportional response or a breakdown of procedural skills which can be performed without stress. Too much on the cognitive side and we hinder our ability to make quick decisions by being overwhelmed by choices and consequences. For peak performance under stress, the two systems are in balance and complement each other, and the elite performers

[15] M. D. Lieberman, M. D., Eisenberger, N. I., Crockett, M. J., Tom, S., Pfeifer, J. H., Way, B. M. (2007). *Putting feelings into words*: "Affect labeling disrupts amygdala activity to affective stimuli." *Psychological Science*, 18, 421-428.

can achieve that balance through experience, training, and mind-set. The question is, what can we do to teach the personnel who don't have the experience, or the mind-set, to get them on the right path for the changing fortunes of a law enforcement career?

If developed in stress-based training and under combat or use of force decision-making stressors, the cognitive system assists in balancing risks, creating strategies, and developing courses of actions even under what to the normal individual would be extreme emotional stress.

The Emotional System

To understand the components of the emotional system, you must go way back in time to when humans did not have access to modern technology and most of their fighting was done with either bare hands or rocks and sticks. The emotional systems of the brain were designed for personal survival and promulgation of the species. The emotional system decides, am I going to eat it or is it trying to eat me? Once that is settled, it's down to who am I going to mate with and how often to move the species along. This portion of the system is geared for survival; it steers you toward reward and away from excessive risk. How you "feel" when under an emotional system response is based on which neurochemicals are released in response to a stimulus. Note the word "feel." As soon as you describe how you feel to yourself or to another, you are engaging the cognitive system to explain an emotional response.

But keep in mind, science has shown it is not a one-way path. Emotions can influence cognition and cognition can influence emotions. For instance, you can be at a funeral and feel an emotional response you describe as sadness and a sense of loss. This would be cognition reacting to an emotional response. You can also sit in a chair and use your cognitive system to imagine losing someone you love, and your cognition can cause an emotional response. The systems are connected, and the deeper connections made over the course of human history are more important than ever.

I have chosen, for ease of discussion and understanding of the material, to divide the brain into the emotional and cognitive systems. You may have heard of the emotional side of the system referred to as the limbic system, and some describe the brain in three systems instead of two. The third portion of the brain usually discussed is the hypothalamus—pituitary pathways of the brain which regulate automatic regulatory things like temperature, blood pressure, and blood glucose. For general ease of understanding this hypothalamic pathway is referenced with the emotional or limbic brain by some neuroscientists. The key functions of the emotional system useful for our discussion are: the interpreting of emotional responses, storing memories, and regulating hormones, as well as involvement in sensory perception, motor function, and olfaction (sense of smell).

For the scientifically minded, the following is a list of the key structures of the brain involved in the emotional system and its connections to the cognitive system useful to our discussion.

1. Amygdala: almond-shaped mass of nuclei involved in emotional responses, hormonal secretions, and memory. The amygdala is responsible for fear conditioning or the associative learning process by which we learn to fear something.

2. Cingulate Gyrus: a fold in the brain involved with sensory input concerning emotions and the regulation of aggressive behavior.

3. Fornix: an arching band of white matter axons (nerve

fibers) that connect the hippocampus to the hypothalamus.

4. Hippocampus: a tiny nub that acts as a memory indexer sending memories out to the appropriate part of the cerebral hemisphere for long-term storage and retrieving them when necessary.

5. Hypothalamus: about the size of a pear, this structure directs a multitude of important functions. It wakes you up in the morning and gets the adrenaline flowing. The hypothalamus is also an important emotional center, controlling the molecules that make you feel exhilarated, angry, or unhappy.

6. Olfactory Cortex: receives sensory information from the olfactory bulb and is involved in the identification of odors.

7. Thalamus: a large, dual lobed mass of gray matter cells that relay sensory signals to and from the spinal cord and the cerebrum (part of the cognitive system).

8. Cerebrum: the largest and most highly developed part of the human brain. It encompasses about two-thirds of the brain mass and lies over and around most of the structures of the brain. The outer portion (1.5mm-5mm) of the cerebrum is covered by a thin layer of gray tissue called the cerebral cortex. The cerebrum is involved in several functions of the body including:

    - determining intelligence
    - determining personality
    - thinking
    - reasoning
    - producing and understanding language
    - interpretation of sensory impulses
    - motor function

- planning and organization
- processing sensory information[16]

A lot of the ideas for addressing the brain as the cognitive and the emotional come from a book written by David Eagleman called *Incognito*. Here is a quote from the book on the brain as a two-party system of reason and emotion:

When trying to understand the strange details of human behavior, psychologists and economists sometimes appeal to a "dual-process" account. In this view, the brain contains two separate systems: one is fast, automatic, and below the surface of conscious awareness, while the other is slow, cognitive, and conscious. The first system can be labeled automatic, implicit, heuristic, intuitive, holistic, reactive, and impulsive, while the second system is cognitive, systematic, explicit, analytic, rule-based, and reflective. These two processes are always battling it out.

Eagleman goes on to describe competing theories but continues with the idea of a dual processing system.

Although psychologists and economists think of the different systems in abstract terms, modern neuroscience strive for an anatomical grounding. And it happens that the wiring diagram of the brain lends itself to divisions that generally map onto the dual process model.

Some areas of your brain are involved in higher-order operations regarding events in the outside world (these include, for example, the surface of the brain just inside your temples, called the dorsolateral prefrontal cortex). In contrast, other areas are involved with monitoring your internal state, such as your level of

[16] Regina Bailey, "Anatomy of the Brain: Structures and Their Function." *Thought Co.*, Updated March 08, 2017 https://www.thoughtco.com/anatomy-of-the-brain-373479

hunger, sense of motivation, or whether something is rewarding to you (these areas include, for example, a region just behind your forehead called the medial prefrontal cortex, and several areas deep below the surface of the cortex). The situation is more complicated than this rough division would imply, because brains can simulate future states, reminisce about the past, figure out where to find things not immediately present, and so on. But for the moment, this division into systems that monitor the external and internal will serve as a rough guide, and a little later we will refine the picture.

After a quick explanation to why he chose the terms reason and emotion, Eagleman concludes with the following:

The rational system is the one that cares about analysis of things in the outside world, while the emotional system monitors internal state, and worries whether things will be good or bad. In other words, as a rough guide, the rational cognition involves external events, while emotions involves your internal state. You can do a math problem without consulting your internal state, but you can't order dessert off a menu or prioritize what you feel like doing next. The emotional networks are absolutely required to rank your possible next actions in the world: if you were an emotionless robot who rolled into a room, you might be able to make analyses about the objects around you, but you would be frozen with indecision about what to do next. Choice about the priority of actions are determined by our internal states: whether you head straight to the refrigerator, bathroom, or bedroom upon returning home depends not on the external stimuli in your home (those have not changed), but instead on your body's internal states.[17]

I hope at this point you are starting to develop an appreciation for each system, what they can and can't do, and the

---

[17] David Eagleman. *Incognito: The Secret Lives of the Brain.* (New York, NY: Vintage Books, 2012), 109.

importance of balance between the two. When in balance, the two systems complement each other. Not understanding this balance accounts for many of the mistake-of-fact shootings involving law enforcement, in my opinion. When an officer's skills match the perceived demands of the crisis situation, they have the best chance at maintaining cognitive appraisal and balance in the systems.

If we accept the fact that the emotional system serves the survival purposes of directing the mechanism toward reward and away from punishment, then we must understand both the fear response and why law enforcement and the military must train personnel to deal with the emotional responses of potential combative situations. For instance, the emotional system will tell you to run from gunshots but if you are a responder to an active shooter situation, then your job is to overcome the emotions directing you to flee to safety so that you may assume the risk on behalf of others. Sound impossible? It's done every day across the country and the world by law enforcement officers, firefighters, and the brave men and women of our military.

The 5% and Peak Performance

In all these professions, we have the "five percenters." These are the people that are the complex problem solvers, the ones who can balance emotions and reason, and can deal with extreme violence. The question is, what if we could take that five percent, and make it ten percent, then twenty percent, and so on, until we were confident we had developed programs to pass on the experience and teach others what the five percent are capable of?

First, we'll explain how threats are interpreted by the brain and then we will put it into the perspective of a law enforcement officer in a potentially life-threatening situation.

Let's start with a sensory input from one of the senses, usually sight or sound. The information travels to the sensory thalamus which acts as a relay station. Imagine two roads moving from the thalamus, one called the low road and one the high road. The low road takes sensory information almost instantly to the amygdala which is involved in threat response and the mapping of emotional memories. The amygdala performs an extremely fast but not necessarily accurate evaluation of the stimuli and can initiate an immediate behavioral response such as freezing, fight or flight, flinching, or the grasp reflex. Not long after the low road is traversed, a secondary signal is sent along the high road to the cortex. This road takes longer to travel but the information is processed more accurately, albeit at a slower speed than the low road response. The low road response is processed unconsciously, while the high road response is a conscious process. It is believed that if excessive amounts of chemicals are released by the emotional side of the house, mainly cortisol, the high road response to cognitive function can be delayed or cut off (amygdala hijack).

Joseph LeDoux is a neuroscientist and professor at New York University. He has extensively studied the amygdala and its role in emotions and mapping of emotional memories. His research on the emotional system and its effect on cognition give us the reason why law enforcement officers sometimes perform poorly under stress. To understand the low road and its importance for survival, in his book, *Anxious*, LeDoux explains the amygdala's role in emotional memories. He correlates a dog bite to how the emotional memory will be stored and then be able to initiate a survival response.

A stimulus becomes threatening by way of its association with something harmful. If you were bitten by a dog, the sight of that dog (or even a different dog) puts you into defensive mode and enables you to begin to protect yourself in anticipation of being bitten again ('once bitten, twice shy'). In order for this to happen, information about the sight and bite has to converge onto the same neurons in the amygdala. This convergence leads to an increase in the strength of the relation between the two stimuli.

In 1949, the Canadian psychologist Donald Hebb proposed that, when weak and strong stimuli activate the same neurons, the strong stimulus changes the chemistry of the neurons in such a way as to enable the weak stimulus to activate the neurons more strongly in the future. In our dog bite scenario, the strong sensation from being bitten modifies the chemistry of the neurons such that the sight of a dog alone comes to strongly activate the neurons in the future.[18]

LeDoux continues with the story of a dog bite and how the amygdala aids in a survival response and in the mapping of the memory for future use. Don't worry about the component parts of the amygdala, there won't be a test.

Before being bitten by the dog, his sight is a weak stimulus (in terms of its ability to activate the defensive survival circuit involving the lateral (LA) and central (CeA) amygdala and periaqueductal gray area (PAG)). While being bitten, the co-occurrence of sight of the dog (weak stimulus) is paired with the bite (strong stimulus). Later, the sight of the same dog, or even a different dog, activates the sight-bite association in the amygdala and thereby elicits defensive behavior, such as freezing, via the PAG.[19]

The weak stimulus triggering a stronger stimulus has links with anxiety issues and PTSD.

Now, back to the low road, the high road, and why it's important for both roads to be traveled and what happens when the emotional response elicited by the amygdala is so

---

[18] Joseph LeDoux. *Anxious: Using the Brain to Understand and Treat Fear and Anxiety* (New York, NY: Viking, 2015), 92.
[19] LeDoux, *Anxious*, 92.

large that the high road is blocked. I'm going to paraphrase a common reference used to explain the low and high road which LeDoux has presented on numerous occasions to ease the understanding.

Imagine you are hiking on a path in the woods. As you are walking, you sense something on the path to your left and you immediately freeze in place, then jump out of the way to your right. When you land, you look over to further examine the object of your concern and see that it is in fact a curved stick. The emotional system, geared to seek reward and avoid punishment, directed by the amygdala, is geared for a fast but not necessarily accurate response. Its job is to make unconscious decisions affecting survivability. The amygdala, if it could talk, would say, "it is better to mistake a stick for a snake and get out of the way, then to mistake a snake for a stick and get bit." The unconscious processing and the reflexive movement are the low road. When the cognitive system evaluates the situation, and recognizes the stick as opposed to the snake and you start to look around to see if anyone saw your movements, possibly hearing sounds come out of you only Michael Jackson could make, you have traveled the high road. As you can see, the two roads traveled are complemented by each other when there is a balanced response. The emotional system through unconscious processing makes the fast but not necessarily accurate moves when required that are then verified or debunked by the slower but more accurate cognitive system. The same thing happens when you turn a corner in your home and are startled by a family member almost running into you from around the corner. The initial startle and flinch or freeze is the emotional response. Recognition of family and a good laugh, the cognitive response. When we say slower, in a balanced system, we are talking milliseconds, but in an extreme emotional response, further delay or a complete shutdown of the cognitive system (amygdala hijack).

For example, an officer is in foot pursuit and is about to catch up to a suspect wanted for aggravated assault with a handgun. The suspect, who may be having a heavier emotional response, reaches toward his waistband, pulls out a cell phone and begins to turn to point it at the officer. Why would he do this? Possibly because he expects the officer to break for cover instead of continuing the pursuit. Or, maybe, the emotional system gives him the hint that now is an important time to call his lawyer. The officer, who knows the suspect is wanted for a gun crime, sees the movement to the waistband and has a heavy emotional response. Without cognitive control what is the emotional hunch of the officer going to be?

For peak performance there must be balance which means we cannot let the amygdala run wild. The heavier the response from the amygdala, the longer it takes for the secondary, high road to be traveled possibly due to an increase in cortisol levels in the blood. That high road is the thinking you, the one that thinks about consequences and conscious control of the situation. Which brings us back to the amygdala hijack and how dangerous it can be for our nation's protectors in law enforcement.

Revisiting the Amygdala Hijack

Earlier we discussed the amygdala hijack—what it is and what it does for the survival of the mechanism experiencing the hijack. Notice I said mechanism. When the amygdala hijack is occurring, the "conscious you" is offline. Fight, flight, freeze, posture, submit, flinch, and grasp are your major choices. The problem is these may not be the choices you need to solve the problem, only your emotional system's best guess. Even if fighting is the answer, without the executive control capabilities of the cognitive system, the response may not be measured, coordinated or proportional. Most excessive force complaints and excessive force violations of policies and the law, I believe, come from an amygdala hijack or at least an excessive emotional response. Remember, until that high road response from the thalamus to the prefrontal cortex occurs, conscious thought, problem solving, and knowing when to stop using force or temper it is effectively cut off until the emotional response subsides or is controlled. Training without the associative emotions and exercising of emotional control renders the user at an extreme disadvantage under real combat conditions, and marks the difference between the poor and peak performance officer. Unfortunately, the veteran officer got to where they can maintain cognitive control by trial and error under real-life extremes instead of quality training. Many officers lose their lives daily because they don't possess the required balance between the emotional and cognitive. Of course, officers should always keep in mind, you can do everything right and still lose your life. There is an element of luck in all confrontations. I may move left to avoid gunfire and walk right into a shot that would have missed had I stood still. Understanding that risk and the fact that you can't do a lot about it, should allow you to focus on the task at hand instead of things you cannot control.

Another analogy: in every fight gym in the world are people who like to hit the bags and do nice easy sparring. When these people spar against seasoned fighters, their skill set falls apart because they are used to hitting things that don't hit back. When you must fight and know you are going to take some hits, the emotional response can be severe if not professionally trained. It seems odd, but the secret to combat is to relax as best you can to keep the emotional system stimulated but not spiked.

Michael G. Malpass

Hunches: Gut Instincts

In his book, *Incognito*, David Eagleman discusses the power of the emotional system to create hunches which steer you toward reward or away from punishment. These hunches turn out to be more accurate than pure chance can predict when they are trained. As it turns out, the more experience you have with a subject and the emotions associated with it, the better the power of your hunches or intuitions will be. The following is an excerpt from the book discussing a study on hunches.

> In 1997, neuroscientist Antoine Bechara and his colleagues laid out four decks of cards in front of subjects and asked them to choose one card at a time. Each card revealed a gain or loss of money. With time, the subjects began to realize that each deck had a character to it: two of the decks were "good," meaning that the subjects would make money, while the other two were "bad," meaning they would end up with a net loss. As subjects pondered which deck to draw from, they were stopped at various points by the investigators and asked for their opinion: Which decks were good? Which were bad? In this way, the investigators found that it typically required about twenty-five draws from the decks for subjects to be able to say which ones they thought were good and bad. [...]

The investigators also measured the subject's skin conductance response, which reflects the activity of the autonomic (fight or flight) nervous system. Here they noticed something amazing: the autonomic (emotional) nervous system picked up on the statistics of the deck well before a subject's consciousness did. That is, when subjects reached for the bad decks, there was an anticipatory spike of activity—essentially, a warning sign. This spike was detectable by about the thirteenth card draw. So, some part of the subject's brain was picking up on the expected return from the decks well before they could consciously say why. This means that conscious knowledge of the situation was not required for making advantageous decisions.[20]

But once again, it is a two-party system and the balance of emotion and reason lead to better decisions. To show this the same study was done again and Eagleman writes:

> Even better, it turned out that people needed the gut feelings: without it their decision making would never be very good. Damasio and his colleagues ran the card-choice task using patients with damage to a frontal part of the brain called the ventromedial prefrontal cortex, an area involved in making decisions. The team discovered that these patients were unable to form the anticipatory warning signal of the galvanic skin response. The patient's brains simply weren't picking up on the statistics and giving them an admonition. Amazingly, even after these patients consciously realized which decks were bad, they still continued to make the wrong choices. In other words, the gut feeling was essential for advantageous decision making.

> This lead Damasio to propose that the feelings produced by physical states of the body come to guide behavior and decision making. Body states become linked to outcomes of events in the world. When something bad happens, the brain leverages the entire body (heart rate, contraction of the gut, weakness of the muscles and so on) to register that feeling, and that feeling becomes associated with the event. [...] Those feelings then serve to navigate, or at least bias, subsequent decision making. If the feelings from a given event are bad, they dissuade the action; if they are good, they encourage it.[21]

When we discuss these gut instincts and the influence

---

[20] David Eagleman. *Incognito: The Secret Lives of the Brain.* (New York, NY: Vintage Books, 2012), 66-67.
[21] Eagleman, *Incognito*, 67-68.

they have on behavior, you can appreciate the importance of behavioral analysis for police officers. Emotions carry behavioral "tells" that when read correctly can influence good decision-making by officers. There are reasons poker player covers their faces with big hats and sunglasses. They want to hide their behavioral responses. These "tells" are what the Left of Bang Program is all about.

Hunches or instincts are based on information gathered. Some instincts are considered inborn behaviors that are also processed unconsciously through the emotional system. Instincts such as the flinch and grasp reflex and the drive to promulgate the species are inborn and part of the emotional system. When a newborn baby hears a loud noise the startle response and flinch reflex ensue. Reach out your finger in front of a baby and they will grasp on. They are not taught to do these things; it comes with the initial programming.

Neuroscientists have shown pictures of just the faces of women with dilated and normal pupils to men. With no conscious awareness of why they are choosing, men looking at the photos, find the faces of the women with dilated pupils more attractive. How can that be? And why? Science says the answer is all about survival. The dilated pupils fool the emotional system to believe these women are in their ovulation cycles. Women in their ovulation cycle are prime for promulgation of the species, so the emotional system of the men tells them the opportunity for the survival of his bloodline is found here. Ever hear of several women living in close proximity to each other getting on the same ovulation cycles? The science is inconclusive, but some scientists believe it's an emotional brain response for competition to the selection of the best mates. Remember, the emotional system has been around a lot longer than the cognitive and the emotional system is geared toward survival. Am I going to fight, flight, eat, or mate? Pupil dilation, skin tone, and a host of other factors are evaluated by the emotional system to bias choice involving survival like the urge to mate to further the species. Pupil dilation through the release of dopamine has also been linked to sexual attraction in several studies.

Joseph LeDoux's research has shown that there are far more connections from the amygdala (emotional system) to the prefrontal cortex (cognitive) than there are connections from the prefrontal cortex to the amygdala. This reiterates the importance of the emotional system and its ability to guide behavior. Law enforcement officers must understand and train the cognitive ability to regulate the emotional response, understanding that, under pressure, the emotional side will attempt to take control and hinder executive control functions by the prefrontal cortex (cognitive side). Since there are more connections from the amygdala to the prefrontal cortex than the reverse, the emotional system has an easier time taking control than the cognitive.

In an article written by Major Andrew Steadman, he writes:

> When the limbic [emotional] system is heavily engaged, as it is during the high threat stress of combat, it will quite literally steal fuel from the prefrontal cortex, thus handicapping a leader's ability to combat the situation with cognition. As successful business consultant and CEO David Rock explains in, *Your Brain at Work*, "the degree of activation of the limbic system is the degree of deactivation of the prefrontal cortex." Brain research has also shown that there are many more neural connections that flow from the amygdala directly to the prefrontal cortex than vise-versa. Therefore, it is easy for our emotions to guide or suppress our rational thoughts. This is a crucial fact because military lead-

ers must preserve cognitive function when leading during combat.[22]

The emotional system through the amygdala, can initiate a survival response without conscious thought involved. This system has been in place long before we were civilized. Your emotional system unconsciously processes an object in your path and you either freeze in place, jump out of the way, or freeze for an instant and then jump out of the way. Whether or not it turns out to be a snake is irrelevant to the emotional system. In the case of immediate potential survival these instinctive responses are vital. When startled, you flinch. When you fall, you reach to grab.

Another quick story from *Incognito* by David Eagleman. This story starts like the beginning of a joke. Several scientists walk into a strip club in New Mexico. Not a joke however, this happened. The goal of the scientists was to see if there were conscious reasons why men chose certain women at the club to dance for them or were there certain unconscious drivers to the male behavior. Their study was based on the tips made by the dancers at the end of the night. Their findings showed that:

> During peak fertility, dancers raked in an average of $68 an hour. When they were menstruating, they earned only about $35 an hour. In between, they averaged $52. Although these women were presumably acting in a high capacity of flirtation throughout the month, their change in fertility was broadcast to hopeful customers by changes in body odor, skin, waist-to-hip ratio, and likely their own confidence as well. Interestingly, strippers on birth control did not show any clear peak in performance, and

---

[22] Major Andrew Steadman. US Army. "What Combat Leaders Need to Know about Neuroscience." *Military Review*, Vol. 91, No. 3, May-June 2011.

only earned a monthly average of $37 per hour (versus an average of $53 per hour for strippers not on birth control).[23]

This highlights the importance of the emotional system and its ability to provide information without conscious awareness involving potential risk and reward.

---

[23] David Eagleman. *Incognito: The Secret Lives of the Brain.* (New York, NY: Vintage Books, 2012), 94.

Michael G. Malpass

CHAPTER SEVEN

THE MEMORY SYSTEMS

It's a poor sort of memory that only works backwards.
– Lewis Carroll

Now let's look at how our memory systems work, how they aid or hinder us in combat, or any situation with high stress levels for that matter. We will also discuss emotion/cognition balance and the influence it has on access to the memory systems.

Short-Term Memory System

The term short-term memory is used to describe how much data can be temporarily stored by the system. Scientists believe that five to nine items can be held in short-term memory at any given time or about four chunks or pieces of information. It is sometimes referred to as working memory but most scientist believe that short-term memory is a subsystem of working memory.

Working Memory

Working memory is referred to as the chalkboard of the mind.

152

The working memory, part of the cognitive system, can use storage from short-term memory, organize, and manipulate information. In the book *Building Shooters,* which is a neuroscience-based approach to firearms training, author Dustin Salomon states, "Working memory is comparable in function to a computer's RAM (random access memory) system. It facilitates the rapid and efficient availability, processing, and utilization of data associated with actively occurring actions or events."[24]

Joseph LeDoux's research in *Anxious* shows a link between long-term memory retrieval and working memory. According to LeDoux, the working memory system has connections to the prefrontal cortex which allow us to observe our own behavior to regulate how we act socially and react to stress. Our emotional intelligence is a measure of how well we regulate our emotional responses to stressors. In the tactical environment and the learning environment, working memory acts as a bridge to the long-term memory systems for faster acquisition of information. Working memory is the reason for the ABC planning from the de-escalation program. By formulating in advance those tactical plans, you are effectively "priming" the system for easier recall once the true stress begins. Obviously, the more experience and training you possess specific to the topic at hand, the easier and more mature your planning will become. The more you develop these ABC plans, the easier it will be for the working memory to chunk information that is new and pertinent to the call at hand and access long-term data for the situations common to almost every tactical situation, such as pre-search for cover, watch the hands, control the people, etc.

----

[24] Dustin P Salomon. *Building Shooters: Applying Neuroscience Research to Tactical Training System Design and Training Delivery* (Silver Point, TN: Innovative Services and Solutions LLC, 2016), 33.

Working memory is also believed to be crucial in forming mental simulations in response to deviations from normal expectations. Working memory and its bridge to both procedural and declarative memory promote "lateral thinking." Steven Kotler in his book *The Rise of Superman* explains lateral thinking:

> Not surprisingly, our creativity lies deeply rooted in the right side of the brain: the side dominated by the implicit system. The reason has to do with the structure of neural networks. When the explicit system (mostly on the left side of the brain) handles a problem, the neurons involved are very close to one another. This much proximity leads to linear connections, logical deductions, and all the other keystones of standard reasoning. When the implicit system is at work, its reach is much broader–far flung corners of the brain are talking to one another. This is known to experts as "lateral thinking" or, to the business executives who so crave this talent: "thinking outside of the box." It means that novel stimuli can combine with random thoughts and obscure memories and the result is something utterly new.[25]

The working memory has heavy ties to the prefrontal cortex within the cognitive system. An uncontrolled or poorly controlled emotional response can inhibit the long road path to cognitive function and inhibit lateral thinking, as well as complex problem solving. The key to lateral thinking and complex problem solving is to control the emotional response and engage the cognitive where working memory is focused on the task at hand and executive function capabilities exist.

---

[25] Steven Kotler. *The Rise of Superman: Decoding the Science of Ultimate Human Performance* (New York, NY: Houghton Mifflin Harcourt Publishing Company, 2014), 39.

Long-Term Memory System

Declarative Memory

The declarative memory system is an explicit system that requires conscious thought to access the information contained within. "The information, skills, actions, and associations stored within the parameters of declarative memory require intentional effort to access. Examples of declarative memory include facts, figures, and procedures that are learned, yet require thought and effortful, conscious recall."[26]

Within the declarative memory system are two types of stored memories called semantic and episodic memories. "Semantic memories involve knowledge you have about a thing or situation that does not involve you. You can learn some facts about what a wedding is like by reading a guide (semantic memory), but you can only know what your own wedding was like after you experience it (episodic memory)."[27]

When performing if/then tactical thinking, which is part of your ABC planning, you are using your working memory to access information in the declarative memory to run simulations in preparation for the situations ahead. LeDoux explains:

> The relation between long-term memory retrieval and working memory is supported by several lines of research. For example, both episodic and semantic memory retrieval are impaired by

---

[26] Dustin P Salomon. *Building Shooters: Applying Neuroscience Research to Tactical Training System Design and Training Delivery* (Silver Point, TN: Innovative Services and Solutions LLC, 2016), 35.
[27] Joseph LeDoux. *Anxious: Using the Brain to Understand and Treat Fear and Anxiety* (New York, NY: Viking, 2015), 182.

damage to areas of the prefrontal cortex that are involved in working memory, and prefrontal neural activity has been correlated with both episodic and semantic memory retrieval. It should be pointed out that episodic memory also engages the parietal cortex which, as we've seen, is involved in attention and working memory. Further, retrieval is impaired by increased cognitive load on working memory (i.e., thinking about something else while trying to remember a particular detail) and improved when cognitive load is reduced.[28]

This is important because overloading the emotional side can lead to distracting thoughts such as, "Oh my God, I am going to die!" Those distracting thoughts during an encounter can diminish working memory and your ability to think your way through the problem when something other than a procedural response is required. Distracting thoughts can also decrease your ability to perform a procedural skill you can perform well when excessive emotions are not involved.

Procedural Memory

Procedural memory is an implicit system, meaning that your brain holds knowledge of something that your mind cannot explicitly access. Driving a car once you have been driving for a while, hitting a baseball, riding a bike, the drawing and firing of a gun in response to the buzzer or target turning, are all examples of movements directed by the procedural memory system once you are past the novice stage of learning the movements. Implicit because, while you can perform the movements, you would find it impossible to describe in detail exactly which nerves and muscles and portions of the brain are firing to make the actions necessarily occur.

---

[28] LeDoux, *Anxious*, 186-187.

Procedural memory exists for the things that need to be done faster than the conscious can process.

Take hitting a baseball. On August 20, 1974, in a game between the California Angels and the Detroit Tigers, *The Guinness Book of World Records* clocked Nolan Ryan's fastball at 100.9 miles per hour (44.7 meters per second). If you work the numbers, you'll see that Ryan's pitch departs the mound and crosses home plate, sixty-feet, six inches away, in four-tenths of a second. This gives just enough time for light signals from the baseball to hit the batter's eye, work through the circuitry of the retina, activate successions of cells along the loopy superhighways of the visual system at the back of the head, cross vast territories to the motor areas, and modify the contractions of the muscles swinging the bat. Amazingly, this entire sequence is possible in less than four-tenths of a second; otherwise no one would ever hit a fastball. But the surprising part is that conscious awareness takes longer than that: about half a second. So, the ball travels too rapidly for batters to be consciously aware of it. One does not need to be consciously aware to perform sophisticated motor acts.[29]

If I sit in a chair and visualize hitting baseballs, I am using the declarative or explicit memory system. If I go to the park to hit baseballs, I need to use procedural memory to hit the ball.

Let's put this into the context of a law enforcement officer contacting a subject on a routine call. You are a law enforcement officer responding to a burglary alarm at two o'clock in the morning at a business that has recurring problems with false alarms. As you are driving to the call you consider canceling your backup, after all it's just another false alarm, right? The declarative memory system accessed

[29] David Eagleman. *Incognito: The Secret Lives of the Brain.* (New York, NY: Vintage Books, 2012), 9.

through working memory kicked in to remind you of the previous false alarms but then another declarative memory kicks in: the story told in your academy of an officer killed on a repeat false alarm shot dead by a suspect. Your working memory now refocuses and you start to quickly formulate your ABC plans. Due to your experience on the job, your working memory is good at chunking material and while your plans are not elaborate, they are priming the system for faster acquisition under stress.

You arrive on scene and while waiting for your backup, decide to walk around the small building to check for any signs of a forced entry or open doors or windows. As you walk around the building you are not complacent, you have chosen to use working memory to stay cautious and prepared instead of complacent because you understand that surprises spike the emotional brain, can lead to an imbalance, and hinder performance under stress. As you reach the back of the building, you can see a car parked in the rear parking lot that you have never seen before. As you move toward the car to give dispatch the plate number, (a conscious decision made by the explicit systems) you sense movement coming from a window of the building (emotional system through the amygdala). You then turn and observe a male subject in all black clothing lowering himself through a window that is about eight feet off the ground. Your heart rate increases, your breath becomes shallow. The emotional system directed by the amygdala is preparing for a confrontation. But you are a well-trained officer, you have a good skill set and you are up on the latest science involving peak performance under stress. You start to use techniques (which we'll discuss later) to settle the emotional side and achieve as much balance with the cognitive that you can under the circumstances.

Cognitive control is important here because we are still left of bang. Your working memory is prepared and primed now to aid in threat identification. You are good with your defensive tactics skills and with your firearm, and those skills are in your procedural memory system for fast and efficient use. But which will you need? Working memory and conscious thought is evaluating the situation and preparing for potential conflict. Because your brain systems are in balance, numerous networks in the systems are working in the background without conscious thought. This primes the unconscious system which is faster at identifying threats and promotes lateral thinking.

As the male subject lowers himself to the ground, he is facing away from you toward the building. Seeing the subject creates a deviation from your established baseline of the situation. You quickly use working memory to form a plan on the fly which includes moving to cover and addressing the subject from behind something that stops bullets. You quickly observe the back of the building has a covered patio which extends around fifteen feet from the building and is supported by brick pillars. You quickly move to one of the pillars as the subject's feet touch the ground and he starts to turn toward you. In a loud, authoritative voice, you command, "Police, don't move!" (cognitive control). The subject continues to turn, and his hands are now moving to his waistband, the area where weapons are kept 90 percent of the time. As you moved to the pillar for cover, you drew your firearm and were prepared with the weapon raised but your focus was on the male subject. You again yell, "Stop!" but his shirt is raised, and his right hand is reaching into his waistband. You have trained for this, you are mentally, physically, and spiritually ready to do whatever it takes to secure the safety of innocents, fellow officers, and yourself, in that order. Your planning and preparation have placed you in a position where the advantage is yours. You understand that action is faster than reaction unless the movement is anticipated and because you are left of bang with your preparation, you are anticipating trouble.

Next, you direct three hundred lumens of light from your flashlight to the subject's eyes and then quickly to his waistband. You still must identify what he is reaching for. If he is reaching for a gun he will find it harder to target you after the light has been directed into his eyes. Your emotional system thinks gun, but your rational system knows that under stress, people sometimes don't do rational things. You remember that his emotional system may be running wild and his rational abilities may be diminished. His right hand is now pulling something from his waistband and your procedural memory kicks in. You are still focused on the suspect, but your gun is now pointed at the subject at a low-ready, so you can still observe his hands. Procedural memory brought the weapon up to a loose focus, but the working memory is focused on the task and you are maintaining cognitive control. The subject's movement is quick and as he pulls an object out of his waistband you secure yourself further behind cover as your finger works its way to the trigger and you prepare for a gunfight. Your firearms training though, was focused on left of bang observations and thousands of decisions made about when to shoot and not shoot the gun.

You are nervous but under cognitive control, as you are preparing for what the emotional side of the house is telling you will be a gunfight. Because of your prior ABC planning, the prep work of the working memory, and because you understand the balanced brain, you have placed yourself left of bang in a good position to resolve this situation effectively. Because you were ahead of the game, your cognitive system recognizes that the subject's arm is not moving toward you, consistent with aiming a firearm and instead is throwing the object to the ground off to his right. You immediately move your finger away from the trigger and readdress verbally and you and your newly arrived backup take him into custody without further incident. The object he threw was a gray money envelope used for making bank transactions filled with cash from the business.

The goal here was to attempt to show the complexities involved with preparing for and effectively dealing with the pre-planning for the call, at the call, the people at the call and the deviations from expectations that occur during these calls. If I failed to do so or have only succeeded in confusing you more, I'll try to clear things up as we proceed.

Here's where it gets interesting. If the only training you have done on the firearms training range is operant conditioning, pure stimulus response without associative decision-making skills included, then the previous example may have ended quite differently. For instance, if your only training involves the target turning or the buzzer sounding, and you fire your handgun every time, then you are priming the procedural, non-conscious system for similar performance. This style of training is all right of bang and is more conducive to competition shooting than training for legal defense of a shooting you are involved in. If the only shoot-no-shoot training you do is a couple of video simulations once a year and the rest of the year is pure stimulus response shooting, you are priming your system for a mistake-of-fact shooting which the county attorney's may find justified under the "lawful but awfuls" or may lead to your indictment.

How do we want the system to work? We want the confidence to know that our procedural system is effectively trained to respond once we have released cognitive control to allow for the correct procedural response. The only way to do this is to place a heavy focus on decisions made in training before the gun is fired. The anatomy of the average police shooting is not pure stimulus response. If you exit your patrol car and see a subject raising a gun toward you, we now have a stimulus response shooting. They do happen, but they are rare. Now, if we want to train effectively for a pure stimulus response shooting then we again better focus on what we train the procedural system to do. For instance, on the average qualification course, you have numerous officers on the line qualifying at the same time which allows for only limited movement on the range. A target turns, representing a lethal threat and you are expected to stand your ground, draw your weapon, and fire to the predetermined target zone. In a study done on stress, it was found that under stress, hormones released into the system "act as a 'switch' that highly favors the procedural memory system."[30]

If most of your training is for the qualifications score, as a lot of police agencies are, then you can expect many of these behaviors as a default system under stress. Remember, what you do the most is indexed in the procedural memory system and may be one of the systems hunches under stress. Instructors tell officers to "get off the X" and move to cover or move to make targeting more difficult, but due to range constraints it is rarely practiced. In training, the target turns representing a lethal threat and officers repeatedly stand their ground and try to out shoot someone who is already pointing a gun at them. Does this make sense? As we have discussed, it takes about a half second under the best of circumstances to process visual information. That means the officer is already at least a half second behind the curve. That is at least a half-second to process the visual information but then at least another quarter of a second, under the best circumstances, to effectively respond. Without training designed to positively train the procedural systems with cognitive override control, the higher the likelihood of a mistake-of-fact shooting, disproportional or non-viable emotional responses under stress, or a dead or wounded cop. Keep in

---

[30] Dustin P Salomon. *Building Shooters: Applying Neuroscience Research to Tactical Training System Design and Training Delivery* (Silver Point, TN: Innovative Services and Solutions LLC, 2016), quoting Schwabe *et al*, 2010, 45.

mind also that most of the law enforcement qualification targets don't even display a lethal threat, just the black or gray silhouette of a human. Why would we want to train the brain of an officer to shoot at a human silhouette they cannot identify that is not presenting a justifiable threat to shoot?

In the law enforcement community, the term "training scars," refers to behaviors expressed under stress, ingrained in poor training, that are not conducive toward the effective resolution of the conflict at hand. Remember, science has shown that under stress the system favors defaulting to the emotional side of the house and the procedural memory system.

The problem is, bad training is still training and what you do the most gets burned into the circuitry. Some training targets for firearms show a picture of a subject pointing a gun at you and some a dark silhouette of a humanoid figure with no weapons present. If the target turns and you are responding to a subject already pointing a gun at you, the odds are not in your favor if you stand still and try to outshoot the shooter. On the range you can't move during formal group training. This can develop a training scar, as the emotional systems "hunch" will be based on what has been performed the most. If the target turns and you are training to shoot a dark silhouette without a weapon presented, what may your default behavior be under stress? The number of examples of this kind of behavior under stress are too numerous to mention, but I will provide a few others. We have several videos showing officers in scenario training, recovering their own weapon back from a suspect who had disarmed the officer, only to hand the weapon back to the suspect. Why would this happen? In the past when training weapon recovery, trainers were trying to get as many repetitions of weapon retention in the belief that more repetitions meant better training. Under stress without some cognitive override, the brain defaulted to the emotional side and the system defaulted to what it had done the most. That was to quickly hand the weapon back to the "bad guy" to get more repetitions.

Here's an example a little closer to home for me. Several years ago, before the explosion of mixed martial arts schools, an amateur fighter who knew I had competitive fighting experience asked for help for an upcoming fight. His problem was when he was taken down by an opponent, he would default and move to a guard or bottom scissor position. If you are not familiar with the position it really doesn't matter; just understand it is a position you would want to know how to get out of to recover to a standing position or to obtain a better-grounded position on your opponent. On short notice with only two weeks before the fight, we opted for repetitions and would do timed rounds with him constantly being placed in the position, escaping, and then immediately dropping down into the position again to get more repetitions.

You can probably guess what happened during the real competition. He was taken down, moved to guard, initiated a beautiful escape, then flopped back down onto his back, and moved right back into a guard position. Fortunately, he was able to escape a second time but after the round ended he apologized and I informed him the fault was mine because of how we trained. This is one of the events that led me to start studying how we learn and perform under stress. At that time, there were theories, but not a lot of hard data on stress and learning. Fortunately for us, more has been learned due to technology advances about the brain in the last five years than all of history before that. This now gives us the science instead of information we only learn through trial and error experience.

One of the key concepts I want any student I teach to understand is that the brain is always learning and most of that learning is done unconsciously through the implicit systems. Under extreme stressors, the system favors the implicit. What skills do you want in your procedural system? If most of your training is only a violent stimulus, then your response will reflect that, and you have missed out on all things you should be doing to place yourself in the best position to either prevent or deal with the violence. In other words, you are failing to do any Left of Bang work. What if, by understanding the brain, its systems, and the balance we hope to maintain, we could start training from day one to be left of bang, making sound tactical decisions to place yourself in the best position to avoid over excitation of the emotional system and a draining of performance levels? This same work would include behavioral indicators expressed subconsciously by suspects whose emotional systems are in a fight or flight response.

Under the stress of violent behavior, the emotional system, including the procedural memory system, wants to take over. Once the fight is on, it's a good idea to be well trained and let the procedural system do its work. But here is the problem: a law enforcement officer, or the average citizen in a self-defense situation for that matter, must have cognitive balance to recognize if it really is a fight, if too many innocent civilians are in the way, or to recognize when the fight is won, and the force can stop. If all of life was the pure battle for survival and promulgation of the species, then letting the emotional system and the procedural memory system take complete control would be the most efficient way to run the brain. Life however has evolved and so has the cognitive systems of the brain. The most beneficial aspect of the cognitive system may very well be its ability to modulate the emotional response when trained.

The problem is that training without the understanding of the balanced brain leads to mistakes of fact, excessive force issues, and poor decision-making left of bang. The emotional side of the brain cares about the mechanism first, not the conscious you, just the component mechanisms. The mechanism can tell you and show you what you need to hear and see to initiate what it perceives to be a survival response. Remember though, these biases and hunches are quick but not necessarily accurate without training sound skills with emotional balance. After that, it cares about the people you have an emotional connection with, like when the house is on fire, but the parents risk all to save their children. What about the stories of parents who flee from a house on fire and forget their children are inside? Sounds a lot like an amygdala hijack with no conscious control. Cognitive control is needed to recognize others are involved in the crisis and need saving, as well as when the fight is over and when to shoot or not shoot.

The goal is to understand the brain balance, establish baselines and look for deviations from these baselines left of bang. This makes it easier to maintain cognitive balance and prevent a situation where the violence is a surprise, risking an extreme emotional response, or worse, a full amygdala hijack. The goal is also to train for the ambush situations where the violence is sudden and extreme for an appropriate procedural response. But keep in mind, the procedural response to someone pointing a gun at you may be to move to cover or move and shoot but without cognitive control you may not see an officer in a crossfire situation with you or innocent civilians in your way. You may also forget to move and attempt to stand your ground and shoot if you have more repetitions of that response in training.

It is my belief, and I think the science supports it, that most of excessive force complaints, mistake-of-fact shootings, and flat out bad shoots, are the result of improper training and an inability to achieve balance between the cognitive and emotional. An overexcited emotional system without cognitive override leading officers to a disproportionate response.

Taming the Serpent

In the book *Incognito*, Eagleman says:

There can be a large gap between knowledge and awareness. When we examine skills that are not amenable to introspection, the first surprise is that implicit memory is completely separable from explicit memory: you can damage one without hurting the other. Consider patients with anterograde amnesia, who cannot consciously recall new experiences in their lives. If you spend an afternoon trying to teach them the video game Tetris, they will tell you the next day that they have no recollection of the experience, that they have never seen this video game before, and most likely, that they have no idea who you are either. But if you look at their performance on the game the next day, you'll find that they have improved exactly as much as non-amnesiacs. Implicitly their brains have learned the game – the knowledge is simply not accessible to their consciousness.[31]

Eagleman then goes on to explain that most of our learning is done unconsciously through the emotional system to interact in our everyday world so that the conscious mind is freed up to focus on tasks at hand.

One more analogy to hopefully ingrain the importance of balance in the emotional and cognitive systems as it applies to procedural memory and working memory. If I was to ask you to go out to your garage get in your car and proceed to drive to the nearest grocery store, other than the finding of the keys and deciding which route you were going to take, the exercise would be almost completely run on procedural memory. As we have discussed, the actual driving of the car, is all done on procedural memory (unconscious system). That is why we can drive and feel free to daydream if we are prepared for violations of expectations like another driver swerving in front of you or coming to an abrupt stop in front

---

[31] David Eagleman. *Incognito: The Secret Lives of the Brain*. (New York, NY: Vintage Books, 2012), 58.

167

of you. Now, let's say that I asked you to do the same exercise except now as you started to drive you realize you and your car have been mysteriously transported to another country. As you realize the rules of the road have changed, the procedural memory can still run your car but the working memory (cognitive system) must be heavily engaged to stay on the correct side of the street and navigate the turns.

It seems that the balanced brain is important for the sake of efficiency in all levels of performance but especially under stress. Cognitive functions like the working memory and the declarative memory system aid us in the development of the ABC plans, as well as from deviations from expectations. Once the violence is on and the decision to use force is made, the emotional/procedural response takes precedent with cognitive executive control available to measure the force response then decide when force is no longer needed. Unfortunately, some police use-of-force shootings have an uncontrolled emotional response with cognitive functions diminished for too long. To be clear, this is not the fault of the officers but instead to their training. To expand on the efficiency of the two systems, we return to the work of Eagleman:

> When the brain finds a task it needs to solve, it rewires its own circuitry until it can accomplish the task with maximum efficiency. The task becomes burned into the machinery. This clever tactic accomplishes two things of chief importance for survival.
>
> The first is speed. Automatization permits fast decision making. Only when the slow system of consciousness is pushed to the back of the queue can rapid programs do their work. Should I swing forehand or backhand at the approaching tennis ball? With a 90-mph projectile on its way, one does not want to cognitively slog through the different options. A common misconception is that professional athletes can see the court in "slow motion" as suggested by their rapid and smooth decision making.

But automatization simply allows the athletes to anticipate relevant events and proficiently decide what to do. Think about the first time you tried a new sport. More experienced players defeated you with the most elementary moves because you were struggling with a barrage of new information — legs and arms and jumping bodies. With experience, you learned which twitches and feints were the important ones. With time and automatization, you achieved speed both in deciding and in acting.

The second reason to burn tasks into the circuitry is energy efficiency. By optimizing its machinery, the brain minimizes the energy required to solve problems. Because we are mobile creatures that run on batteries, energy saving is of the highest importance.[32]

Emotional Intelligence

Emotional intelligence is a measure of your cognitive appraisal skills. It involves your ability to recognize when emotions are getting spiked and when they may not be spiked enough. Pure boredom with a task, then a sudden surprise, will excite the emotional side of the house. An already excited emotional system that is suddenly surprised, can throw the system into severe anxiety or panic. Emotional intelligence involves knowing your balance between the emotional and cognitive and maintaining homeostasis. It also involves the right amount of cognition in standby mode for the violations of expectations. Emotional intelligence is the key to maintaining a healthy life, both on and off duty, as the stressors from the job and personal life can build up. This elevates the emotional side of the house and without the ability to

---

[32] Eagleman, *Incognito*, 72.

detect deviations from your own emotional baseline, you may not know the stressors are affecting you until your health or physical well-being is impacted. Mindfulness meditation, which will be discussed later, is one of the keys for learning to manage the emotional system and increase cognitive appraisal and thus emotional intelligence.

CHAPTER EIGHT

STRESS, PRESSURE, AND THE DIFFERENCE BETWEEN THE TWO

No man is worth his salt who is not ready at all times to risk his body, to risk his well-being, to risk his life, in a great cause.

– Teddy Roosevelt

Stress and Pressure

The book *Performing Under Pressure* relates the difference between stress and pressure and the influence that each can have on performance when performance really matters.

> We experience feelings of stress when the demands (stressors) of the environment in which we are working outweigh our ability or perceived ability to respond to them. Think about all the demands made on you in the course of a day, from paying the mortgage, to doing well at work, to parenting, etc. Stress refers to the situation of too many demands and not enough resources— time, money, energy—to meet them.[33]

---

[33] Hendrie Weisinger, and J. P. Pawliw-Fry, *Performing Under Pressure: The Science*

So, let's say you are a law enforcement officer who is currently off-duty, but it is your workday. You are due at work in five hours, but in the meantime: you have bills that need to be paid, you have to pick up your uniform from the dry cleaners, your spouse wants to talk about taking time off for the family and your current attitude around the house which they believe is work related. You do the best you can to tackle these issues while also handling unexpected phone calls, including the principle of your kid's school who needs a meeting with you and your spouse due to their behavior. You barely make it to work on time and are still worried about the school meeting, the bills, your attitude, and what the hell you are going to do about them. Your first call after briefing involved terrible things done to a child. You leave that call emotionally upset and angry at the in-custody suspect. Then, you must deal with a drunk individual trespassing at a business, when your boss informs you that you are taking calls too slow and he is investigating a complaint against you from your previous shift. You feel—overwhelmed; you feel stress. The difference between stress and pressure can be described this way:

> Those who study pressure and its effects describe pressure as a situation in which you perceive that something at stake is dependent on the outcome of your performance. Typically, the outcome either advances your chances of success or sets you back. For our earliest ancestors, these moments were related to survival. Often their lives were dependent on the outcome of their performance. Success would allow them to live another day. Today, a stellar presentation to your boss is apt to advance you; mismanaging a mission critical project can set you back.

> While in a stressful situation there are (nonspecific to the task)

---

of Doing Your Best When It Matters Most (New York, NY: Crown Publishing Group, 2015), 36.

multiple ways to respond that can help you manage stress better, in a pressure situation there is only one response requirement: that you get the job done correctly—whether that means safely landing a helicopter, delivering a persuasive presentation, or, in basketball, making a game winning free throw. In other words, while there are multiple ways to manage pressure, the end game is always task-specific; you are trying to successfully do something to meet the demands of the situation. In a stressful situation, reduction is the goal. In a pressure moment, success is the goal. Thinking that you must be successful all the time means you are under pressure all the time."[34]

To elaborate on the previous example of the officer at work and the events of his day, the day-to-day things leading up to going to work and the details of the beginning of his workday, caused stress in his life. At the end of the day, how he reacts to those stressors will not have a significant effect on his immediate survival, unless he allows those emotional stressors to build up throughout the course of his shift. Pressure is when the officer on a call sees a subject aiming a gun in their direction. Pressure because in this moment the response must be demand specific to solve the immediate problem. The challenge for law enforcement officers is that both stress and pressure can tax the emotional system, and without a way of dealing with stress, the spiked emotional system can be left behind the curve when dealing with pressure. The stress we bring to work can hinder our ability to deal with pressure situations at work.

In a stressful situation, practicing a relaxation technique might help us feel less overwhelmed and help us regain our perspective and composure. In a pressure moment, relaxing might help us, but we also have to deliver on the required

---

[34] Weisinger and Pawliw-Fry, *Performing Under Pressure*, 37.

behavior or we don't advance.[35]

Keep in mind, to an unbalanced emotional system, stress and pressure are one and the same and can place an individual in a constant perceived survival response. Therein lies the major problem. You must address stress in your life because the build-up of multiple stressors or one major stressor can start to overexcite the emotional system. With the emotional system already spiked, the application of a true pressure situation requiring the balanced brain, will already have the balance tilted heavily toward the emotional side. The further the balance is broken to the emotional side, the more you must do to spend precious energy to find balance. Balance is where good decision-making and sound procedural responses with cognitive/executive control are found.

Factors Affecting Performance Under Pressure

In *Performing Under Pressure*, Weisinger and Pawliw-Fry state there are truths about pressure that we need to know and understand:

There are three basic and powerful truths about pressure. They are powerful because they influence our life every day, often in ways that we are not aware of, and almost always to our detriment.

The first is that pressure disrupts what we value most: our relationships, our careers, our parenting effectiveness, and our core ethical and moral decision making. The consequences of pressure can break a marriage, derail a career, and cause children to pull away from their parents or feel the need to cheat to meet

---

[35] Weisinger and Pawliw-Fry, *Performing Under Pressure,* 38.

their parent's expectations. And it can compromise our very integrity.[36]

However, in a law enforcement career, it can cost you your life or your freedom.

The second truth is that people who handle pressure better than others do not 'rise to the occasion' or perform statistically better than they do in non-pressure situations. If you are a sports fan, you've been fed a myth by the media that some athletes are 'clutch' performers who do better under pressure. Or maybe you've heard that some people at work do more creative work, are more productive, work better as a team, or add more value to a client under pressure. But it's not true. Moreover, perpetuating this fiction only exacerbates poor performance under pressure.[37]

The book goes on to mention research performed by David Grabiner on athletes in professional baseball and professional basketball. Their findings show that while any athlete can deliver a clutch performance under pressure, statistics show athletes in both sports perform no better over the course of their careers in clutch situations that they do on any other occasion. The fact is, they are consistent in their performance while a lot of athletes' performance degrades to an extreme when under pressure. This fact alone should be liberating. Anyone can deliver a clutch performance when it matters. When your life is on the line ... it matters a lot.

The third truth, confirmed by our study of more than twelve thousand people and conducted over a ten-year period, is that you simply need to leverage the natural pressure management tools each of us already possesses to counteract pressure's inju-

---

[36] Weisinger and Pawliw-Fry, *Performing Under Pressure*, 16.
[37] Weisinger and Pawliw-Fry, *Performing Under Pressure*, 16.

rious effects. When it comes to handling pressure, most individuals fail to leverage these tools, and thus handicap themselves.[38]

What do these tools do? They help you to maintain the balance between the emotional and the cognitive. We'll discuss the tools in the section on biohacks.

Choking Under Pressure

We have briefly discussed what can happen when either the cognitive or emotional systems are too far out of balance. Too much cognitive and we risk "paralysis by analysis," where the mind is bogged down with too many possibilities and too many consequences for those possibilities. Thinking cognitively of a skill burned into the procedural memory can cause you to overthink and forget how to perform an already mastered skill. Too heavy a response from the emotional side and we risk at most, the amygdala hijack or at the least a degrading of the procedural skills we need to solve the problem.

In my twenty-five-year career, I have heard people teach that officers need to learn how to manage their "shit" under stress and I'm guilty of saying it in the past to officers whose performance was placing everyone involved at a scene, including other officers, at risk. But in my career, I have never heard anyone take on the challenge of explaining exactly how to get that done. Recent findings in neuroscience and performance psychology have started to tackle these issues and it's time for these important findings to translate to law enforcement.

So, what do we know about what causes people who already have a certain skill level in a job or task to perform

---

[38] Weisinger and Pawliw-Fry, *Performing Under Pressure*, 16.

poorly under pressure?

A complex interaction of three factors is the heart of the human performance system: (1) physical arousal, (2) thoughts, and (3) behavior. These factors operate as a system, and each of them influences the others; a change in one stimulates a change in the others. Think about a recent time that provoked strong emotions in you—and you will recall how quickly the physiological effects showed up in your body and the impact they had on your behavior and decision-making.

In order to perform effectively under pressure, you need to leverage these factors to your advantage. That is, you need to be able to regulate your physical arousal, think clearly, and execute the appropriate response to your capability.[39]

Putting these contributors to poor performance into the context of a law enforcement officer in a potentially violent situation, we will be able to see the interaction between physical arousal, thought, and behavior. If you remember, at the beginning of the book we talked about an officer responding to an active shooter situation and they believe they are going to be the first officer on scene. The fight or flight response can be quite extreme based on their experience, levels of training, and confidence in their abilities. As the officer is arriving on scene and without any cognitive control, their heart rate could be as high as one hundred and ninety beats per minute. Keep in mind that research done by Dave Grossman and Loren Christensen for their book, *On Combat*, shows performance starts to degrade after one hundred forty-five beats per minute unless the body is trained to perform while in those ranges. Numerous studies of Special Forces personnel show them at peak performance with heart rates of up to one hundred seventy-five beats per minute, but

---

[39] Weisinger and Pawliw-Fry, *Performing Under Pressure*, 58.

this is a trained response. NASCAR drivers can keep one hundred and seventy-five beats per minute sustained during a race. Untrained, if the average person tried to sustain one hundred seventy-five beats per minute for four hours they would risk serious health problems, but NASCAR drivers do it on a regular basis.

The untrained officer responding to the active shooter may not recognize their heart is racing, and their breath is becoming more shallow and rapid. The physiological response of the elevated heart rate and breath affect the emotional system which can then cause the physiological effects to worsen. With the emotional system becoming increasingly excited, cortisol levels in the blood increase and working memory now suffers. With the working memory inhibited, your mind becomes filled with distracting thoughts and your ability to use the working memory for pre-planning and priming the brain for peak performance are negatively affected. Distracting thoughts of one's impending doom then further excite the emotional side of the house and performance at all levels is diminished. They may be an expert shooter on the range, but without decision-making training under pressure, skills burnt into procedural memory can fail. Without left of bang training, an officer may not even understand how to place themselves in the best position to solve the problem. In these situations, the officer must feel their skill set is up to the challenge. The only way to do that is to train under pressure with an understanding of the science introduced in this book. Or, you can rely on luck, or enough time under real pressure and the risks associated with it to hopefully train the system.

Stress and pressure can hinder decision-making. In the book *Sources of Power, How People Make Decisions* Gary Klein argues that while stress/pressure can play a role in decision-making, the role is not what we previously believed.

I am not arguing that stressors do not have an effect. My

claim is that stress does affect the way we process information, but it does not cause us to make bad decisions based on the information at hand. It does not warp our minds into making poor choices. Stressors such as time pressure, noise, and ambiguity, result in the following effects:

- The stressors do not give us a chance to gather as much information.

- The stressors disrupt our ability to use our working memory to sort things out.

- The stressors distract our attention from the task at hand.[40]

Decision-making skills are the key to solving complex, potentially violent situations faced by law enforcement. Without decision-making skills, which require focused working memory, the officer is left with stimulus/response skills. Stimulus/response could be a suspect resisting arrest by burying his hands underneath him; your overstressed emotional system's hunch is to fight and strike the suspect in the head, leading to an excessive force complaint. This would be a pure right of bang response and an incorrect one at that. For those not in law enforcement, judges are making it clear that law enforcement agencies must increase their competency in control tactics which enhance the ability to control suspects who are resisting arrest but not trying to hurt the officer. Control tactics do not involve striking the suspect unless that level of force can be articulated. Left of bang concepts place you in the best positions with the best resources to observe, act, and solve problems before the violence begins, including controlling the spike in the emotional response.

------

[40] Gary Klein. *Sources of Power: How People Make Decisions* (Cambridge, MA: The MIT Press, 1999), 275.

CHAPTER NINE

COGNITIVE APPRAISAL SKILLS: THE SECRET

All great discoveries are made by men whose feelings run ahead of their thinking.

– C. H. Parkhurst

Earlier, we gave the definition of cognitive appraisal from the book *Performing Under Pressure*. "The mental process we engage in that helps us to define what is happening to us or around us is called cognitive appraisal."[41] Cognitive appraisal works from the inside out and from the outside in. The cognitive appraisal process involves understanding your physiological reactions to the initial stressors and how to control those stressors. It involves loading your working memory based on the incoming information and developing your ABC plans. Constantly analyzing the need for further resources and evaluation of who is creating the exigency in the situation is also part of the process. Other factors include driving conditions, establishing the baseline of the initial scene, your left of bang observations, and being mentally prepared for

---

[41] Hendrie Weisinger, and J. P. Pawliw-Fry, *Performing Under Pressure: The Science of Doing Your Best When It Matters Most* (New York, NY: Crown Publishing Group, 2015), 16.

violations of expectations. In other words, cognitive appraisal is everything we have already discussed and everything we are about to discuss. Proper cognitive appraisal is the secret to problem solving when the pressure is on.

In the basic law enforcement academy setting, students get anywhere between five hundred to eight hundred hours of instruction in the law, patrol procedures, use-of-force policy, shooting, defensive tactics, community-based policing, racial bias training, and a host of other training designed to load the declarative memory system with information they hope you will be able to consciously recall when needed. If you have evaluated as many use-of-force incidents as I have during my career, you would see in most cases the success or failure of the officer came down to left of bang observations and the decisions made leading up to the use of force. Cognitive appraisal and the good decisions that come from effective cognitive appraisal are vital in the day-to-day functions of a law enforcement officer. As far as I know, no academy in the country teaches the science of the brain in conflict, the memory systems, and the concept of cognitive appraisal. Having all the individual skills without knowing how they come together is like learning auto repair from books and PowerPoints without ever having touched an actual engine.

If there is one major lesson I could give after all these years on the job and numerous lethal and less-than-lethal force encounters, it's that enhancing your cognitive appraisal abilities, while effectively training the procedural skills for combat situations, are the secret to peak performance and survival in the law enforcement field or any other field were life is on the line. "Cognitive appraisal is one of the most effective tools we have to manage pressure because it is a mediator between external events and our internal brain, our bodies, and our behavior."[42]

Cognitive Appraisal; The Rookie and The Veteran

The lack of any formalized training in emotion, cognition, and cognitive appraisal puts a rookie officer behind the curve in the day-to-day decisions that must be made in a law enforcement career. In the current system, expertise is reached through trial and error and some rise to become good decision-makers and sound tactical officers. But, if we are being honest, there are plenty of officers with eight to twenty years of law enforcement experience who are no better tactically or in their decision-making skills than they were coming out of the academy. For now, let's focus on some of the differences between the cognitive appraisal skills of the novice and of the expert.

There are many things experts can see that are invisible to everyone else. Patterns that novices do not notice:

- Anomalies: Events that did not happen and other violations of expectancies.

- The big picture (situational awareness).

- The way things work.

- Opportunities and improvisations.

- Events that either already happened (the past) or are going to happen (the future).

- Differences that are too small for novices to detect.

- Their own limitations.[43]

---

[42] Weisinger and Pawliw-Fry, *Performing Under Pressure,* 75.

[43] Gary Klein. *Sources of Power: How People Make Decisions* (Cambridge, MA: The

Patterns

In any tactical or potential tactical environment, pattern recognition is essential to forming situational awareness, which includes the establishing of baselines and deviations from baselines. Veteran officers look at the big picture, whereas rookie officers have problems because their training focused on policy and procedures and their focus is on putting that information to work instead of on the immediate task at hand.

For example, emotions are behavioral drivers, they have unconscious behavioral tells that rookie officers and officers who are not controlling their emotions sometimes miss. I have seen myself, and heard countless stories told by officers, of a person they were contacting looking past the officer and around their environment. The tell: the person may be looking for an escape route or may be looking to see if there are any witnesses. Is this a guarantee? No, just a deviation from expectations that should be noted and ready to act upon. Numerous accounts exist of veteran officers telling a subject being contacted to have a seat on the curb, because the officer noticed the unconscious behavior of the person pulling their leg up behind them and switching to the other leg as if stretching for a quick run. The funny part, they don't remember doing it. It was a behavioral expression of emotional energy.

A person being contacted who rolls his head in wide circles as if to stretch the neck and shoulders or rolls his shoulders and clenches and opens his fists may be gearing up for a fight. The look on their face when you point out that behavior while taking control of them is priceless because they had no conscious idea they were doing it. Simply put, pattern

---

MIT Press, 1999), 148.

recognition aids in establishing baselines and recognizing deviations from baseline and violations of expectations. Like a poker player, by trying to read the emotional ticks of another player, you are attempting to get left of bang by making smart decisions about your hand and the other player's perceived hand.

Anomalies

The term "routine call" has received a bad rap from the law enforcement community because any call can become dangerous and, therefore, is not routine. I agree wholeheartedly. Here, I use the term from the point of view of learning and decision-making. Experienced officers have seen more calls for service and heard more about how others have handled different calls. In the ABC planning we talked about the plans that work across the different calls. This similarity between the tactics and strategies "chunks" material into the working memory and frees up space in preparation for the anomalies which can occur. The veteran officers "can size up a situation in a glance and realize that they have seen it, or variations of it, dozens or hundreds of times before. Their experience buys them the ability to recognize that a situation is a typical case. The opposite side of the coin is noticing when a pattern is broken, or an expectancy is violated."[44]

Imagine an expert veteran shooter and a novice shooter are both at the range and both experience a failure to fire, meaning the trigger was pulled but the gun did not go bang. The expert shooter has dealt with this situation so many times before that he requires no conscious, explicit response. The response is burned into the procedural, implicit circuitry. Tapping the bottom of the magazine to make sure it's seated

---

[44] Klein, Sources of Power, 151

right and the racking of the slide to ensure a round is in the chamber are done on autopilot. For the novice shooter, he has classroom training or declarative knowledge of a failure to fire but limited experience tapping the magazine and racking the slide. For the novice there is a time lag where consciousness kicks in and they realize something is wrong. The working memory focuses and accesses knowledge from the declarative memory system and the novice now remembers to perform a tap and rack. The difference in time to finish the task between the expert and the novice would be noticeable even to a spectator who has never shot a gun before.

The Big Picture: Situational Awareness

When we discuss left of bang strategies, observations, and violations of expectancies, we are talking about situational awareness. An officer with limited or poor decision-making experience is usually emotionally driven with a reduction in cognitive abilities due to the heavier emotional response. With the decrease in cognitive ability comes the smaller focus on only what is perceived as the threat and not the environment the officer and a suspect may be operating in. For example, an inexperienced officer may see a subject wanted for aggravated assault with a firearm walking down the street. Their emotional system may spike, and you get one of two typical responses. A young, inexperienced officer may get on the radio, advise what they see, then wait for someone to tell them what to do and to develop the plans for how to safely take this suspect into custody. In this case, while you would like to see young officers already have an idea for how to handle this situation, you at least give kudos to the fact they understand it's something they can't handle on their own.

An aggressive, overconfident, yet inexperienced officer may see the same situation as an opportunity to make a name for themselves and show that they can handle something like this on their own. Their brain is now in the "rabbit runs and the dog chases" mode. This officer is so focused on the task at hand, getting the suspect into custody, that they fail to see the suspect is walking in front of a schoolyard filled with kids, and several businesses in the area have people out in their parking lots. Sometimes knowing what not to do is just as important as what to do and the decision to confront the suspect in this environment can lead to disaster. Again, going back to de-escalation, if a running gunfight ensues from contacting this individual in this environment and several innocent people including children get hurt, who created the exigency here? That is situational awareness and what can happen when you fail to see the big picture.

The Way Things Work

Klein describes the way things work in the book *Sources of Power.*

> Experts see inside events and objects. They have mental models of how tasks are supposed to be performed, teams are supposed to coordinate, equipment is supposed to function. This model lets them know what to expect and lets them notice when the expectancies are violated. These two aspects of expertise are based, in part, on the expert's mental models.

> Since the experts have a mental model of the task, they know how the subtasks fit together and can adapt the way they perform individual subtasks to blend in with the others. This makes their performance so smooth. They do not even feel that they are performing subtasks because the integration is so strong. If they must explain what they are doing to novices, they may have to stop and artificially break it down into subtasks. Often, they feel uncomfortable teaching the separate steps because they know they are teaching some bad habits. They are teaching the novices

to do the task in a choppy way. In the short run, though, this task decomposition makes it easier for the novices since they do not have to worry about the big picture. They just have to remember the steps. As part of their mental model of the task, experts know various tricks of the trade, along with the conditions for using them.[45]

Mental models are the secret to using any skills necessary to navigate a potential lethal force situation whether with a weapon or with empty hands. We will discuss this more in the training section, but the method of training used currently in the academy setting, and in advanced training for that matter, does not promote mental models, it is simply "if this happens, then do this" training. The study of defensive tactics will illustrate the point I am trying to make. Defensive tactics programs, for the most part, are cookie-cutter programs where everyone learns the same techniques and is expected to put them to effective use. Effective in that you should be able to demonstrate the technique on call regardless of whether it works for real under pressure.

I have fought competitively in boxing, kickboxing, and mixed martial arts. I have been studying martial arts and combat systems for thirty-eight years. I have been teaching some form of unarmed combat for thirty-four years. Over the course of my career, I have used my knowledge to diffuse situations with minimal force, fought with violent offenders, and brought them in alive. On several occasions, due to the weapon and manner used by the suspect, I have been forced to kill to save myself, my partner, or innocent people. Many officers have; I am not saying all of this to toot my own horn. My point is, based on my experience, cookie-cutter lesson plans just don't work. How am I going to teach a one hun-

---

[45] Klein, *Sources of Power*, 152

dred-pound female to fight like me? And why would I? Understanding and teaching the principles that work across the spectrum of techniques allows for adjustments to be made to take the focus away from technique and onto principles. In the end, does it matter if the technique an officer used to control a subject came from the lesson plan if it was done safely and in an objectively reasonable manner? Going back to some of the elements of force and *Graham* v. *Connor* considerations, you will see the rules of engagement for use of force are different for each officer based on size, experience, the suspect's size and experience, and a host of other factors. Knowing this, why would we try to teach officers with body-weight disparities up to and over one hundred pounds to fight in the same manner?

Understanding of the principles of human structure and how to break that structure to establish control, allows the officer to formulate ideas based on their level of experience, the suspect's perceived level of experience and size, weight, and height differences. This allows the officer to form mental models for how to establish control, as well as the ability to readjust when the mental model isn't working. When all you have is a technique that starts to fail, emotions will spike. When a principles-based model starts to fail, you adjust. I will elaborate more on this concept in the training section.

Opportunities and Improvisations

In *Sources of Power*, Gary Klein describes leverage points as "a small difference that makes a large difference, a small change that can turn a situation around—to create a new course of action, notice something that may cause a difficulty before there are any obvious signs of trouble, and figure out what is causing a difficulty."[46]

Law enforcement officers newer to the job are lacking the skill of spotting leverage points, while experienced officers see and capitalize on them. For example, I remember responding to a rookie officer who was out with a subject who was suicidal and pointing a gun at his own head. I had probably eighteen years of experience as a police officer at the time and had been to an excellent SWAT negotiators school put on for all SWAT officers newly assigned to the unit. When I arrived on scene, the rookie officer couldn't move past the fact the guy had a gun and was repeatedly yelling, "Drop the gun, drop the gun, drop the fucking gun!" The suicidal subject was non-responsive to the commands and the officer indicated the subject had not acted like he understood or even heard the officer, who was standing at good cover about fifteen feet away.

Keep in mind, while I attended the negotiator school, I was not a practiced negotiator. I tried establishing different openings, but I was not having much success. I noticed a Marine Corps tattoo on his forearm and asked him if he was a Vietnam veteran. He turned his head toward me and said that he was. I had found a leverage point. I thanked him for his service and asked if we could talk a little. The whole time this was going on I had my rifle at a low ready from behind cover and felt comfortable with my temporary position, knowing the rest of my team was on the way. After getting his attention, I was able to get him to carefully place the gun pointed to the ground alongside his leg. We were able to find out that he was upset the Veterans Administration doctors wouldn't listen to him when he told them repeatedly that the drugs they gave him made him feel like a "zombie." We negotiated for a while and he agreed that if I would drive him to the VA

---

[46] Klein, *Sources of Power*, 111

and speak with the doctors then he would give up the gun. After transporting the subject to the VA, the initial officer asked to speak with me wanting to know what he could do better next time.

First, hats off to him for asking and wanting to know where he could improve. At the time we used the word "hooks" as in you are looking for hooks which are leverage points. When dealing with the mentally ill, it's basically anything that gets them talking. The officer admitted that he was stuck in a loop of "drop the gun," and not focused on problem solving and he answered most of his own questions. Looking back, both the officer and the suicidal man's brains were heavily engaged on the emotional side. Observation skills and the ability to ask and answer questions are found only when the cognitive side is re-engaged. That's why in the de-escalation program I helped write, we taught officers that, if you want to find out how heavily engaged the emotional system is in someone you are contacting, then ask them a question. If they are non-responsive, chances are the emotional side is too heavily engaged and we recommend containing the scene and waiting until the emotional side of the brain cools off. Heavy emotions burn a lot of energy and sometimes, especially when dealing with the mentally ill, you wait it out. When they become responsive, the cognitive system is engaged, and there lies the opportunity to convince the thinking brain of the best possible choices for a good outcome.

The Past and The Future

In aviation, there is a term to describe people who are so wrapped up in what they are doing that they are insensitive to what lies ahead: flying behind the plane. It describes people who are either too novice or so overworked or have such poor situation awareness that they are not generating expectancies; they are not preparing themselves properly.[47]

Young cops love to drive fast. While they are trained in pursuit driving, and how to effectively handle the car; they are poorly trained in decision-making and the science of decision-making in a car going 90 to 100 mph. Experienced officers can remember the many dead cops killed in accidents, as well as their own driving limitations discovered through training and practical experience. I remember when one of our officers was shot during a foot pursuit and a citywide "officer down, needs assistance" was broadcast over the radio. My partner and I responded to that call and later found out that at two different intersections in the area there were accidents involving responding police cars. At one intersection, two police cars ran into each other and the other intersection involved an officer's failure to control his own vehicle. Fortunately, in both cases, no innocent people were hurt. Experienced officers who are tactical thinkers always learn from the past, their own and others. They are also able to think into the future and run mental simulations to create expectancies.

Your ABC planning loads the working memory for faster access to the long-term memory systems. Looking into the future allows you to perceive possible outcomes while preparing for violations of expectancies that may lead you on a new path. In pursuit driving, young officers are driving faster than their brain can process information. If you genuinely wanted to excel at driving and making rapid decisions at 90 mph, the number of hours required would exceed the number of hours allotted for the whole basic academy. The more experienced officers understand they can only help in any given situation if they can get there safely.

The two police cars that hit each other, in the previous example, were one block away from where their fellow officer

---

[47] Klein, *Sources of Power*, 155

lay bleeding. Fortunately, that officer survived his horrific injuries, but the fact of the matter is, help was delayed by what would have been the first officers on the scene crashing into each other. Experienced officers are using the past and the future to run simulations that guide their behavior. For example, in a foot pursuit of a suspect, inexperienced officers are in a pure emotional brain response; rabbit runs and dog chases. Experienced cops are projecting into the future. Does this suspect have friends in the area? Where might he be headed? Is he armed or potentially armed? Are there innocent people around he could injure? While in foot pursuit, they are preparing to move quickly to cover if the suspect stops and turns.

Remember, the suspect's brain is almost guaranteed to be in an emotional response meaning his cognitive function is diminished. Suspects will sometimes turn with nothing or an object, not a weapon, in their hands, believing a good cop will break for cover thus allowing them time to expand their lead over the officer. Officers either lacking experience or failing to control their own emotions, will sometimes default under the stress and stand their ground to outshoot the potential threat. Even if it is found to be an objectively reasonable shoot, the fact is, they still shot an unarmed individual. To be honest, you would probably be lucky they were unarmed, as standing your ground to outshoot someone already going for a weapon can lead to disaster. Because both the officer and the suspect have failed to control their emotional response, sometimes the tragedy of a mistake-of-fact shooting occurs. It is vital to learn that when the emotional system is spiked, it will tell you and show you what you want to hear and see. It's an extreme survival mechanism. Experienced, well-trained cops know this and in the same situation they get off the "X" and move to cover, or with no cover immediately available, move to buy time to identify what's in the suspect's hands.

The ability to use the past, project into the future and rapidly access mental simulations gives an officer every possible chance of staying either left of bang, or already perceiving bang so quickly, it appears your reaction was faster than the action. It is vital that we start introducing these concepts in the basic academies, so that instead of trial and error learning, the officers can borrow the trials and errors of others. This loads the declarative memory with ideas and when introduced into training, conditions the procedural memory for a trained response. This will then aid in the development of mental simulations run by the conscious system and educated hunches developed by the emotional system.

Fine Discriminations

In any field of endeavor, there is an enormous difference between a novice, an experienced person, and an expert. Experts have seen more, felt more, anticipated more, and learned to read situations the novice and sometimes even the more experienced can't see.

In the fighting sports, be it boxing, mixed martial arts, wrestling, jujitsu, etc., there is an enormous difference between the novice and the expert. The novice is trying to think of combinations of punches or punches and kicks, takedowns, etc. The novice is burning cognitive energy thinking about how to fight. Good fighting comes on the other side of thinking and great fighting is taking the developed techniques, strategies, and lessons learned and applying them while relaxed, instinctively, and with just enough cognitive override capabilities for the violations of expectations.

What if you had the fighting capabilities of an expert but now we added a few new dimensions to the mix? What if you knew how to fight but instead of the sporting agreement to participate in a fight, you would never know when the fight is to begin or how many people you would be fighting? But wait, there's more. Along with not knowing when or where the fight begins, or how many opponents, let's add the fact that any of your potential opponents are free to arm themselves with knives, guns, or any other weapon system they can think of. These are the problems presented to law enforcement officers every day. Part of the fine discriminations is taking what you have learned in the past, such as fighting skills, and applying them to job-related tasks. For instance, sportive techniques must be adjusted for the fact that the officer is wearing a gun and must protect it at all costs. Firearms training, defensive tactics, practical job knowledge to enhance mental simulations, and evaluating any skill set to see how you want it trained into procedural memory are all factors in the development of an experienced officer. Unfortunately, that training responsibility currently lies with the officers themselves as the agencies are not providing training based on science to enhance officer performance.

Managing Our Own Limitations

Experienced people are constantly involved in cognitive appraisal while performing tasks related to their field of endeavor. Part of the inside analysis is understanding their own strengths and weaknesses and using that knowledge to their own advantage. Part of the outside-in cognition appraisal is always seeing the big picture and incorporating plans that work to the officer's strengths while considering and working around their weaknesses. Experts are critical of their own performance and are constantly evaluating ways of improving their performance based on what they have learned in the past and projected into the future through mental simulations.

In law enforcement, the young, inexperienced officers are usually only focused on the task at hand and not the big picture. To expand on a previous example, when an officer is down and needs help and the "all call" is broadcast on the radio, officers who lack cognitive appraisal skills are only focused on getting to the scene as quickly as they can. The officers with sound cognitive appraisal skills understand the need for speed balanced with the safety of innocent people in traffic, and their own safety. Many of the on-duty accidents caused by officers are caused by speed and a lack of cognitive appraisal of their own driving abilities balanced with their own self-control.

Cognitive appraisal skills are the key. All skill sets matter not at all, if the individual cannot bring them into play under pressure. The practice of skills without cognitive appraisal work is the major focus of current law enforcement training and the reason we are not getting the expected performance results from some of our officers in high-pressure situations.

CHAPTER TEN

DECISION-MAKING

In the middle of difficulty lies opportunity.
– Albert Einstein

Novice decision-makers are stuck on procedures. They are usually so focused on performing skills and procedures correctly, they fail to see the big picture, to establish baselines, to make observations left of bang, and thereafter place themselves behind the curve for making sound, rapid decisions in high-threat environments. Experienced officers, whether consciously or unconsciously, understand the law, policy and procedures, sound tactics, cognitive appraisal, left of bang, can see more, process more, and use all this information to make sound decisions and decisions under compressed time and high threat.

When we look at the science involving emotion, cognition, and decision-making it becomes apparent that the decision-making process is a byproduct of everything that came before the decision was made. An experienced officer with excellent observation skills places him/herself in the best position to observe and absorb information. They process left of bang and are anticipating trouble before it begins. By observing, processing, and anticipating trouble, they are in a good position to respond to violent actions tactically. They have prepared mentally, physically, and spiritually to perform at their best under pressure. The anticipation of trouble has them concerned, but not overly emotional, as they know this will downgrade his performance. All these factors make them confident, relatively calm, and prepared. These factors give the ability to attempt to diffuse the situation from a strong position and even give time for identification of weapons or dealing with situations that could lead a less-experienced officer to a mistake-of-fact shooting.

If most training involves the standard methods we have used in the past, then you are training the brain for stimulus response only and not the micro decisions that are made to make every attempt to prevent the violence from happening in the first place. Training must include a discussion and application of cognitive appraisal skills. The more decisions made in the context of tactical applications and strategies the better the critical-thinking skills become.

In the book *Stealing Fire*, authors Kotler and Wheal discuss the default mode network of the brain. "Responsible for mind-wandering, and daydreaming, this network is active when we're awake but not focused on a task. It's the source of a lot of our mind chatter, and with it, a lot of our unhappiness."[48] The default mode network is the enemy of a high performer in potentially violent situations. Without focus, the mind wanders and a wandering mind under pressure is not focused on performing the task at hand. Thoughts of family, of lost time, intrusive thoughts that make no sense at the time, and thoughts of what you believe to be your impending doom, are all examples of default mode actions which can negatively influence your performance under pressure-filled

---

[48] Steven Kotler and Jamie Wheal. *Stealing Fire: How Silicon Valley, the Navy SEALS, and Maverick Scientists Are Revolutionizing the Way We Live and Work* (New York, NY: HarperCollins Publishers, 2017), 125.

circumstances. Forming ABC plans, communications strategies and left of bang observations with good procedural response training will aid in focusing on the problem at hand. This gives the conscious you a task to focus on and will aid in shutting down the default mode network.

While reading the book *The Rise of Superman*, the research done by Dr. Leslie Sherlin on decision-making under stress caught my attention. In the book, Sherlin describes his research. We are going to get a little technical here, but this research, based on the data collection characteristics of EEG technology, make it possible to set up the research study we are looking to do by providing a way to train the brain for better decision-making.

> Whenever you encounter stimuli or have a thought, explains Sherlin, the brain has an electrical response. EEG measures these responses down to the 1/1000 of a second range, which allows us to track how the brain changes across time. When someone is decision making—and this can be an athlete solving a physical problem or an artist solving an aesthetic one—we can see everything that leads up to a decision, the decision itself, and everything that happens as a result. No other technology can do that.

> As those electric responses occur in bursts, they create waves—technically 'brain waves'—which is what an EEG actually measures. There are five major brain-wave types, each correlating to a different state of consciousness. 'Delta', the slowest brain wave (meaning the one with the longest pauses between bursts of electricity), is found between 1 Hz and 3.9 Hz. When someone is in a deep, dreamless sleep, they're in delta. Next up, between 4 Hz and 7.9 Hz, is 'theta' which correlates to REM sleep, meditation, insight, and (as is often necessary for insight) the processing of novel incoming stimuli. Between 8 Hz and 13.9 Hz hovers 'alpha' the brain's basic resting state. People in alpha are relaxed, calm, and lucid, but not really thinking. Beta sits between 14 Hz and 30 Hz, and signifies learning and concentration at the low

end, fear and stress at the high. Above 30 Hz there's a fast-moving wave known as 'gamma,' which only shows up during 'binding' when different parts of the brain are combining disparate thoughts into a single idea.

EEG has another feature that makes it useful for decoding decision making: it is very good at detecting networks. While it doesn't have the detailed spatial resolution of functional magnetic imaging (fMRI), the technology can see which parts of the brain are talking to one another at any given time. Thus, when decisions are being made, EEG can help determine the structure of the network involved in the process. In fact, it was this network detection ability that gave us our first neurological insights into flow.[49]

"Flow" is a term which came into usage in the 1970s based on research by Mihaly Csikszentmihalyi. The term, which is gaining popularity due to the book *The Rise of Superman*, and work done by the Flow Genome Project, is synonymous with a peak performance state. If you're looking for great examples of athletes in a peak performance or flow state, hit the internet and watch Luke Aikens jump without a parachute, Laird Hamilton's famous ride of the Teahupoo waves, and Danny Way jumping the Great Wall of China on a skateboard with a broken ankle. All three, feature amazing self-control under life-threatening pressure.

Now, as we have been discussing the difference between the beginner and expert in decision-making and the balance between the emotional and cognitive brain, research done in the 1970s provides insight into the brain of the expert.

Back in the 1970s, Csikszentmihalyi used EEG to examine

[49] Steven Kotler. *The Rise of Superman: Decoding the Science of Ultimate Human Performance* (New York, NY: Houghton Mifflin Harcourt Publishing Company, 2014), 33.

the brains of chess masters mid-game. He found a significant decrease in activity in the prefrontal cortex, the part of the brain housing most of our higher cognitive functions. This may seem surprising. Chess is a game of reasoning, planning, and strategy, three things that appear to require higher cognitive functions. But this isn't the only way the brain can make decisions.

Human beings have evolved two distinct systems for processing information. The first, the explicit system, is rule-based, can be expressed verbally, and is tied to conscious awareness. When the prefrontal cortex is fired up, the explicit system is usually turned on. But when the cold calculus of logic is swapped out for the gut sense of intuition, this is the implicit system at work. This system relies on skill and experience, is not consciously accessible, and cannot be described verbally (try to explain a hunch). These two systems are often described as "conscious" versus "unconscious," or "left brain" versus "right brain" but neither comparison is entirely accurate.

"Think of a factory," says Sherlin. "If all the workers are broken into little pods and they're all doing unique things at unique times, that's the explicit system. On an EEG, it shows up as beta. Replace those pods with a giant assembly line, one where the work is extremely rhythmic, fluid, and collaborative—aimed at a collective goal—that's the implicit system. It's usually denoted by a low alpha/high theta wave."[50]

Earlier we discussed work by David Eagleman in his book *Incognito*. If you recall, Eagleman described the advantages of the implicit system as speed for faster decision-making and efficiency because while the brain makes up approximately 2 percent of our body weight, it accounts for around 20 percent of our energy usage. The explicit system requires

---

[50] Kotler, *The Rise of Superman*, 34

a lot of energy to use and the split processing system allows us to free up energy, holding the cognitive in reserve for those violations of expectations that can occur in the decision-making process.

This is also why Csikszentmihalyi found little activity in the prefrontal cortex of chess masters. After years of playing, they'd internalized board patterns and move sequences and didn't have to rely on their conscious mind to work through every option. Instead, their explicit system went offline, and the implicit system turned on. Since low alpha/high theta is the dominant brain wave produced by the implicit system, this frequency has long been considered the signature of both high performance and flow states. But this idea is now starting to change—and Sherlin is part of the reason why. [51]

The book goes on to explain more about Dr. Sherlin, the company he works for, and an association with the Red Bull high performance research team headed by Dr. Andy Walshe, and research done on peak performers.

Their goal was straightforward: use EEG to figure out what the brains of top action and adventure athletes were doing and help them do more of it. To this end, thousands and thousands of subjects were analyzed. Bat and ball athletes were compared to action and adventure athletes. Amateurs against elites (top 5 percent) against super elites (top 1 percent). In the beginning, they examined resting states, but beyond more low alpha/high theta in the baseline experts—which for the aforementioned reasons, was to be expected—there wasn't much to see. Once they got the athletes moving, though, that story started to change.

For this portion of the study, Sherlin used a simple target acquisition task. Subjects had to stare at a screen as images

---

[51] Kotler, *The Rise of Superman*, 35

flashed by. If the image was a target (twelve pink squares arranged as a cube), they had to react. If the image wasn't a target (eleven pink squares arranged as a cube, with the center square missing), they had to suppress the reaction. "It sounds really simple," says Sherlin, "but there's actually a lot going on. It requires speed, stamina, focus, and really good decision-making abilities.

When any of us make decisions, our brains go through a six-stage cycle. Before the novel stimuli shows up (which is what starts the whole process), we're in a baseline state. Then we move to problem-solving analysis, pre-action readiness, action, post-action evaluation, and back to baseline. Each of these stages requires different parts of the brain and produces different brain waves: theta for processing novel stimuli, beta for analysis, alpha for action, etc. When Sherlin and his team examined the data, what became clear was that the best athletes moved through this entire cycle fluidly, seamlessly transitioning from step to step.

"That's the secret," says Sherlin, "extremely fluid brain control. Most people can't make it through the whole cycle. They get hung up somewhere. They either can't generate all the necessary brain states, or they can't control them. Elite performers can produce the right brain wave at the right time, vary its intensity as needed, then smoothly transition to the next step. Mentally, they just take total charge of the situation."

Flow states, which can be considered elite performance on overdrive take this process one step farther. "In the zone," says Sherlin, "you still see this same fluidity in the transitions between states, but you also see even more control. Instead of producing all these other brain waves, really great athletes can transition smoothly into the zone, creating that low alpha/high theta wave, and then hold themselves there, sort of in suspended animation, shutting out the conscious mind and letting the implicit system do its stuff." [52]

Law enforcement experts are masters of pattern recognition at the subconscious level, leading to fast, accurate decisions under the pressure of condensed time frames. Experts leverage experience, mental simulations, and biohacks to accelerate their learning and they understand that they are always learning. The novice must invest much more cognitive control to problem solving and decision-making because of their lack of experience in problem solving related to law enforcement. The novice lacks an understanding of training and controlling the emotional system and usually has low confidence in their procedural skills yet to be ingrained into the implicit procedural memory.

The Quiet Eye

In 2007 Joan Vickers authored a book called *Perception, Cognition, and Decision Training*. The book describes a visual process known as "quiet eye" and how this concept differentiates the novice from the expert and the expert from the elite. Vickers provides the scientific definition of the quiet eye as:

> A fixation or tracking gaze that is located on a specific location or object in the visuomotor workspace within 3 degrees of visual angle for a minimum of 100 milliseconds. The onset of the quiet eye occurs prior to the final movement of the task; the quiet eye offset occurs when the gaze moves off the location by more than 3 degrees of visual angle for a minimum of 100 milliseconds. The

---

[52] Kotler, *The Rise of Superman*, p. 36

quiet eye is therefore a perception-action variable, in that its on-set is dictated by the onset of a specific movement in the task.[53]

Vickers performed extensive research on athletes and found the quiet eye principle at work in all the elites across numerous sports. Her research verified that when the elite performers were successful in a targeting task (e.g. shooting free throw, shot on goal in hockey or soccer, handgun shoot-ing and rifle shooting, etc.), the quiet eye was present and when those elites missed their target, the quiet eye was not present. Her research showed a lack of consistent quiet eye in novices and more experienced but less consistent per-formers. Her research with biathlon athletes and their perfor-mance under stress sparked the interest of training officers of the Calgary Police Department in Alberta.

In 2012 Joan Vickers and Bill Lewinski, of the Force Sci-ence Institute, conducted a study using police officers from across the experience spectrum. The focus of the study was to see if the quiet eye was present when good decisions were being made and if the quiet eye improved accuracy of the police shooter along with better shoot/no shoot decisions.

The officers were placed in a scenario where they were observing a man in a jacket approach a desk where a female was seated. The male subject had his back towards the offic-ers performing. The male subject begins arguing with the fe-male and reaches into his coat and begins to pull an object which is either a cellphone or a handgun from his waistband. When given commands, the subject begins to pull out the object and turn around toward the officer leading with the arm holding either the gun or cellphone extended. Eye gaze technology inside of a pair of glasses worn by the officers records all the action and exactly where the officer's eyes are

---

[53] Joan N. Vickers, PhD. *Perception, Cognition, and Decision Training: The Quiet Eye in Action* (Champaign, IL: Human Kinetics, 2007), 234.

looking throughout the scenario. For this study, rookie officers were compared to SWAT trained officers to compare performance.

The following is an abstract from the study by Vickers and Lewinski published in *Human Movement Science*:

Gaze of elite (E) and rookie (R) officers were analyzed as they faced a potentially lethal encounter that required use of a handgun, or inhibition of the shot when a cell phone was drawn. The E shot more accurately than the R (E 74.6%, R 53.8%) and made fewer decision errors in the cell (cellphone) condition when 18.5% of E and 61.5% of R fired at the assailant. E and R did not differ in duration of the draw/aim/fire phases, but the R's motor onsets were later, during the final second compared to the E's final 2.5's. Across the final six fixations the E increased the percent of fixations on the assailant's weapon/cell to 71% and to 86% on hits, compared to a high of 34% for the R. Before firing, the R made a rapid saccade to their own weapon on 84% of trials leading to a failure to fixate the assailant on 50% of trials as they fired. Compared to the R, the E had a longer quiet eye duration on the assailant's weapon/cell prior to firing. The results provide new insights into officer weapon focus, firearms training and the role of optimal gaze control when under extreme pressure.

So, you may be asking, what does all that mean? For starters, the experts were more accurate with their weapons and made better decisions. But just as important, the experts learned faster and got better as the trials continued. The best performers fixed their gaze on potential locations of weapons reference to the subject's hands and on the turn, anticipated where the hand and weapon would be to aid in the identification process of either a gun or cellphone. The rookies had no method to their gaze fixation, failed to anticipate the turn, and the location of the hand holding either the cellphone or the gun. Experts anticipated trouble sooner and were already prepared to fix their gaze on the anticipated location of the hand as it turned with the object. This gave them more time on target to correctly identify and then either inhibit their response or engage the threat. Interestingly, when the experts made mistakes and failed to identify, they failed to anticipate and fixate on the hand as the subject turned toward the officer. During the final 700 milliseconds before the rookies fired, their eyes made a rapid movement called a saccade back to the sights of their gun to verify alignment. Experts stayed target-focused and brought their sights into reference while staying focused on their target.[54]

If you recall, there was no time difference in the times of the rookies and experts to draw, aim, and fire their weapons indicating the primary limitations of the rookies were not physical but the cognitive ability to maintain focus and concentration under fire. By remaining target focused, the expert officers performed in a similar fashion to elite, Olympic-level shooters studied by Joan Vickers in previous studies.

While all shooters are initially taught to superimpose their sights on the target and then fire, expert Olympic-level shooters and expert officers maintained target focus and brought the sights of their weapons into a reference on the target while maintaining a quiet eye focus on the target. This quiet eye, the at least 100 milliseconds of gaze on target, allows the competitive shooters to achieve higher scores and the expert officers the ability to identify the threat correctly and have greater accuracy.

Now, prior to the extensive studies done by Joan Vickers, elite athletes and police officers figured out how to achieve elite status unconsciously, without really understanding

---

[54] Joan N. Vickers, PhD. and William Lewinski, "Performing Under Pressure: Gaze Control, Decision Making and Shooting Performance of Elite and Rookie Police Officers." *Human Movement Science*, Volume 31, Issue 1, February 2012, 101-117. https://www.ncbi.nlm.nih.gov/pubmed/21807433

what they were doing to get there. The quiet eye studies revealed the secret no one at the time could explain. Experts see more, process more, and make better decisions because they know what to look at, where to look, and how to fixate for at least 100 milliseconds on their target before pulling the trigger or taking the shot in sports.

If you have ever done Simunition (bullet projectiles made of soap) training in law enforcement or run live-fire shoot house training on paper targets, you will know when acting for Simunition training or observing paper targets in the shoot house, a lot of rounds end up in or near the hand holding the weapon. This is the quiet eye in action without the conscious knowledge of the individuals taking the shots. In the process of making good shoot/no shoot decisions, the officers are fixating their gaze on the hands to properly identify weapons. With this fixation of gaze, the first rounds fired are where the gaze is fixated. On paper, inexperienced officers can make decent shoot/no shoot decisions because they don't necessarily experience a time crunch and usually transition from the threat identification to their center of mass shots on the chest. But when the inexperienced officers use Sims rounds to go against live opponents, they panic, fail to identify, and make a lot of mistakes trying to transition back and forth from target to their gun sights. Experts use their eyes, bring their gun sights to their eyes on target, and shoot their way to center mass from the first identified target area. Knowing the quiet eye method, we can now add drills to training to enhance proper identification and response to threats. We'll enhance our discussion of the quiet eye and its introductions to shoot/no shoot decision-making in the training chapter.

Scientists of quiet eye research believe a contributing factor to poor performance under stress is pressure, which triggers anxiety, which degrades attention. The result is you don't look in the right place at the right time and instead the eyes are usually rapidly moving while desperately attempting to gather data. Science also done by Vickers and the Force Science Institute have shown that when the eyes are moving in saccades it's easy to miss information because the eyes don't have time to gather the data before they have moved on to the next gaze point. The *Merriam-Webster* dictionary defines saccades as, "a small rapid jerky movement of the eye especially as it jumps from fixation on one point to another (as in reading)."

In the quiet eye study, you will notice the experts still made identification and shot accuracy mistakes. I believe and soon hope to test a theory on some of that data. In the study, the officers were only allowed to move within a boxed off area. I believe, had they been allowed to move to cover or move further, we would have seen even better numbers from the experts. Movement buys time. Time to identify. Time to target. Time to problem solve. Standing your ground means you are out of time. Movement means the suspect must reacquire and target you. You have made him reactive instead of actively attempting to kill you. Not a guarantee of success but better than nothing.

A famous experiment conducted in 1999 illustrates the point of missing information when the eyes are moving rapidly from point to point.[55] Viewers were asked to watch a video of six people passing a basketball, three in white shirts and three in black. Viewers were asked to count the passes of only the people wearing white shirts. Within the time frame of the video, a person in a gorilla suit walked between the six subjects. Half of the people who viewed the video failed to notice the gorilla in the video. Why? Selective attention; they were so tasked focused and making rapid eye movements to follow the ball while observing what color shirt the passer was wearing, their eyes failed to see what would be obvious to anyone without a specific task. The results of this test also explain why an officer cannot observe and control more than one person at a time and why they may find themselves right of bang if they attempt to do so. Remember, the quiet eye is knowing where to look, and at least 100 milliseconds of fixation to make a proper decision. Without the relevant experience of left of bang observations and anticipation of threats, along with a quiet eye fixation at time of identification, relevant cues can be missed or only processed right of bang. Selective attention can also account for why a video can clearly show pertinent facts the officer states they did not see. Could the officer be lying? Sure, but is it also likely that, under pressure, the officer is so focused on what they feel is important, that they fail to see other things. This is also called inattention blindness.

CHAPTER ELEVEN

THE BIOHACKS

Compared to what we ought to be, we are only half awake. We are making use of only a small part of our physical and mental resources. Stating the thing broadly, the human individual thus lives far within his limits. He possesses power of various sorts which he habitually fails to use.

– William James

Before we get into training the brain systems for better performance under stress or pressure, it's important to discuss what we can do in our everyday lives to balance our cognitive and emotional systems. This aids in directing the unconscious learning that is always going on along with the cognitively directed training that we hope will get burned into the procedural circuitry. The added benefits of the biohacks are numerous to not only work and its stresses and pressures but also to our personal lives. They also aid in teaching us not to bring our personal stresses to work and vice versa.

If you were to ask what I think the number one thing anyone could do to improve the quality of their work and personal lives and receive the greatest benefit with the least amount of effort, my answer would be mindfulness work. Here is why. One: it's hard to screw up. Two: results can come from as little as ten minutes of work a day. Three: the benefits on heart rate and blood pressure alone are beneficial to your overall health. And four: mindfulness work teaches you to take cognitive override and tame the emotional system when it wants to run wild.

The following is from an article written about a study performed at the University of California-San Diego, titled *War and Peace (of Mind): Mindfulness Training for Military Could Help Them Deal with Stress*. The article was printed in *Science Daily* in a 2014 issue. The summary of the research stated:

> Mindfulness training—a combination of meditation and body awareness exercises—can help U.S. Marine Corps personnel prepare for and recover from stressful combat situations. The study suggests that incorporating meditative practices into pre-deployment training might be a way to help the U.S. Military reduce rising rates of stress related health conditions, including PTSD, depression and anxiety, within its ranks.

Within the study it was found that "personnel who received mindfulness training had reduced activity in a region of the brain known as the insula, also known as the insular cortex, which acts as the brain's connector strip. Meditation appears to change how people's brains respond to and recover from highly stressful events."

Drawing on the teachings of Zen Buddhism, scientists describe mindfulness as a mental state characterized by 'full attention to the present moment without elaboration, judgment or emotional reactivity.' Mindfulness training, traditionally practiced through sitting meditation, attempts to cultivate this mental state by quieting the mind of extraneous thoughts.

In the study, Marine infantrymen in four platoons at Marine Corps Base Camp Pendleton took an eight-week course in mindfulness, tailored for individuals operating in highly stressful environments.

The course included classroom instruction on meditation and homework exercises, as well as training on interoception—the ability to help the body regulate its overall physical equilibrium (homeostasis) by becoming aware of bodily sensations, such as tightness in the stomach, heart rate, and tingling of the skin.

"If you become aware of tightness in your stomach, your brain will automatically work to correct that tightness," Paulus explained.

Participating Marines, along with others who had not undergone mindfulness training, then spent a day in mock immersive combat at a 32,000-square-foot training facility staged to resemble a rural Middle Eastern village. During the day's exercises, Marines patrolled the village, met village leadership, and responded to a highly realistic ambush.

The scientists found that the heart and breathing rates of those who had received mindfulness training returned to their normal baseline levels faster than those who had not received the mindfulness training. Blood levels of tell-tale neuropeptide suggested that the mindfulness-trained Marines experienced improved immune function as well.

Subsequent magnetic resonance imaging (MRI) scans revealed that the mindfulness-trained Marines had reduced activity patterns in the regions of the brain responsible for integrating emotional reactivity, cognition and interoception. Lori Haase, a postdoctoral fellow in Paulus' lab and a co-author of the study, said similar brain activity patterns had been observed in high performance athletes and Navy Seals. High activity levels in these areas of the brain, she noted, are associated with anxiety and mood disorders. The scientists hypothesize that reduced brain activity in the anterior insula and anterior cingulate may be characteristic of elite performers in general.

"That we can re-regulate the activity in these areas with so little training is this study's most significant finding," Paulus said. "Mindfulness helps the body optimize its responses to stress by helping the body interpret stressful events as bodily sensations. The brain adds less emotional affect to experiences and this helps with stress recovery."[56]

I'm not going lie to you. I was introduced to mindfulness work roughly thirty years ago and scoffed at the idea. Several years ago, I was teaching at a seminar in Montreal with Kevin Secours and Alex Kostic and was reintroduced to the idea and then began really evaluating its benefits. Since then, I have added some form of mindfulness work every day, and have noticed benefits in blood pressure, mood control, and ability to make faster and more consistently correct decisions in the compressed time frames of combat conditions. With the amount of free mindfulness apps available to all, it is not hard to find ten to twenty minutes a day to just sit and breathe.

Remember when we discussed working memory and its importance in pre-planning, as a bridge to long-term memory systems and its ability to aid in emotional regulation? Knowing its importance in combat conditions, why wouldn't you want to make your working memory more efficient?

Research done at the University of California, Santa Barbara showed that working memory could be improved through mindfulness training, as well as reducing mind wandering (default mode network mentioned earlier.) In the study *Mindfulness improves reading ability, working memory, and task-focus* published in *Science Daily* in 2013, it states, "many psychologists define mindfulness as a state of non-

[56] University of California-San Diego, "War and Peace (of Mind) Mindfulness Training for Military Could Help Them Deal with Stress." *Science Daily*, 16 May 2014, https://www.sciencedaily.com/releases/2014/05/140516092519.htm

distraction characterized by full engagement with our current task or situation. For much of our waking hours, however, we are anything but mindful. We tend to replay past events—like the fight we just had or the person who just cut us off on the freeway—or we think ahead to future circumstances, such as our plans for the weekend. Mind-wandering may not be a serious issue in many circumstances, but in tasks requiring attention, the ability to stay focused is crucial."

As it relates to the study, Michael Mrazek, a graduate student researcher stated, "This is the most complete and rigorous demonstration that mindfulness can reduce mind-wandering, one of the clearest demonstrations that mindfulness can improve working memory and reading, and the first study to tie all this together to show that mind-wandering mediates the improvements in performance."[57]

Sit, relax, breathe, and don't think. As you get older it almost sounds like bliss. Try it, stay with it for at least three weeks and you will be pleased with the benefits. While mindfulness work at home has health benefits and working memory benefits, which will aid in law enforcement work, there are also mindfulness breathing techniques you can use to maintain or regain cognitive control when a heavy emotional response is present.

Square Breathing

Square breathing keeps the same count for each phase of breath. The count doesn't matter as much as the consistency.

---

[57] University of California-Santa Barbara. "Mindfulness improves reading ability, working memory, and task-focus." *Science Daily*, 26 March 2013, https://www.sciencedaily.com/releases/2013/03/130326133339.htm

When first using square breathing, it's best to begin with three or four seconds, but depending on the time available and the amount of emotional response happening to you, that number can be increased. To square breathe, pick your number, say four seconds, and then inhale for four seconds, hold breath for four seconds, exhale for four seconds and then hold again for four seconds. This breathing should be done through the nose. This patterned style of breathing calms the emotional system as its effects are being driven by the cognitive system. Remember, blood goes where the action is and by taking cognitive control of breathing, the conscious systems continue to get blood flow and you are basically telling the amygdala to relax. Obviously, during combat, square breathing is not going to work. This breathing method is done before your shift starts, when you are feeling stressed but not in combat, or it is used as a cognitive override of normal breathing on the way to calls as a wake up for working memory while you are formulating your ABC plans.

Doctors at the Mayo Clinic have recommended deep breathing techniques. On their website, it lists some of the benefits such as lowering blood pressure, providing a sense of calm, and taming the fight or flight response. They also list stress reduction and mood improvement. Research has shown benefits to deep breath work for people suffering from anxiety disorders, PTSD, depression, and pain management.

Burst Breathing

During dynamic conflict the square breathing method will, of course, not work. Square breathing is for before the action and recovery from the action. Burst breathing is for the midst of combat when tension in the body is increasing and your breath is either becoming shallow or you are out of breath from exertion or emotional stress. Burst breathing is taught to women giving birth for pain management and dealing with the emotions of the introduction of a new life to the world. In combat, it helps for pain management, emotional regulation, and keeping you alive in this world. Burst breathing requires cognitive control just like square breathing and this cognitive control aids in taming the amygdala.

To perform a burst breath, inhale quickly through the nose like you are sniffing a flower then forcefully exhale through the pursed lips like you are blowing out a candle. This shorter breathing cycle mimics the natural breathing cycle of a shorter inhalation and longer exhalation and recent studies have shown this to be a biohack to fool the amygdala into calming the fight or flight response. I have used this technique in combat sports, during exercise, in training, and on real-life high-risk search warrants, hostage rescues, and active shooter responses to remain in cognitive control of my brain and physical control of my body. When you are out of breath, burst breathe until you can recover normal breath and when you are under stress, burst breathe to overcome the shallow breathing that stress can compound. Remember, when the fight or flight response begins, the emotions start to run wild. Excessive emotional response necessarily means less cognitive control. Watch video after video of police performance where the officer's response is in question and you will see in most of these cases, an officer in an extreme emotional response which causes an inhibition of cognition. Knowing this, why have we chosen not to look to science to see if we can do something to aid in the control of the emotional response, decision-making, and overall performance in life-threatening circumstances?

I like to grapple and use my grappling time as an exercise in breath control. I want to be able to grapple and maintain endurance while maintaining cognitive control capabilities by consciously using breath to my advantage. Deep breaths when I can and burst breaths when I need them. When doing gun work and moving, burst breathing calms down the emotional system and prevents you from holding your breath. Just these two factors alone will aid in the decision-making process by enhancing cognitive executive control. I could write on and on about the benefits of these breathing techniques, but the easiest way to see it for yourself is to perform a series of exercises with burst and without burst breathing. As an experiment, run a 200-meter sprint and track how long it takes your heart rate to recover to normal. Rest for a while. Then run the 200-meter sprint again, but this time burst breathe as you cross the finish line for twenty to thirty breaths. Your recovery time will be drastically decreased.

Labeling

Law enforcement trainers used to teach that you should ignore fear and anxiety by putting it in a "box" and not recognizing fear's existence. As it turns out, science does not support this obviously ridiculous assertion. A study performed by Dr. Matthew Lieberman showed that by naming an emotion such as "fear," activity in the ventrolateral prefrontal cortex increased while activity in the amygdala decreased.[58] Instead of ignoring how you are feeling in any given situation, label it, which switches to cognitive control and serves to tame the amygdala which drives an excessive fight or flight response. A simple concept when you think about it. Engage cognition by labeling the emotion you feel, thus taking back some control from the emotional system. To admit to yourself, you feel fear, requires cognition. Get some cognition online

------

[58] Matthew D. Lieberman, et al. "Putting feelings into words." *Psychological Science*, vol. 18, issue 5, May 1, 2007, 421-428.

and the emotional system's response will decrease. Instead of thinking as the place you store your emotions as a box, consider it is more like a balloon. The balloon can only hold so much air and then? Your excessive emotions are the air in the balloon.

Understanding What Causes Choking Under Pressure

Ever had to give a presentation in front of a group of people and after a massive amount of preparation and rehearsal, failed at your task? Chances are, if your preparation was sound, you engaged your working memory with thoughts of failure, looking bad, and forgetting key thoughts. Working memory acts as a bridge to the long-term memory systems and you clogged your bridge with numerous obstructions. This is a choke involving your own working memory.

Do you score well with your firearm when there is no pressure, but perform poorly when it matters, like in force on force training or actual real-life shootings? If the skills are sufficiently ingrained in the procedural memory, but under stress you are failing to control excessive emotion, procedural skills can fail. This represents a procedural choke. Remember, cognitive override tells us shoot/no shoot and with cognition online the opportunity to recognize when you need to move before you shoot because innocent people or other officers are in the way. Once it's time to shoot, we want procedural memory running the show until we get a violation of expectations where the cognitive systems take over from standby mode. By understanding these choking patterns, we can design training programs which allow participants to learn how to manage and deal with the stressors of combat and high-pressure situations.

A helpful hint: take cognitive control of your breathing

patterns and it calms the emotional system down allowing you to keep the working memory online. Technically speaking, there are two distinct cognitive chokes. One, you overthink a skill already ingrained in the procedural memory system. This is the choke that usually occurs on the firing range during yearly firearm qualifications if you train regularly. The second is when your procedural skills are sound but your critical-thinking skills are not and you shoot well at the wrong thing or in the wrong circumstances. A procedural choke is when you have the skill set without pressure but have not sufficiently trained under pressure to control procedural skills. This is a choke common with well-prepared athletes facing enormous pressure in big competitions such as the Olympics.

Mission Focus

The following is from the book *Performing Under Pressure*. It stresses the importance of focusing on the problem and not distracting thoughts of failure.

There is probably no easier pressure solution to use before and during a pressure moment than this:

This solution suggests that you stay clear on what you are trying to accomplish – your mission. It could be to shoot a clean round of golf (regardless of score), have a strong interview (independent of how other interviewees do), or just be an excellent employee. Increasing your awareness of your mission before and during a high-pressure moment helps to depressurize the situation quickly.

First, it prevents distracting thoughts generated by consciousness or external distractions. Such thoughts can derail your efforts.

Second, focusing on the mission keeps you on track because it cues you to do the things you need to do to achieve the performance you are looking for. [...]

Remember, focusing on your mission is different from focusing on the outcome. Focusing on the outcome steers your thinking into whether or not you will suffer negative consequences if you do not succeed; worrying over failure can distract and derail you.

In contrast, focusing on your mission creates a mind-set that helps you recognize the best way to accomplish your mission is to simply do your best on each task. In this way, you stay anchored in the moment.[59]

Pain Shared Is Pain Divided

One officer alone, under life-and-death pressure, does not possess the cognitive abilities to monitor a suspect(s), the environment, other people in the environment, and deviations from baselines established for each. Don't try to do it alone! As soon as you realize a situation is becoming too complex, ask for help. There's nothing more reassuring than knowing that people who care about you are willing to stand shoulder to shoulder with you when the pressure is real, and lives are on the line. More sets of eyes, more opinions on tactical plans, more hands ready to respond, all decrease the cognitive load thus reducing the emotional response. We should only go it alone when the exigency is so extreme, like an active shooter, that the risks are worth the benefits. We risk a lot to save a lot when it is dictated by the suspect or

[59] Hendrie Weisinger, and J. P. Pawliw-Fry, *Performing Under Pressure: The Science of Doing Your Best When It Matters Most* (New York, NY: Crown Publishing Group, 2015), 117.

Reframe Your Perspective

Do you see the pending situation as a challenge or life-and-death situation where you might die? Does it matter? Science says it absolutely does. A 2014 article on Forbes.com by Amy Morin explains the difference.

> The initial response to stress occurs unconsciously and automatically based on our initial rapid evaluation of the situation. Some people are able to respond in a manner that helps their performance, known as challenge state. But, other people enter into a threat state, which hinders their performance.
>
> A challenge state reflects a positive mental approach to pressure situations where our mental resources meet the demands of the situation. We endure physiological changes—like an increased heart rate and decreased blood vessel constriction—that allows blood to be delivered to the brain efficiently. This helps us concentrate, make decisions, and have control over our thoughts and emotions.
>
> Those who don't enter into the challenge state, enter a threat state. During the threat state, the heart rate increases like in the challenge state. But this time, the blood vessels constrict, which means, the blood pumped from the heart remains largely unchanged. As a result, the delivery of glucose and oxygen to the brain—which is essential to peak performance—is inefficient and our ability to focus and make decisions is hindered.[60]

For me, this has always been the "if not me, then who"

---

[60] Amy Morin. "Why Successful People Don't Crumble Under Pressure." *Forbes*, August 7, 2014.

mentality. As in, I am here, I am trained, and I am ready. If not me then who? I train hard, I prepare mentally, physically, and spiritually for the worst the job has to offer. When faced with life-and-death struggles and decisions, I try to look at it as another test, a challenge. By seeing these situations as a challenge instead of an "oh my god, I'm going to die" experience, the brain is primed for better performance. Primed, because science shows the brain is receiving more blood flow in a challenge state. In that challenge state, the balanced brain is receiving the right amount of flow to the cognitive and emotional sides for the best shot at peak performance. Current science shows that while the front and rear portions of the prefrontal cortex are shut down during peak performance, the medial prefrontal cortex is online and assists with creativity and unique problem solving.

A quote attributed to the famous Japanese swordsman Miyamoto Musashi illustrates this point of turning off the portions of the prefrontal cortex that act as our nagging critic and impulse control. "To win any battle, you must fight as if you are already dead." Translation? Don't focus on the outcome, focus on the process. If you fight as if you're already dead, then you don't think about what you stand to lose or how hopeless the situation is, you just ... fight!

Which brings us to one of the most ridiculous concepts I have seen taught. Trainers for years have been saying, "Think about your family, your friends, and what you're fighting for!" These thoughts are not pertinent to the matter at hand and will probably lead to an emotional dump and lack of cognitive override. Sound mean-spirited? Well, on my way to work, I think about my family, friends, my faith, and why I do what I do. Once the shift starts, those thoughts are put behind me. At best, they will only serve as a distraction, and at worst, they will only produce an extreme, unthinking, unbalanced response where even the good procedural skills are lost. During shift, it's all about "in the deep now." This is the whole point of doing mindfulness work, to keep you in the deep now focused on the problems at hand and not the past or the future.

Chapter Twelve

Training the System

Failure to prepare is preparing to fail.
– John Wooden

Law enforcement training today bears a striking resemblance to training from twenty-five years ago. Sure, there have been some cool innovations like the Taser, bullet projectiles made of soap for force-on-force training, and the addition of competition-style training for firearms, but the methods of how these are taught and the expectations from the training are still the same. That is the problem. The training methodologies haven't changed. We aren't getting the results we are looking for and we continue to do the same things over and over expecting improvements. The missing piece has been the understanding of the operating systems of the brain, how they perform under stress and how these systems can be trained for better decision-making. Advancements in technology make it easier than ever to study and train the brain for better performance, but the use of this new knowledge will require a paradigm shift in how training is conducted.

While developing a new principles-based handgun retention lesson plan, I decided to do some experimentation while teaching in Arizona and outside of the United States. I asked officers what they would do in certain situations by showing them what I was going to do to go after their handgun. I asked them what their response would be without physically performing the action. I noted each of their responses to the posed problem on paper. Later in the training, but before I presented any of my handgun retention principles, we would do a quick test. In the test, an actor would go after the officer's gun in precisely the manner earlier described to them. Safety gear was supplied to all participants and the officers were told it would be an extremely physical confrontation. Asking them what they would do, was a test of their declarative knowledge of the subject. Later when presented with the same problem but asked to give a physical response, their declarative solutions and procedural responses were not the same. To make matters worse, the procedural responses were in most of the cases, ineffective.

As I started teaching the new handgun retention program based on some of these findings, I would repeatedly hear officers say they would do something different. For the record, I don't have a problem with that if you have tested the methodology you are using. They, of course, had not. When pressure was applied, their fantasies of what they would do went out the window and uneducated, uncoordinated responses ensued. Why the disconnect? Shouldn't we be able to use our declarative memory system which allows us to run simulations to do exactly what we can think of without stressors to perform better with them? If you have absorbed the information previously presented, then you probably already know the answer.

Let's say you are at a party watching an American football game for your favorite professional team and they are in the playoffs. Your team is down by six points, but in position to score and take the lead with little time left on the clock. On the next play, your favorite receiver dives for a pass on the outside corner of the end-zone, but the ball slips through his fingers and the pass is incomplete. One of your friends screams, "Come on! I could have caught that damn pass!" And the million-dollar question is ... could he? And the answer, of course, is no, he could not. Declarative knowledge of the game of football and maybe some high-school experience lets him run a mental simulation where he in fact does catch the ball in front of sixty thousand people and millions watching worldwide, but without practiced procedural knowledge, emotional control, trained reflexes, and physical conditioning, that mental simulation is a fantasy.

Civilians, police administrators, news reporters, and activists sometimes do the same thing when they see a video of a police officer involved in a use-of-force incident. I'm not here to comment on underlying intent or to question motives, just to provide the facts. People who are not in law enforcement and watching these types of incidents are using their declarative knowledge of law enforcement, which is usually limited, to run mental simulations/fantasies of what they think they would do in these cases. In most cases, there is no ill intent in what they are doing. They are using cognitive abilities to find rational ideas for what officers should have done in the situation in question. But once again, declarative knowledge without procedural memory skills and emotional control to back it up, is a fantasy. Which brings us back to the problem at hand: law enforcement trainers have been selling that fantasy to officers for years. In the past, because they didn't know any better, but now we do know better and what will we do with that information? Make it better or pretend it doesn't exist?

Here's another example of the disconnect I show when presenting information on the neuroscience of performance under stress. On YouTube, you can find a video of Rob Leatham and Rob Pincus called, "Worlds Collide – Forcing Variation into Training." If you are not familiar with the two Robs; Rob Pincus is a firearms instructor specializing in training ci-

vilians for self-defense situations using firearms. He is an excellent instructor and is innovative with his training methods.
On his worst day, Rob Leatham is one of the top fifteen competitive shooters in the world. Rob Leatham takes speed and
accuracy to another level and is fun to train with. In this video,
Pincus is discussing the difference between shooting for
speed against a clock and the micro decisions that must be
made before, during, and after a potential lethal-force situation. The drill does not use a clock but instead relies on decision-making to direct the shooter to the targets which are a
series of numbers on several pieces of cardboard around
seven yards from the shooter. Leatham is directed to walk in
a figure eight pattern parallel to the targets to simulate walking in a mall. While Leatham is walking, Pincus yells out a
number and Leatham must orientate himself to the target
and put anywhere from three to six rounds, Leatham's choice,
on the targeted number.

After several rounds of this, Leatham is walking his figure
eight pattern and Pincus calls for "half of eight." Leatham
should shoot the number four, but in the immediacy of the
situation and the new type of problem to solve (half of eight
= four), Leatham is at first frozen in place. Then, he begins to
shoot several different numbers, none of them being the
number four. At the completion of this round, Pincus asks
Leatham what half of eight is and Leatham responds with the
correct answer. This simple but effective drill shows the difference between stimulus-response style firearms training
and the decision-making like, who to shoot, do I need to
shoot, can I shoot, or should I move.

Of course, the weakness of his drill is that the shooter
knows they are going to shoot in every case. There aren't any
no-shoot situations built into the drill. I believe competition
training has numerous advantages when put into the correct
context. Context must include decision-making, not just the
timed response to a buzzer. Why? Because in the real world,

you must identify your target and whether they are holding a weapon, what your backdrop is, how many innocents are present, if it is a shoot situation, and a host of other factors before you fire the gun. If we add left of bang indicators to the training like recognizing indicators that either prevent the violence, recognize the threat is gone, or place yourself in the best position to deal with the unavoidable violence, then we are truly modernizing law enforcement training.

Currently, most police departments' firearms training is designed around their state qualification course. So many officers have problems passing their qualifications that most of the training time is spent trying to reduce the number of failures. Qualification courses are not training, they represent a basic test of fundamental marksmanship. Administrators, without a working knowledge of the brain, try to include what they call training into the qualification courses because that may be the only training some of the officers get during the year. This is ridiculous and contributes to the problem. Remember, procedural memory can be trained by you or by circumstances. For peak performance, we prefer an educated response from the procedural memory and not a best guess based on what you have done the most. Done the most, like standing your ground and trying to out shoot a target on your qualification course representing a lethal threat already pointed at you.

During a qualification course, numerous people are placed on the firing line, thus reducing any movement that can be made by the shooter. The buzzer sounds, the target turns, and the officer must place the given number of rounds to the target area in the given time frame. Due to movement and time constraints, the officers must stand their ground and attempt to out-shoot what represents a lethal threat already directed at them. If the procedural memory system is always learning and defaults under stress to what it has either done the most or a best guess for the circumstances, what are we teaching our system to do?

Let me digress for a moment. I understand I have mentioned firearms training on several occasions in this book. If you understand the science, then you can see why I am so passionate about this subject. If we want better decisions, we need to make more decisions! Standing your ground to make decisions when a suspect already has an advantage is bad business. In most of the mistake-of-fact shootings on video, the officer is lucky the suspect didn't have a weapon because the odds would favor the suspect. The fact is though, an unarmed individual was shot by mistake whether lawfully justified or not.

Marksmanship is necessary, but it does not represent gunfighting. Gunfighting requires left of bang observations, cognitive appraisal, and numerous decisions before the gun is fired. The Leatham video represents some of the differences. Leatham knows how to shoot a gun quickly, accurately, and efficiently. His procedural memory is trained for how to game a contest for the fastest time, not the best decisions. For a police officer, expert marksmanship, while important, is nowhere near as important as expert decision-making. The focus of rounds fired over decisions made does not translate to real-world use-of-force encounters. I believe that is one of the reasons law enforcement officers miss so much in real gunfights. Think about it, most officers have the procedural memory down of pointing, aiming, and firing their handguns. However, the "anxiety" of not performing well, or racing the clock to get shots off in time, is not the same anxiety as facing someone who is trying to kill you or an innocent person you are trying to defend. I am not offering an uneducated opinion here. I have been there on numerous occasions and can make the comparison and so can thousands of others.

Skill building without stress is a smart way of getting procedural skills burned into the circuitry. Under stress, those procedural skills can fail if the emotional system is too heavily engaged, so once basic competency is attained, the pressure testing can begin. Layered training to include skill building with light, moderate, and heavy pressure testing under stress, as part of a structured training program, has the science to back it. I believe it is the reason for the large gap that exists between the average patrol officer and the more heavily trained officers of the departments' tactical units. But, my friends, the most dangerous law enforcement job is not the job of the SWAT officer, statistically speaking, it is that of the patrol officer. So why do we sign off on substandard training when the cost of just one excessive or unreasonable use-of-force lawsuit could fund years of training?

The following is from the book *Building Shooters* by Dustin Salomon:

> It is intriguing that one of the standard benchmarks for the quality of a tactical training program and its resulting operational skill is often the amount of ammunition expended per trainee. The Federal Bureau of Investigations, widely considered the leading law enforcement organization in the world, once had an informal mantra associated with its academy firearms training program: "Ten thousand rounds per man." In fact, the liability considerations associated with this standard assumption result in an often-voiced (justifiably) administrative objection to reducing round counts in organizational firearms and tactical training programs. What administrator wants to accept responsibility for voluntarily reducing the round count associated with a tactical training program?

> In light of our training experiences and research, we challenge the assumption that associates the number of rounds fired with training quality. Instead, we propose an alternate mantra for any training program that is intended to produce operational tactical competence: 'Ten thousand *decisions* per man.'

> Reviews of both law enforcement and civilian use of deadly force show that the need for extremely high levels of fundamental

technical skill (as compared to competitive shooting or special-missions-unit requirements) is extraordinarily rare, so rare as to be statistically insignificant. In contrast, even a cursory glance at today's news headlines shows that extremely high levels of associative judgment and decision-making skill are of the utmost importance, no matter the job title or relative skill level of an armed professional (or civilian).

If we accept that expert-level decision-making skills are more important to both operational success and organizational liability mitigation than expert-level technical shooting skills, then it follows that the ultimate quality of a tactical training program should not be directly associated with the number of rounds fired. Instead, it should be judged by the amount of times that the human-stimulus-based recognition and decision-making neural-networks are linked (successfully) with the neural-networks representing the performance of the physical skills for applying the varying levels of the force continuum.[61]

In my career, I have known expert range shooters who have fired multiple rounds at a real-life lethal threat and missed them all. I have also known mediocre range shooters who have never missed against a real lethal threat. There is absolutely a disconnect between most law enforcement range training and real-life gun work. I could not agree more with the above idea presented from *Building Shooters*. The disconnect is the decision-making process, the observations and cognitive appraisals which should occur left of bang. Very rarely, so rare as to be "statistically insignificant" are police shootings pure stimulus response without decision-making involved.

The problem is, if you don't train the brain to perform

---

[61] Dustin P Salomon. *Building Shooters: Applying Neuroscience Research to Tactical Training System Design and Training Delivery* (Silver Point, TN: Innovative Services and Solutions LLC, 2016), 155.

cognitively during the evaluation process, and then release cognitive control to procedural memory when needed, there will always be a disconnect. When control is released to the procedural memory system, training should include the cognitive executive control capabilities. This would include evaluating if lethal force is necessary, when to stop using force, civilians in the way, or identifying mistakes of fact before they become a potentially lethal accident. More decisions made in all aspects of law enforcement training from ABC planning on the way to calls, deciding what resources are needed, and if exigency exists. Evaluating what tactical strategies to use including setting yourself up for best chance of control when it's time to go hands on. Of course, this also includes when to back out of the situation, if you can, when you realize you have bitten off more than you can chew.

These are just some of the myriad of decisions that must be made on every single call for service. Most decision-making training in the academy setting or in advanced training is geared toward a couple of videos done in a simulator once a year. Videos that occur in two dimensions and can be gamed by waiting until well after the suspect fires to return fire. Good for passing a video test; horrible for surviving in the street. Even most scenario training is geared toward testing policies and procedures instead of tactical decision-making.

The real difference between great cops, good cops, mediocre cops, and rookies is the ability to make sound decisions under stressful and pressure-filled situations. The skill sets themselves are not that different, although tactical officers have of course received a lot more training. The real difference is in the set up for the call, the resources brought, the cognitive appraisals, and left of bang observations. When the situation does take a turn for the worse, the experienced cops have placed themselves able to more effectively deal with the violence.

So, how do we do it? What are the best methods for getting to where we should be when it comes to effective, lawful, and modernized police training? Let's break it up into the different disciplines and then bring them all together to show how the same concepts apply across the spectrum of police training.

First, a quick disclaimer: Never, and I mean not ever, take information given to you and assume it is true, accurate, and all you are ever going to need. When it comes to training, and in life for that matter, people have their own agendas based on their own implicit bias system. Politicians, activists, administrators, cops, lawyers, doctors, etc. We are, after all, human and subject to the biases of the unconscious systems. Thus, we educate the cognitive to understand these biases and take personal responsibility for our training. After all, the life on the line, is yours.

We have gotten so out of hand in our discourse with politics, religion, interpersonal communication, the media, and this list could also go on and on. Sometimes, I think that we would primarily rather complain about the way things are than produce workable solutions to fix it. Our default selves are driven by the emotional system, where we like to know what we know and sometimes believe what we want to be true is more important than the truth. This is of course a bias within the system. When we start to understand this, we can choose to start looking for solutions to problems rather than live with the problem. As a trainer, the greatest gift I think I can give to any student I teach is how to be their own meter for the level of usefulness of some of the training currently being taught around the country. Examples in defensive tactics, firearms, de-escalation, etc., abound. Which goes back to this simple concept; is what I am currently learning useful to my job? Can I perform it with my gear on? Does it put me in a bad position tactically or legally? Is it something that works fine for some and not for all, and am I part of the some?

See where I'm going here? Take nothing at face value. Look it up for yourself to verify information and check to see if you can make it work for you, especially "techniques" taught in defensive tactics and firearms.

As a prime example, recently Keanu Reeves was featured on YouTube training for his part in the *John Wick 2* movie. The video was posted by the training company that was working with Reeves. In the clip, Reeves is working the gun like a champ, engaging numerous targets at fast speeds. Comments like, "That dude is a badass," and "Wow, I wouldn't mess with that dude," filled the internet. Fact Check: Keanu Reeves is an actor playing a scripted role with scripted bad guys. Entertaining? Sure. Real? Not a chance.

Hint, if twenty people with guns are facing you and you try to out shoot them, you are under-trained for reality and will very soon be dead. Rarely does one shot fired from a handgun bring a subject off their feet, and if you take the time to grapple with one bad guy while several other armed bad guys are in the room, one of them is going to shoot you! If the pressure is not real, then the simulation is not real. No simulation is even close to the real thing. It is what my friend Kevin Secours calls the "acceptable lie." How close to reality you choose to train and push yourself makes the lie smaller, but it is still a lie. By the way, I like the John Wick movies as entertainment understanding that there isn't the slightest dose of reality involved in its production. I also like Reeves as an actor. It's not personal. It's also not real. If you are a cop and your mental simulations look like a Hollywood movie; you are engaged in purely mental/tactical fantasy.

Violence is ugly and the closer it is to your proximity, the nastier it is. Killing is ugly and so are its after effects. No need to glamorize it because there is nothing glamorous about it. We don't need more fantasy in training. We need a heavy dose of reality, understanding the best we can do is make the acceptable training lie smaller. Learn to become your own teacher. Decide what you want in the procedural memory system and work at it. Filter out the crap, because in the end ... the life you win or lose may very well be your own.

My first recommendation is to introduce the de-escalation and tactical planning or a variation of each to your personnel as a primer for the series of training sections to follow. This primer would include the science of the brain and how it performs under stress. This could also introduce the mindfulness work that will aid in training and performance under real pressure. Next, I would adopt the cost-effective Left of Bang Program to introduce behavioral recognition and the concept of all the things you can do before the bang to anticipate the violence and plan your response. These concepts would serve as the foundation of the training to follow over the course of a year to include an end-of-the-year review, lessons learned and planning for the next year. Tactical communication strategies, ABC planning, understanding the balanced brain and incorporating these concepts into training primes the six inches of real estate between your ears for peak performance under the worst of circumstances.

Firearms Training

First and foremost, although I am a firearms instructor, I do not routinely train officers in the use of their firearms reference marksmanship. Basic marksmanship is the ability to hold the firearm, sight the firearm, and hit what you are aiming at. With basic marksmanship the only stress you feel is the stress you place yourself under. The only pressure comes during qualifications because you must pass these tests in order to continue working the street. Basic marksmanship is not gunfighting. If you can pass the qualification with whatever skill set you are using, then check that box and get on with training for a real gunfight. I teach how the gun comes into play from a close-quarters combative perspective. How to maintain better control of your suspects to protect your firearm. How to move when things aren't going your way and how to target, using science, with your handgun at close quarters, and most importantly, the realities of real-life violence without the fantasy. In other words, I prefer to train how to handle real-life pressure by teaching skill sets that are then pressure tested making the pressure as real as I can given the training environment.

If you only train in large groups, you will hinder your ability to displace yourself from the last place the suspect fixed your location. An instructor telling you to move in real life but not on the range or in a defensive tactics scenario, is loading your declarative memory with knowledge it will be unable to access under pressure. Fortunately, you can find range time or training time for defensive tactics, and instead of focusing on an arbitrary time to target, focus on being behind the curve due to the suspect's action and moving to cover, to identify, or moving to shoot as options instead of standing your ground.

Prior to going to the SWAT team, I was assigned as a tactical training officer for advanced training at the academy along with Officers Chris Trapp, and Chris Ray. During the time there, we had the opportunity to conduct several experiments to see the differences between standing your ground, shooting on the move, and moving to cover to return fire. By running informal experiments, we tested what worked and what didn't work.

The key idea being, if you can't at least beat the three hundred feet per second of training rounds, how are you going to beat something faster? Without a doubt moving immediately to cover when faced with a firearms threat was the best option. Attempting to shoot on the move was less successful than moving to cover, but should be trained, as it may be the only option available given the circumstances. Standing their ground and attempting to outshoot a threat already presented was the most catastrophic. To date, no formal study has been conducted, but it's easy to set up an informal study to see for yourself and I highly suggest you do so.

It is vital that you train your procedural memory system to seek cover when faced with a firearm threat you did not anticipate left of bang. It is just as vital that at close quarters you learn to shoot on the move against the sudden draw of a firearm by a suspect. The only way to do this (until the departments across the nation start considering the most effective way to train) is to start with yourself and set the example that influences others. Here's the big secret: if you think your academy training or whatever yearly training your department provides is enough to save you in a real gunfight, you are probably living a fantasy.

Projectile or Laser Training

Most training for the real-world gunfight will necessarily be performed off a live firing range for cost, safety, availability, and a host of other reasons. But, if you believe as I do that decision-making is the most under-trained skill set in modern law enforcement, then the problem isn't due to lack of live trigger time or an abundance of live fire. Again, I will say, most law enforcement uses of force aren't a pure stimulus response ambush. The things the officer does to place themselves in the best position to deal with conflict, the observations the officer makes left of bang, and the preplanning for what to do once bang occurs, all matter. I will tell you from my experience that I believe these are the most important skills influencing your performance in a real-life gunfight.

Most people think of scenario-based training when they

think of Simunition, Airsoft, or any type of laser training. My take is, scenarios can act as a test of the skills you are trying to ingrain, but do not qualify as training. Scenarios are a pressure test of all the skills trained put together. Without adequate training on the skills themselves, the scenarios don't tell us much. I'm not against scenarios *per se*, but the way I have seen them used is not supported by science and usually has little or no training effect. Scenarios, when used as a test after skill work or refresher work, can be used to measure the training effect, and adjustments can be made to training from what you learn. But, if personnel perform poorly in a scenario and you do nothing with the poor performance, what really was the point of the scenario?

To me, the skill building work that can be done with training tools like lasers and training projectiles is invaluable and necessary to supplement the amount of range time spent standing your ground and shooting. Elements of skill building should include, at least, the following topics.

Suspect moves for gun when officer attempts to control subject. Options vary but breaking contact and trying to outdraw someone already drawing at touch distance, does not pressure test well. This, incorporated with defensive tactics training, makes the skill building more realistic and aids in the pattern recognition we are looking for in our cognitive appraisal and left of bang observations.

Suspect makes a move for concealed object while officer is at varying distances from touch to fifteen to twenty feet away. This will incorporate either attempt to control at touch distance, moving to cover, when provided, or moving and shooting to test accuracy when shooting is required and suppression of fire when situation becomes a no shoot.

Suspect making left of bang indicators like turning the body to keep a concealed weapon away, touching areas where weapons could be to make sure they are concealed and accessible, shifting body weight back and forth, furtive glances over officer's shoulder or toward escape routes. The sky is the limit with possibilities. Use your imagination, your experience and the experience of others, and script your role players well to get the desired training effect.

Suspect goes for officer's weapon. To include situations where officer is grounded, suspect has officer's gun, officer must retain then fire at close quarters, and the gun in the officer's hands but suspect trying to take the gun.

Every cop should understand the principle of angulation. The person who takes the angle first, owns the angle. An example is the corner of a building. If a fleeing suspect runs around the corner of a building, the suspect owns that corner. If a chasing officer takes the same corner at speed, they could walk right into gunfire. Training should include foot pursuits where corners are taken by the suspect and the officer must slow down and use a tactical movement to see around the corner with a gun at the ready. Limited techniques which teach limited exposure to what can't be seen should be taught and put into context.

Identification drills which allow you to teach the "quiet eye" concept and aid officers in how they respond to furtive movements made by suspects. This drill builds on the drill where officers are deciding to either establish physical control of the suspect or move. In this case, the drill involves the actor concealing fifteen to twenty different combinations of weapons and ordinary things likes cellphones, wallets, lip balm container, etc., the average person my carry around with them. This should include purses and knapsacks to aid in identification of implements drawn from them. The more specific the training, the better the training response. For each implement drawn, the officer should be trained to move then identify and only engage the lethal threats. If the trainee makes a mistake, address it, talk about the quiet eye concept and get back to work. This drill should be done on an ongoing basis as it develops the quiet eye, pattern recognition, and proper identification. To build on the quiet eye concept, students can be taught at close quarters to start shooting the lethal threats where the threat is identified and not losing focus to chase the sights to the center mass of the target. If you do enough role playing as the bad guy, you will get hit a lot with training rounds in the hand and arm holding the weapon. This is good quiet eye identification but now you must add shooting your way to center mass. By training the quiet eye concept and building on it to include shooting skills you are aiding in helping the officer to maintain the cognitive executive control capabilities that will help identify when the subject is down or out of the fight, when civilians are in the way, or any other variable that would indicate they should stop shooting.

As new equipment is introduced into patrol functions it must be trained with, to include skill building under stressors to improve performance In real-life conditions. A prime example is the introduction of ballistic shields to patrol officers and details other than the SWAT team. Handing out shields and not training in their use, limitations, advantages, and disadvantages can lead to problems during real-life violence. I have seen "training" put on by departments, including my own, which is scenario based and Spielbergesque in grandeur and ridiculousness.

In these scenarios, an officer with a ballistic shield is attempting to shield twelve or more officers as they attempt to walk in a slow perfect straight line toward the front of a house. First, a shield can protect the holder where the shield covers and possibly one or two others depending on the situation. As part of any training, a realistic evaluation of whether you can pull off what you are attempting to do should be incorporated. Supervisors must be forced to make decisions to include: recognizing that with the given information and available resources, a crisis entry, or whatever tactical movement is being considered, should not be attempted. It should also include decisions based on available information of whether you even have the criteria met for a crisis entry into a location. As tactical gear is introduced to patrol functions, tactical training must also be introduced, or you may not get the results you are looking for. If you're going to teach about tools you have never used, then be careful and honest about how you present the material. Entry tools are also being introduced at the patrol level.

I'm all for it, if training is conducted properly and we are as focused on when not to use them, as well as when and how to use them. Without training, tools get misused and that misuse can cost lives if you're not careful. You cannot pretend to ram a door in practice and expect someone to do it under a real crisis. Breaching is a skill. To assume it's as simple as hitting the door with big piece of metal is the height of ignorance. This includes window-breaking tools. I have heard instructors say that anything laying around can be used as a breaching tool. Oddly enough, these instructors have never actually broken a window under crisis conditions and are making assumptions. Now, even if you could get the glass of the window broken, you still must get curtains out of the way as we are trying to get eyes and a gun on a potentially hostile suspect. Window breaching is also a skill and must be trained. Pretending to clear a fake window and moving pretend curtains out of the way is not training to win, it is training to fail. Again, training should include when you should not take windows and the proper, tactical way to set it up.

I was on a hostage/barricade situation that went on for over ten hours. SWAT officers were rotating our positions to keep fresh people in the shooting spots. I was assigned to breach a window when the call was made to launch a hostage rescue. The suspect started firing rifle rounds inside the house where he was holding several hostages when the call was made to initiate the rescue. While multiple breach points were being made into the house, the suspect fired over fifty rounds in a 180-degree arc at the entry teams. Rounds passed between me and my cover officer and some hit the shield being held off the corner of the window. Glass had to be broken and three layers of curtains moved out of the way while under fire. Each entry team faced the same problem due to his continuous targeting of the entry points. The only thing that saved us was good training, good communications, some luck, and the tactical plans we brought to the incident. The hard truth is that the suspect had a say and his say halted our initial entry. I cannot even imagine what it would be like to do that entry without the training, discipline, and experience that came from breaking multiple windows and breaching multiple doors before a crisis entry.

To train people without accounting for the pressure of violent situations, is ignorant and carries liability for "training not adequate to the task." Tactical officers with real experience should be teaching shield work, entry work, and how to safely use them in a tactical environment. Officers who are instructors, but don't have tactical experience, should be very clear in what they do and don't say and set up skill building so students can see what does and doesn't work against Simunition or paintball rounds. If your tactics can't beat three hundred feet per second, then you're out of luck at 900 and above. Please, remember that tactical teams bring equipment they train with all the time, plans they use all the time, and team movement and efficiency because they train together ... all the time. Throwing tools at the problem without proper training may create an even bigger problem when the exigent rush is made worse when one or more officers are shot who now also need rescue.

Training Tips

The following are some ideas for adding pressure testing to your training. If you are not in law enforcement and not really interested in the training aspect, please feel free to skip to the next section.

Low Light or Dark Environments

Operating in low light or completely dark environments should be including with force-on-force training. For example, you may have a legitimate reason to breach a door or a window, but if you have more light behind you than the person inside of the house does, then you are backlit and easy to target. If you are standing outside in broad daylight and breach into a darkened home, all advantage goes to the person whose eyes are already adapted to the environment. Using Simunition, Laser, paintball or any other force-on-force training rounds, these learning experiences have emotion attached to them and become easier to ingrain in the memory system. Low light also includes light discipline while moving within an environment. Pointing your flashlight at the back of an officer in front of you, backlights the officer and makes them easy to target. Low light combatives to include force-on-force with training projectiles is also a skill set. Learning when to use and not use your gun-mounted light or a hand-held flashlight are essential skills. You aren't going to learn it procedurally from reading a book. You want the stress and emotion of pressure testing once the foundational skills are set in place.

Ambush Training

Counter ambush training can be enhanced using training projectiles, but this training should include all options, not

243

just the ones focused on the available training environment. If you are in a car and receiving fire, you have been targeted. The suspect knows where you are probably going to exit the vehicle, and this is easy to target. Proper training with the patrol vehicle involved should include accelerating through the ambush, when practical, and bailing out of the vehicle to cover positions, when necessary. Of course, you must put this skill building into context and do so safely, but it can and should be done. It's easy to say, when ambushed do this, or "if I was ambushed that way, I would do this." As I have hope-fully established, this is declarative memory indicating what may not be your true procedural response when the violence is sudden and real.

Officer Grounded by Suspect Drills

A simulated ground engagement where the officer is grounded and underneath an attacking suspect. Safety gear is essential. Put the officer in situations where their handgun might come in handy and then they will learn how hard it is to get the gun in combat conditions while the suspect has a say in the matter. Procedural response training should be principles-based and indicate how to get to the gun and when not to introduce it into the fight.

As part of any skill building or pressure testing, con-stantly remind your personnel to train to use performance breathing, tactical planning, communication, and de-escala-tion strategies to aid in the cognitive appraisal and evalua-tion of who is creating the exigency to aid in decision-making. These are the skills that may prevent or at least set the officer up tactically if the situation is going to go from bad to worse like an ambush or officer taken to the ground.

Use of Cover

Skill building work to show how a position off your cover is better than one right up on the cover. Rounds that hit hard surfaces at an angle may deflect several inches off the surface and move parallel to the surface. This has been demonstrated using live fire to a target hugged up to a hard surface and occasionally happens if the paintball or Simunition round is hard enough. If you stand directly next to your cover instead of moving off the cover, the round that injures or kills you may be a deflected instead of a direct hit. Why improve the other guy's odds of hitting you? Being off your cover also improves your ability to see when the bad guy may be flanking you, a concept used against Dallas officers during the ambush watched on television from around the world in 2016. The more you can safely move off cover, the better your view of the suspect. The more you hug up to cover the smaller your field of view reference to what may be hunting you. Of course, the situation may dictate that you must stay closer to cover, but an understanding of the difference can improve your chances of success.

Shooting While Moving

Training should include situations where both the suspect and the officer are moving and shooting and, for instruction purposes, a series of drills where the officer cannot move but the suspect can and vice versa to "feel" the difference and not just be told the difference.

Vehicle Stops

When training with vehicles include traffic stops where the attack occurs at different portions of the stop. Officer in the car, just out of the car, walking up to the suspect's car, at the window, and on the return to his patrol car to write the ticket.

This can include shoot/no shoot, defensive tactics to control multiple passengers, multiple attackers, and innocent people in the area affecting angles of fire.

This is by no means an all-inclusive list, just ideas for how to take the concept of the brain science and incorporate it into training to achieve desired training results. Now, there are also things you as an individual can and should do to improve your performance with your firearm under pressure and we'll address those issues next.

Individual Firearms Skills and Training

Dry-Fire

If there is one piece of advice I could give anyone to become a better shooter on the range and under real pressure, it would be to burn into your procedural circuitry your grip, draw, presentation, sighting, and trigger control. The fastest, easiest, and least expensive method of doing so is to make dry-firing a part of your training. If you only fire live rounds, you had better have a lot of money on hand as the level of rounds required to establish and maintain efficiency is costly. Dry-fire training allows you to perfect the draw and presentation of the weapon until you can't get it wrong. It allows you to practice the quiet eye principle of maintaining target focus and superimposing your sights on target instead of finding your sights and then reacquiring the target. With extensive dry-firing you learn to feel structural alignment which lets you know at certain distances that your sights are aligned even if you can't see them. Under extreme stress and at close quarters you may not be able to see the sights, but procedural memory, if trained correctly, can lead to proper alignment and success in a close-quarter violent confrontation. The fact is most people, including cops, don't feel comfortable with a gun in their hand. If the only time you handle the gun is for qualifications, it's no surprise why. Dry-firing overcomes this issue, as well as drastically improving shooting skills. Most people who dismiss dry firing because there is no bang and recoil, fail to understand the bang and recoil don't change where the round goes if the sights are aligned when the bang goes off. If you want to be faster, then grip and draw faster so you have more time on target with alignment to hit what you are aiming at. The following is from the book *Navy SEAL Shooting* by Chris Sajnog, which discusses the science of dry-firing as it relates to learning.

There are three phases to learning a new motor skill: cognitive, associative, and autonomous. We all start off at the same place, but how quickly we get to the finish line depends on how efficiently we train. Cognitive learning is very slow. You're often using self-talk to work through each step. This requires lots of brainpower to think through each move while you find out what works. This stage is inefficient but necessary to move on.

In associative learning, the basic movement pattern is understood. The learner makes more subtle changes and movements become more efficient. The last phase is autonomous learning, consisting of fluid, effortless movement. When you get to this phase, your movements are consistent and accurate, with very few mistakes. This is where experts are, and where you want to get as fast as possible. How do you do it? Dry-fire!

Dry-fire improves the neuroplasticity of your brain. Every time you train, you create neural pathways in your brain. Do the same movement enough, and you'll create perfect muscle memory – your brain knows only one way to do the task, and it can't make a mistake. That's why it's critical not to practice a whole technique from start to finish and then decide it wasn't right.

This is a big mistake I see many instructors commit in letting students make mistakes. Why? To teach them a lesson? Unfortunately, it does teach their brains that what they just did was one way to perform that skill, but your learning brain doesn't know right from wrong. Each mistake, no matter how small, teaches your brain one option, even if it's not the option you want to imprint.

What most people call "muscle memory" is really the process of myelination. Think of myelin as insulation around your nerves that your body puts there so it can send messages faster. Practice builds myelin around the nerves responsible for your movements so that the next time you do those movements they will be faster. This happens slowly, but it happens no matter what your movement is – so even if you're training something wrong, you're still building myelin around the pathway, teaching your body the wrong way to do something. To build myelin the fastest, your movements need to be flawless. The speed you move at has no effect on myelin, so the best way to learn and reinforce motor skills is through slow, perfect practice.

With consistent perfect practice you pave the path to perfection. As in the metaphor with the rider, the elephant, and the path, dry-fire is the best way to clear the new path quickly. If your goal were to get from one side of a dense forest to the other as quickly as possible and you had as much time to train and prepare as you'd like, how would you do it? Would you just keep running different patterns as fast as you could, seeing which route was the fastest? Or would you plot out the best course, remove obstacles along the way, and pave the ground so the path is smooth and fast? Wasting rounds at the range is the first course, dry-fire is the second.[62]

---

[62] Chris Sajnog. *Navy SEAL Shooting: Learn How to Shoot from Their Leading Instructor* (San Diego, CA: Center Mass Group, 2015), 48-49.

The point is simple: burn in the procedures you want to be there for you when you are under pressure. The system will default to what it's done the most if your training includes emotional control under stress and pressure. By understanding how the brain operates under stress and pressure, the cognitive you can maintain executive control over the subconscious systems. Sajnog, who is an ex-Navy SEAL, is a firearms instructor who also relies heavily on neuroscience in his teaching methods. With the abundance of scenario training with training projectiles, most agencies run training around these "pressure" tests. The problem, again, is that scenarios test what you already know. They don't build new skills. When you want to add new skills, start with slow and methodical training until you can't get it wrong and then speed will start to develop and then the pressure testing can begin. Without the methodical skill build up, the system defaults and performance can be dramatically decreased.

Movement Work

Movement work can be part of your dry-firing and I like to mix it up and work them together and separately. When I separate them, I am focusing on the mechanics of shooting; the grip, draw, re-grip while presenting, finding the sights on target, and firing. When I do both together, I am usually working on identifying and using points of cover to reinforce those habits. By moving quickly to cover off a threat command or prompt and then slowing down to properly align the sights on target, your brain becomes the throttle that decides when to speed up and when to slow down. Under an untrained default with extreme pressure, the system will default to fast, uncoordinated movements to the gun, and you may even forget to move to cover. Movement training should also be part of your close-quarter combatives. Knowing when you are close enough to the threat to attempt control and when to move and move again to identify threats are invaluable tools which aid in decision-making and performance when it matters most.

Laser Dry-Fire Systems

There are several dry-fire laser products on the market; the one I chose for myself is the iTarget Laser Training System. Dry-fire training works, and works well, but laser dry-firing scores your hits, can provide the start stimulus, and can record your times from stimulus to fire to track improvements. Dry-firing is my primary handgun and rifle training method along with movement work. Dry-fire laser training tracks development. I want efficiency and speed, but speed will only come consistently at the other end of efficiency. The laser training aids in your skill building and develops confidence. Those skills can then be tested on the live-fire range. (Any equipment you purchase is also a tax write-off, so make the investment in yourself and your future skill set.) Dry-fire laser training also allows you to focus on the most important round you fire in a gunfight: the first one. You can't miss fast enough to win a gunfight. Focus on scoring your first hit and it's easier to stay on target, assess, and finish the fight.

Defensive Tactics and Subject Control

The Four Physiological Factors and Strategy for the Fight

1. Breath

Our goal, when we can, is to inhibit a suspect's ability to take deep meaningful breaths and to maintain our own ability to breathe under control. By taking conscious control of our breathing, the cognitive system becomes engaged, working memory is enhanced, executive control is present, and problem-solving capacity is increased. It is amazing to see how many people hold their breath while involved in physical conflict. In the conscious learning phase of any skill, it is vital that performance breathing is discussed and regularly practiced, or else you will have to retrain breathwork back into your skill work after the pressure testing fails. I suggest that initial skill work is done slowly and methodically with breathwork, so you get it right the first time and don't have to go back to the beginning of your training.

Remember, the brain is always learning and only the cognitive system cares whether what you are learning is right. Part of breathwork is the understanding of the differences in breath patterns and which pattern fits with each circumstance. For instance, on the way to a call, which already carries a certain level of excitation of the emotional system, use square breathing to enhance cognitive control and the ability to ABC plan and run mental simulations. During intense bouts of exertion, burst breathing, to mimic a normal breath pattern and attempt to tame the amygdala of the emotional system. After the call, to aid in recovery, deep meaningful breaths in through the nose until the belly is fully expanded and out through the mouth with the mental focus on breath to calm the emotional system. The most important factor here is that you have trained yourself to take control of your breathing in preparation for, during, and recovery from, stress and pressure.

2. Structure

The human body is fastest, most perceptive, and most mobile when it is closest to the "anatomical position." Martial arts or sportive stances favor one-to-one conflict and an "agreement to participate in combat" mentality but are not conducive to a multiple opponent or weapons environment.

Our goal is to take as much structure away from our sus-pects while maintaining our own structure to establish con-trol. Structure, when maintained, supports breathwork. Structure when broken, inhibits good breathing and restricts movement. When you fundamentally understand this princi-ple, the "techniques" used are not as important as the princi-ples that allow them to work. Understanding the underlying principles of a technique, turns one technique into several. When the subject you are against has their structure broken, their first priority is to recover structure. While their mind is occupied with recovering structure, your mind can focus on problem solving to establish control of the situation.

3. Continuous Movement

Movement is life. When the body becomes fixed in conflict, so does the mind. If all else fails, move. Move to cover, move to shoot, move to control, move to escape, or move to think. When all else fails, move. When in a physical altercation, but not clinched up with the suspect, move to make yourself harder to hit. When clinched up with a suspect and you fail to move, you are making it easier for the suspect to formulate a plan of attack, because his mind is free to focus on attack. By using continuous movement, the suspect must move with you or risk losing position. While he is occupied by moving with you instead of moving you, his ability to hurt you, by formulating a good plan of attack, is diminished.

4. Referenced Relaxation

You can't be tense in structure and movement in a fight. It wastes a lot of energy and telegraphs your actions. Tense body leads to tense mind which leads to decreased perfor-mance. By focusing on breath control and labeling the asso-ciated emotions, you are inviting the cognitive brain into the fight. Fighting without the cognitive brain is fine in an extreme survival situation requiring only blunt force trauma and an "animalistic" approach, but that is not the anatomy of a law enforcement encounter. We are required to know not only when force is appropriate, but how to use that force, when to use it, and when to stop it. Cognitive control tells you when the handgun, or any other tactical tool, is the proper tool and how to function with it in dynamic circumstances.

For instance, if you fail to control the emotional system and cognitive control is cut off, you may not see another officer in crossfire, or a civilian in the way, or a suspect who has now submitted. Lack of cognitive control is also what leads to the mistake-of-fact shootings which are becoming more prevalent, or at least reported more by twenty-four-hour news, across the country. When you focus on breath control, movement, and the idea of decreasing tension in the body, you are telling the emotional side of the brain to calm down and allow some executive control where needed. That is the secret to peak performance under pressure.

Subject Control

For years, I have heard different police defensive tactics instructors from around the country teach that body-to-body contact should be avoided at all cost, so there is no need to train it. Here is the problem with that line of thinking. The grasp reflex is ingrained in the procedural memory system. A baby will grab a finger in front of their face and when a person falls, they reach out to grab something to prevent the fall. Under pressure when you are hit, you will grab onto what hit you. If you hit someone and they are under pressure, they will grab onto you. You must learn the clinch, use it to your advantage, and against the suspect. Keep in mind, clinching is illegal in boxing, but when a fighter is stunned by a punch or doesn't know what to do at close quarters, they clinch.

For simplifying clinch work, we divide the human body into three zones, three levels, and three positions on the ground where we will move a suspect to establish control. The purpose of dividing the human body into zones, levels, and positions is to enhance the idea of always beginning with the end in mind and what this situation looks like when it is over. It simplifies the fight or attempt at control and aids in pattern recognition which we will discuss shortly.

Zones, Levels, and Positions

Zone One

Zone one is in front of a suspect. The zone extends out 45 degrees from the point of the suspect's shoulders in front of him to whatever distance the weapons he has available can hurt you. If the action breaks, we don't want to be in zone one. In zone one, you are either verbally establishing control, moving to physical control, moving to cover, moving to identify or moving and shooting. When we are getting left of bang indicators, these are the only options that lead to success. Standing still or trying to control a human being in zone one is a bad idea. Remember, you must control them and both of their hands or you will rarely see the weapon coming in a zone one close-quarter confrontation.

If, for whatever reason, we either place ourselves or the suspect places us in a zone one clinch, our first objective is to get out of zone one and move to either zone two or three. If we are standing at any distance outside of arm's reach of the suspect and the suspect moves for a weapon, we still don't want to be in zone one. Moving to cover is priority one but may not be feasible given the circumstances. If it's not feasible, you may have to move and shoot at close distances or move to identify the threat while still trying to get to either cover or zone two or three. At greater distances, moving out of the 45-degree area forces the suspect to move and track and can buy you time to get to cover.

Zone Two

Zone two is directly behind the suspect's elbow of what you believe to be his primary arm. The arm is controlled using your own body against the back of the suspect's elbow and variations of grips on the suspect's upper arm and wrist. I have heard numerous instructors over the years talk about always moving so your gun side is away from a suspect. This has caused right-handed officers to move to their own right to establish initial control of a suspect. The problem with this, of course, is that it leaves you attempting to control the non-dominant hand of ninety percent of the population.

Try this as a quick test: Conceal a training gun or knife positioned for your dominant hand to easily get to it. Have a partner attempt to control your non-dominant hand and see how easy it is to lift your shirt and access the weapon even if your non-dominant hand is in a control hold. Next, have your partner control your dominant hand with the weapon concealed for the dominant grab. See how much more effort is required and how many "tells" there are for your partner to witness when using the off-hand to attempt to gain access to the weapon. Is it possible, a suspect could be good with both hands? Of course, but what then have you lost? When we test this with actors who don't know what's coming and use training guns which fire projectiles, we see time and time again, our "suspects" are not expecting their dominant hand to be controlled and are taken by surprise. Why not try to take every possible opportunity to turn the fight, if there is going to be one, to your favor?

Position two also provides easy access to the brachial

plexus origin, located just under the ear and down to the base of the neck. The brachial plexus origin is the key to attempting to control the dominant hand of the suspect as it is the primary target for strikes, stuns, and manipulations, as well as bracing to prevent the suspect from closing the distance on your handgun. Zone two work is vital also to weapon retention and protecting yourself from a knife at close quarters. As this book is not intended to be a full defensive tactics manual, I'll leave these ideas out there for you to explore.

Zone Three

Zone three is directly behind your suspect, ideally with some variation of either body control or head control of the suspect. From this position we have several principle-based techniques for bringing a resisting subject off their feet and to one of our grounded reference positions. We also have several default take-downs we teach from this position.

Level One

Level one extends from the top of the suspect's head to the base of the suspect's neck. Any attempt at head control of the suspect, is a level one technique.

Level Two

Level two starts at the top of the suspect's shoulders and extends to the suspect's waist. Body harness techniques are attempts at level two control of a suspect.

Level Three

Level three starts at the suspect's waist and extends down to where their feet touch the floor. Most of the level three work is default work with a higher risk of injury possible to the suspect. Officers are taught they must be able to articulate the need for the default work in zone three.

Position One

Position one, as a reference point, has the suspect seated in front of the officer with the officer behind the suspect and pushing the suspect forward 45 degrees while controlling one of the suspect's arms and the suspect's head.

Position Two

Position two has the suspect on his side with the top arm controlled and the head held in place by the officer placing either their forearm or their knee into the brachial plexus origin (directly under the ear). Our system teaches handcuffing methods from here, as well as team arrest tactics from this position.

Position Three

Position three has the suspect facedown with one of their arms secured behind their back. The suspect's head is secured by bracketing it with the officer's knees and squeezing tightly. Unseemly, yes, but it allows smaller officers the ability to use their strongest muscles against the isolated head of the suspect. It also allows the officer the ability to quickly regain their feet before the suspect if the need arises.

Pattern Recognition

When we discuss intuition, these ideas or quick insights that sometimes guide our behavior, we are really talking about the ability of the emotional system to recognize patterns and provide those quick but not necessarily accurate ideas. The more experience you have in the field or procedure where the insights are provided, the more accurate they turn out to be. In his book, *Sources of Power*, Gary Klein describes this connection between pattern recognition and intuition:

> Intuition depends on the use of experience to recognize key patterns that indicate the dynamics of the situation. Because patterns can be subtle, people often cannot describe what they noticed, or how they judged a situation as typical or atypical. Therefore, intuition has a strange reputation. Skilled decision makers know that they can depend on their intuition, but at the same time they may feel uncomfortable trusting a source of power that seems so accidental.

> Bechara, Damasio, Tranel, and Damasio (1977) found that intuition has a basis in biology. They compared patients who were brain damaged to a group of normal subjects. The brain damaged subjects lacked intuition, and emotional reaction to anticipated consequences of good and bad decisions. In the normal subjects, this system seemed to be activated long before they were consciously aware that they had made a decision.[63]

Here is a quick example of intuition or pattern recognition in action. The examples from Klein's book are numerous, as well as examples I could give from personal experience, but for the sake of brevity without too much back story, I will use one of Klein's.

It is a simple house fire in a one-story house in a residential neighborhood. The fire is in the back, in the kitchen area. The lieutenant leads his hose crew into the building, to the back, to spray water on the fire, but the fire just roars back at them.

---

[63] Gary Klein. *Sources of Power: How People Make Decisions* (Cambridge, MA: The MIT Press, 1999), 31.

"Odd," he thinks. The water should have more of an impact. They try dousing it again and get the same results. They retreat a few steps to regroup.

Then the lieutenant starts to feel as if something is not right. He doesn't have any clues; he just doesn't feel right about being in that house, so he orders his men out of the building—a perfectly standard building with nothing out of the ordinary.

As soon as his men leave the building, the floor where they had been standing collapses. Had they still been inside, they would have plunged into the fire below.

"A sixth sense," he assured us, and part of the makeup of every skilled commander. Some close questioning revealed the following facts:

- He had no suspicion that there was a basement in the house.

- He did not suspect that the seat of the fire was in the basement, directly underneath the living room where he and his men were standing when he gave his order to evacuate.

- But he was already wondering why the fire did not react as expected.

- The living room was hotter than he would have expected for a small fire in the kitchen of a single-family home.

- It was very quiet. Fires are noisy, and for a fire with this much heat, he would have expected a great deal of noise.

The whole pattern did not fit right. His expectations were violated, and he realized he did not quite know what was going on. That was why he ordered his men out of the building. With hindsight, the reasons for the mismatch were clear. Because the fire was under him and not in the kitchen, it was not affected by his crew's attack, the rising heat was much greater than he had expected, and the floor acted like a baffle to muffle the noise, resulting in a hot but quiet environment.[64]

To a novice firefighter, lacking the experience and time under tension of the above commander, this situation could have played out quite differently in a monumental tragedy. After the fact, the lieutenant could rationalize through what was happening, but in the pressure-filled situation itself, the subconscious, emotional system was providing information based on training and pattern recognition which did not require the conscious and slower thought process. Again, we are looking for a trained, subconscious emotional system to make fast and more accurate decisions based on training, instead of fast but not necessarily accurate information provided by an untrained emotional system.

Which brings us back to our zones, levels, and positions, which are reference points to aid in pattern recognition and quick decision-making while engaged in combative circumstances.

Reference Points

As we have discussed, the emotional system is very good at pattern recognition, when trained. Reference points are positions, platforms, or repeated experiences that can train the emotional brain in pattern recognition and problem solving.

We continuously analyze positions that officers find themselves in and then educate them on problem solving relative to those positions. The variations are endless, but usually include: subject control, ground control, shooting stances, use of cover, movement to cover, and movement to

---

[64] Klein, *Sources of Power*, 32.

shoot, etc. Reference points can be positions that occur naturally during conflict or those we create to aid in problem solving.

One of the first reference points I teach is the initial test for compliance. Regardless of the compliant handcuffing method an officer uses, under stress there is a tendency to become fixated with why the technique is not working and doubling and tripling down on its use, instead of a transition to non-compliant handcuffing methods. I have seen in training, and out on the street, officers attempting to repeat the same handcuffing procedure when the first fails due to the suspect's non-compliant actions to include attempting to regain a handcuff control while the suspect has started to strike them. This is another example of emotional system overload. I teach an initial test for compliance which places the officer in the best position to effectively deal with resistance. This test allows the officer to rely on tactile instead of visual information to establish initial control.

As part of referencing, it's important to understand your initial approach and objectives. If my goal is to move in and control a subject while protecting myself against violence, then why would I want to establish control, the way most police officers in the world do, by moving to first control the left arm of the suspect? We have discussed previously that 90 percent of the humans on this earth are right-handed. What good has an officer done in protecting themselves from the suspect's primary arm and weapons accessible by the primary arm? In the initial interview stance, I like to address this topic and see what the student's objections are to move to control the primary arm of the suspect. Remember, we don't assume everyone is right-handed, we look for indicators like stance and what arm their watch is on to help gauge their strong side. But if all else fails, you will be right 90 percent of the time by controlling the right arm first. If I could take you to Las Vegas and guarantee you would be right in your bets

90 percent of the time, wouldn't we all be headed for Vegas? I have heard instructors say that standing to interview a suspect in a manner consistent with establishing control of the right arm places the officer's gun where the suspect could grab with either hand. Okay, but if this is a reference point and I train my reference points, I have fast and accurate ideas for how to counter those movements to the gun.

The initial test for compliance is simple. If the officer is moving to control the suspect's right arm, while facing the suspect, then the officer's right hand is placed on the front of the suspect's right shoulder near the collar bone. The officer's left hand is placed with the wedge between the officer's thumb and index finger pressing lightly into the area just above the suspect's right elbow. This is not a position of control. It is a starting reference point to test for their compliance to your attempt at control. This allows you to train for responses based on pattern recognition of the suspect's actions. If the suspect is compliant, the officer's right hand, which was on the suspect's shoulder, can slide down the suspect's arm and establish the compliant handcuffing method of choice. Most important, by contouring, or sliding the hand down the suspect's arm, the officer can move to compliant control without looking to see where the suspect's wrist or forearm are located. If the suspect starts to resist, numerous options are available to quickly attempt to establish control.

By using our ABC planning and beginning with the end in mind, reference points aid in pattern recognition and training to recognize positions which can quickly be turned into control situations. Options include, but are certainly not limited to, using the officer's right forearm to brace against the suspects brachial plexus origin (side of the neck) to prevent the suspect's attempt to establish body-to-body contact or to grab the officer's handgun. The forearm can then be vigorously rubbed into the neck area as a distraction to create an opportunity to move to a zone two or zone three control.

Zone one is a reference point and serves to remind the officer to stay out of the suspect's reach while communications are going on. Thinking about what you are going to say and listening for their answers while trying to watch the suspect's hands and the overall environment is the ultimate in multitasking. This understanding of zone one and the dangers associated with it, remind the officer to move when the suspect makes a movement toward their waist, where 90% of concealed weapons are kept. Once the decision to take the suspect into custody is made, zone one should remind the officer to quickly establish control while having a backup plan in mind if the suspect resists.

If we understand the dangers of zone one, then zone two and three are reference positions because they make it harder but not impossible for the suspect to launch an attack. Just being in zone two or three doesn't end the confrontation, it only improves the officer's odds if they have a plan. Giving multiple principles-based options for bringing a suspect under control to the ground aids in simplifying options and providing insight on how to end the confrontation.

The levels of the human body also act as reference points based on where the officer's hands are while attempting to control the suspect whether standing or on the ground. Level one controls are important because where the head goes, the body will follow. Head control gives a smaller officer an opportunity to control a suspect and aid in holding them in place on the ground for handcuffing.

Level two acts as a reference because if you can't get control through the head you may have an opportunity to manipulate the subject's center of gravity. This can change the focus of the suspect's central nervous system from active violence against the officer to trying to regain balance. When balance is lost, the central nervous system focuses on finding it, and this creates an opportunity for the officer. The primary data centers for balance (horizon line and vestibular fluid between the ears) of the subject are being manipulated. Level one and two manipulations are your A or B plans when you are attempting control and each officer will usually favor one level over the other, but it is important to remember that nothing works 100 percent of the time. The easiest way to prevent the emotional system from spiking under stress is to plan and prepare for what happens when things aren't going exactly as planned. The only way to get competent at this is to practice against resisting partners and getting comfortable with being uncomfortable.

Level three is usually a default level as the techniques used to bring the subject to the ground are more sportive and technique based, rather than principles based. They also have a higher potential for causing physical injury to both officer and suspect, so their use must be articulated using the Objective Reasonableness Standard of *Graham* v. *Connor*. The level three take-downs usually fall under your C plan as an emergency when A and B plans have failed, or the immediate need arises.

The ground positions act as reference points. Officers should be learning to bring a subject resisting arrest down to the ground under control into position one, two, or three. When you bring a subject to the ground, there are only a limited number of ways they can land. Understand this and you have an opportunity to take advantage of the position and attempt control. Understand the similarities to how someone lands when taken down and someone already grounded trying to get back up and you can train ideas for how to manipulate the suspect into these reference points.

Referencing simplifies the fight. It allows you to quickly assess the situation and use pattern recognition to hasten an accurate response. Reference points can be created in training to establish quicker trained responses in any form of combatives, including working with a firearm. For instance, in training when a suspect is reaching for a weapon at greater than touch distance, you can reference this situation and train to move to cover or move to shoot if cover is not available. It can include close-quarter combatives work to show the officer that introducing their handgun to a close quarter zone one crisis is hazardous. Remember, the suspect has as much incentive to stop you as you may have to shoot to stop them. Training to get offline and behind the suspect's primary elbow before introducing the handgun pressure tests better than the zone one engagement as it is harder for the suspect to get ahold of the gun when the officer is in zone two.

Reference points can be established off cover to show officers how to use cover effectively to prevent crowding cover and losing necessary angles on your opponent. These are all examples, but the limit to the number of reference points that can be created and repeated in training are only limited by the imagination of the instructors.

While I was on the SWAT team with Officer Dave Norman, we developed a class that used referencing, emotional control, and ABC planning to resolve close-quarter crisis situations involving weapon retention and firing the handgun at danger close distances. The first part of class involved defensive tactics instruction in weapon retention. Students were then dressed in Simunition gear and given Sim guns which fire projectiles. The students then pressure tested what they learned in the defensive tactics room against live opponents. Officer Dave Norman is one of my go-to firearms instructors when I have ideas about shooting, along with Officer Mike Linn and Officer Bob Pinkerton. We had the idea of taking the students at the end of class to live fire at close distances while manipulating a dummy usually used for defensive tactics work. Of course, the idea created some controversy. We did however get approval and the students had the opportunity to control their emotions while firing a handgun into a dummy they were connected to.

That class, which was put on several times for over five hundred students, was one of the most well-received classes and we still are asked when we are going to start teaching it again. What was the point of the class? To train the brain and the emotional system to effectively deal with close-quarter crisis. Close-quarter crisis is the hardest to deal with emotionally, so why not start with the worst distance and work your way out? This training also connected worlds. Normally, you have defensive tactics training separate from firearms training. By building a bridge between the two, the training became more realistic with a lot of the associated emotions. For example, almost all the students said they had never fired their weapons at close quarters in a manner that simulated holding onto a live suspect. Should the first time you perform an action be in real life?

After introducing ABC planning and de-escalation strategies to officers, the next step is to introduce those concepts into every level of training. The problem in the past has been we train individual skill sets as if they are not connected to other aspects of training. Communications strategies, declarative knowledge of the law, policies and procedures, firearms skills, defensive tactics skills, tactical decision-making skills, and de-escalation skills are interconnected. It is crucial they be trained together instead of separately. In this way, training is layered, so each skill builds on the other and they work together, the way they are supposed to, when the violence and associated emotions are real and in your face.

In the future, as we develop research opportunities to enhance tactical training, I hope to expound more on how to develop training programs related to putting it all together.

For now, I hope you've been provided with enough ideas to get started. Remember, it all starts with the brain training. Without that understanding from instructors, as well as your personnel, nothing else will make sense as to why you train it the way you do. Next come the de-escalation and tactical planning strategies because these aid in pattern recognition and dealing with violations of expectations. Training should steer more toward skill building and hold scenario-based training as the final exam once the skill sets have been trained and established.

Never waste an opportunity to learn from your own behavior and the behavior of others. Review use-of-force incidents and look for left of bang indicators. In law enforcement, we tend to not want to second-guess or bad-mouth officers who lost their lives or were seriously injured in the line of duty. Understand this: we are all human. We all make mistakes and, at times, fail to perform at our best. Even professional athletes, who get paid a lot of money to perform, fail to achieve success 100 percent of the time. They are paid for their consistency and not a perfect success rate. Looking at use-of-force incidents is not Monday morning quarterbacking (judging using 20/20 hindsight for my non-American friends) because I'm not trying to say what I would have done. I'm only looking for borrowed experience based on the broader view with no stress that analysis provides. If we are being honest, you can do everything right and still lose your life. Each of these experiences offers us a window into the brain under the most intense pressure it can experience. By not looking and learning from these experiences, I feel we do more to disparage their memory than by honestly evaluating what we can learn from them. If not, then what did they die for?

In the case of an accusation of excessive force, mistake-of-fact uses of force, or an all-out bad use of force, we, and the people who investigate these issues, can now look not only at an individual case, but what we can all learn from the case and add to our training. Knowledge is power if knowledge is applied. Knowledge is useless if it isn't shared, adapted to training, and passed on to the people who are making these critical decisions under life-threatening pressure.

In addition to the information provided, you can now also begin adapting decision-making into all your training. Most importantly, including decisions with every aspect of firearms training, so you train the emotional system to anticipate decisions being made before, during, and after you fire your firearm. This can only be accomplished through skill building with problems that need to be solved involving cognitive executive control for the violations of expectations. It doesn't have to be complicated. Look up the Pincus-Leatham, "When Worlds Collide" on YouTube and tailor your drills specific to law enforcement, moving to cover, and violations of expectations. The more decisions you must make in training under some pressure, the better you will be when the violence is sudden and real.

I have been a cop since 1992. In that time, I have seen incredible acts of courage, as well as all aspects of human performance from a complete performance shutdown by officers to peak performance under life-threatening pressure. I could tell story after story until the pages of another book were filled. Some would make you laugh, some would make you angry, and some would break your heart. Others would motivate you to believe that humans are so much more capable to do great things then we ever thought possible. Some would make you wonder what on earth is wrong with our species. Buy me an Irish whiskey and I will tell you those stories, until I decide it's time to fill the pages of another book.

If we can take the five percent peak performers and make it ten percent and so on, the job will be the better for it, society will be the better for it, and hopefully the community will be even more grateful than they have already shown to our profession. It's easy to think through social media that the perception of law enforcement is at an all-time low, but I don't find that to be the case. We are constantly thanked for our service, we must constantly turn down people from buying our meals, and when one of our own has fallen, the outpouring of emotion from the community is amazing to see. But, why can't we make it even better, by showing we are on the cutting edge of making the most resourceful, calm, quiet, professional police force we possibly can. In the process we would find that many of the things we can do to train the brain for peak performance also protect us from the dangers of PTSD and emotional issues from seeing way too many horrible things during our careers.

CHAPTER THIRTEEN

A LANDMARK NEUROSCIENCE STUDY

When a man knows he is to be hanged in a fortnight,
it concentrates his mind wonderfully.

– Samuel Johnson

If you recall, earlier I talked about Dr. Leslie Sherlin and his research into how elite performers can do what they do on a consistent basis. After reading *The Rise of Superman* and the work done by Dr. Sherlin, I contacted him about his research and how it applies to law enforcement. I was curious to see if he would be interested in doing a law enforcement study on the effects of training the brain for better performance under stress. Dr. Sherlin utilizes a product called Versus to perform an assessment on the user's brain and then trains the brain to achieve more balance in the operating systems. The Versus headset performs a NeuroPerformance Assessment (NPA) and measures three constructs related to stress and three related to focus. The Stress Constructs measure:

1. Activation Baseline: A measure of mental activity during the non-task portion of the NPA, which reflects how "busy" the brain is during a restful period.

2. Stress Regulation: Reflects the stability of brain activation and the stability of response time during the varying demand levels of the test.

3. Max Activation: The change in brain activation between the resting and the performance portions of the assessment.

The Focus Constructs are as follows:

1. Focus Capacity: Reflects the ability to create a focused brain state.

2. Focus Endurance: Derived from the task portion of the assessment and reflects attention and errors over an extended period of time.

3. Impulse Control: Reflects the speed and accuracy of responses during the performance task portions of the assessment.[65]

Now, here's my favorite part. After the performance assessments are made, the system designs a training program for you, which can be done on an iPad. The cool part is, the same headset that was used to perform the assessment is now used to measure what portions of the brain are firing during the training. Your brain is the joystick. If the right portion of your brain is firing in response to the prompts, you are rewarded on the screen. The system has a database that includes elite performers from extreme sports and military Special Forces. The system then trains your brain to be more like these elite performers in the measured areas. Now don't get me wrong, I like doing mindfulness work and training that requires me to control my emotions during tactical events, but how do you know when you are where you want to be? The Versus system provides you with a measure against peak performers and training for how to make your brain's performance more like theirs. The goal of the study would be to take a pre-training assessment, then a tactical test to

---

[65] Leslie Sherlin, PhD. *Brain Performance Assessment Education and Training Proposal Letter*, 2016

measure correct decisions under time, sight, and sound pressure in a series of shoot/no-shoot situations. After this initial assessment is complete, the Versus training system takes over for a series of sessions up to three times a week for approximately twenty sessions. We would then perform another tactical test like the first to compare good decisions and the number of bad decisions to see if there is an improvement. A second neuro assessment is also performed at the end of the study to measure results from the first assessment. As of the final edit of this book, we have tentatively received funding and will hopefully start the study in December, 2018. I believe this will be one of the most important studies ever conducted for law enforcement and the results could change the future of law enforcement training. Sure, I'm biased in this case, but I think the results will show this type of training is vital to teaching the brain how to perform better under stress.

The following are two paragraphs from a brief written by Dr. Sherlin discussing the study and his proposal.

Stressful situations are abundant in our lives today, but none so much as in the lives of police officers. The negative impacts of stress on health, interpersonal relationships, and general well-being are widely accepted. All systems of the body are impacted by stress through the autonomic nervous system (ANS). This means that breathing, heart rate, sweat, muscle tension, every part of the body is altered to meet the demands of each stressful situation. Importantly, the brain is responsible for interpreting events, for classifying situations as potential or actual stressors and for the behavioral and physiological responses we have to them. (McEwen, 2009) Therefore, it stands to reason, that the brain should be a primary target for maximizing the experience of stress and maximizing the reaction to and recovery from stress.

While stress often has a negative connotation, it is necessary for handling emergencies, as well as, attaining peak performance. Those individuals that are able to use stress to their advantage to increase performance are often described as having commitment to self, the belief they can control or influence events, and ability to set goals and priorities. Additionally, they often demonstrate strong impulse control and good decision-making that supports internal balance.[66]

So, when it comes to using tech to borrow experience form elite performers, I am all on board and can't wait to do this study.

Here are some other Technology Sources that could be used in future studies:

Neuropriming is the process of using electrical stimulation (such as transcranial direct current stimulation, or tDCS) to increase plasticity in the brain prior to an activity. This process decreases the amount of input required for neurons to fire, and helps neurons fire together, enabling more rapid strengthening of connections in the brain. When paired with quality training, this results in increased strength, explosiveness, endurance, and muscle memory.

Your training, whether it is lifting weights or playing the piano, provides input that causes your neurons to fire. As this happens, your brain fine-tunes the connections between the neurons used to control your movement. Whether Neuropriming or not, no communication and no learning occurs if there is no input. No training means no benefit! So, you need to train while in the hyperplastic state to see benefits from Halo Sport.[67]

I own a Halo Sport headset and have used it for about a year now. After Neuropriming with my headset prior to working out, my workouts are better, and I am stronger and more

---

[66] Versus EEG Headset for NeuroPerformance Assessment, https://getversus.com/

[67] Halo Neuroscience Neuropriming Headphones, https://www.haloneuro.com/

powerful than I have been in a long time. Priming before skills work turns off that inner nagging critic that Jamie Wheal, the executive director of the Flow Genome Project calls, "our inner Woody Allen." After priming, I have sixty minutes of a quiet mind geared toward learning. I'm a big fan and found the cost worth the results. I believe a ton of new research will be conducted on Neuropriming and athletes from professional, extreme sports, and military special forces are already experimenting with the technology.

I have recently started experimenting with the Muse headband for guided mindfulness meditation. I like it. From their website, "It gently guides your meditation through changing sounds of weather based on the real-time state of your mind. This allows you to obtain a deeper sense of focus and motivates you to build a highly rewarding practice."[68] I like the idea of using tech to gain feedback. There are also plenty of free apps available that can guide you. The Muse system allows me to track my progress and that is why I'm a fan.

---

[68] Muse Brain Sensing Headband, http://www.choosemuse.com/

CHAPTER FOURTEEN

RECOVERING FROM VIOLENCE

We must combine the toughness of the serpent and the soft-ness of the dove,

a tough mind and a tender heart.

– Martin Luther King Jr.

In law enforcement work, a good amount of your time is spent seeing human beings at their worst and being constantly amazed at the evil we can do to one another. Then, there is the violence you must participate in as part of the job to include taking the life of another human being. Add the stress of dealing with friends severely injured or killed in the line of duty and the politics of the profession. You then have a perfect conglomeration of emotional bookmarks which can and will adjust your emotional control off baseline. We all want to believe we can handle it because it's part of the job and part of being a good cop. But listen carefully here, we are all human and while our emotional baselines are different, the systems operate the same. If we don't account for the deviations away from our emotional baseline, then our performance, our relationships, our very mental well-being, can be negatively influenced. Every individual on the face of this earth is carrying emotional scars (bookmarks). Love lost, loved ones lost, money struggles, family struggles, and past

275

traumas are only a few of the issues that can negatively influence our emotional baseline. We can and must, for the sake of ourselves and everyone we care for, take control of our emotional selves before things spin out of control.

First and foremost, I am not a doctor. What I offer is from my experience when it comes to preventative care, and recovery from violence and trauma whether physical or mental. Please, do your own research and if you are already experiencing anxiety, what you believe to be PTSD but have not received a diagnosis, or are experiencing suicidal thoughts, please seek professional help. Flashback memories, agitation, feelings of impending doom, and anxiety for known or unknown reasons can spike the emotional system. Showing up for work with a spiked emotional system is a recipe for disaster. I was one of those cops who thought that seeing the shrink after a shooting was a waste of time. But, what started as psychological theories, now has neuroscience-based methods and studies to effectively deal with the deviations from emotional baseline. Every day across this country police officers and military personnel are committing suicide because they feel like no one gives a damn and life is hopeless. My dear friends, if you take nothing else away from this book, if I have failed completely as a writer and teacher, know this; your emotional system will lie to you. When the systems are out of balance, it will deceive you to believe you are not good enough, nobody likes you, you are worthless. It is one big lie and I promise you there is a way out that starts with one deep breath, one step forward in blind faith that with one more ounce of courage you can and will see your way through this. It all starts with pre-loading your brain, starting now, to understand the brain and deviations from balance between the emotional and cognitive systems.

Before the Violence—Preventative Care

If you haven't done so after reading the biohacks chapter, install a mindfulness app on your phone or tablet and spend at least ten minutes a day using it. When you get used to the feeling of being in the "deep now" after several weeks of practice, everything can become an exercise in mindfulness. I now do mindfulness work daily involving sitting and focusing on breath. What I have noticed is now my dry-fire practice, writing, exercising, and combatives training is all an exercise in mindfulness. Mindfulness, the deep now, is a regulator of the emotional system in that mindful focus tames over-reactions from the amygdala. Anxiety issues, PTSD, and some forms of mental illness all have links to a spiked emotional system without cognitive override.

I believe you will start seeing results in a short period of time. Once the mindfulness becomes part of your daily life, you will still have bad days and days where you don't feel like being mindful. That's okay. On those days, I find ten minutes and go back to breath work. The problems don't go away but you are better equipped to deal with them. As part of your daily practice, begin to develop your cognitive appraisal skills on and off duty. Simple exercises like if someone was going to ambush me, where would the best position be for them to do it from. If they did, how would I respond? In crowds, look to see who stands out and how some people blend in and figure out the difference. The observations in the deep now also serve to tame the amygdala response and the more you practice the better your appraisal skills.

During the Stress or Pressure

Remember the burst breathing method. A sip of air quickly

into the nose and a quick exhalation through pursed lips like you are trying to blow out a candle. This method mirrors the normal breath of shorter inhalation and longer exhalation and studies have indicated it serves to tame the emotional response. Incorporate the other biohacks into your training and keep the working memory online for problem solving and as a control over an excessive emotional response. I have used this breathing method on hostage rescues, high risk search warrants, high risk arrest situations and still use it when I am practicing my fighting or shooting skill sets. It works!

After the Violence or Extreme Emotional Incident

Recovery from extreme fight or flight response from the sympathetic nervous system can have a wide range of extremes. A good rule of thumb is to go back to square breathing as soon as possible, and back to mindfulness work as soon as practical. Violence is ugly and the closer you are to it and the more you must participate in it, the more extreme the responses can be. The best advice I can give you is to try not to spend too much time trying to figure out what normal is. You are going to run through a spectrum of emotions, remember the emotional side of the house is going to want to make some emotional bookmarks to aid in future decision-making. Memories can be triggered by sight, sound, touch, taste, smell, or unconscious impressions. You may feel elated for surviving, then guilty for feeling elated for surviving. You may have some paranoia and feelings of certain trouble. You may feel nothing at all. What is normal anyway?

Normal is whatever you are experiencing, as long as those thoughts don't include hurting yourself or another. My best advice is to sleep as soon as possible after a heavily

emotional event. Avoid the urge to consume alcohol immediately after the event. After waking up from the best sleep
you can get, exercise using your favorite method to get the
blood flowing and to move the metabolites still in your system from the breakdown of all the chemicals initiating and
sustaining the fight or flight sympathetic nervous system response. If you remember nothing else from this section, remember this: there is no standard normal for how you feel or
should feel. I have used this advice and have given it to others involved in critical incidents and have received positive
feedback on not trying to define normal.

Side Note: After an incident everyone wants to gather all
the facts. This is understandable. When you are attempting
to remember details of the encounter immediately after the
fact, memories have not had a chance to consolidate in the
system. Due to questioning, you may feel the urge to fill in
the blanks to leading questions. You may feel as if your answers will be interpreted as deceptive if you don't answer.
Under a fight or flight response, the emotional system is not
working in a conscious, logical manner to index memories.
It's looking for emotional bookmarks to index for future reference related to survival. Facts and observations important
to an interviewer, the media, and to anyone else not immediately involved in the violence, may not have been important
to your emotional system at the time of the incident. It is important for not only the officers themselves, but investigators, county attorneys, and the community at large to understand this before they accuse someone of lying, appearing
deceptive or making comparisons between a video and the
officer's interview.

There is an enormous difference between remembering
a pleasant experience or even a neutral one, for that matter,
and an incident that carries with it heavy emotional baggage.
This concept is so important to understand, because when
we understand how the emotional system indexes memories,

we can understand the difference between sitting in a chair and waxing philosophical on what we would have done and participating in a violent emotional event. What I can tell you is the more you train in the balanced brain, the better your performance at all levels including recall memory and dealing with the trauma itself.

Profiles of Courage and Resilience

Officer Jason Schechterle

On March 26, 2001, Phoenix Police Officer Jason Schechterle's Ford Crown Victoria police vehicle was rear-ended by a cab at a speed estimated by accident reconstruction experts to be 115 mph. The police cruiser with Jason inside burst into flames. There is an incredible book about Jason's survival written by Landon Napoleon called *Burning Shield*. I highly recommend this book for anyone who thinks they have it bad and there is nothing they can do, or for anyone who wants to be inspired by one of the most amazing human beings it has ever been my pleasure to call a friend.

In Jason's own words in the foreword to the book he writes:

> It has been more than a decade since March 26, 2001, the night I was burned alive and, by all measures, should have died. Few people, if any, have survived fourth degree burns, which are burns that leave nothing except bone; all the skin layers, muscle, tissue, and tendons are vaporized. That I'm here to write about such trauma is inexplicable. As I would discover, something intervened for my larger purpose. It was simply not my time to go, and the unlikeliest collection of circumstances had to transpire to save my life.

My partner, Mike Yatsko and I, along with a host of officers from 500 Precinct, offered to stand guard at Jason's hospital room door during his recovery. All I can say is, every time I stood at the door and got an opportunity to talk with him or his family, I was deeply moved and inspired. Jason found the courage to reframe his perspective and see opportunity where others may have seen hopelessness. His burns were horrific and his prolonged chances for survival were not good. But not only did he live, his lawsuits against Ford Motor company made it safer for police officers around the world and he now is a motivational speaker who continues to inspire people in and out of law enforcement with his kind soul, sense of humor and purpose, and relentless courage.

Jason continues in the foreword,

The subsequent journey has taken me to some remarkable places emotionally, mentally, physically, and spiritually. I needed these intervening years to recover, rebuild, and mentally process everything that had happened and was happening in my life. I had to relearn how to live in a disfigured body, including my horribly damaged hands and eyes, the latter of which continue to provide daily challenges. Time has given me a new perspective. Only now am I ready to share my story.

My message here is simple. We all face challenges in this life. Call it the hazards of living, but from normal hurdles to all-encompassing adversity—a cancer diagnosis, the loss of a loved one, getting laid off, financial calamity, and all the other smaller and daily grinding annoyances—we are all being regularly tested in this journey. Unfortunately, the tests never end. Fabulously rich, poor or somewhere in between as most of us are, there is no destination where all our problems magically disappear.

Despite it all, how do we get out of bed and face another uphill day? How do we slog forward when the urge to just quit is so appealing? Ultimately, how do we let our human spirit shine brighter than we ever thought possible?

We all get to make one simple choice, day by day, when yet another roadblock gets dropped in our path: to quit or to keep going. In retrospect, our life becomes the story of how we overcome the adversity we face. It is never easy, and we never do it perfectly. But the important stuff—our determination, integrity, loyalty, love, and family—is ours to keep. It is a bad cliché, but there's one tenet I try to follow: Life is 10 percent what happens to you and 90 percent how you react to it. Being burned alive was my 10 percent; how I reacted has been my ninety.[69]

Jason rebuilt himself. He figured out how to shoot and qualify with disfigured hands and he came back to work as a detective for a while to show that he could. Every time I hear him speak I am inspired and moved to tears.

Officer Rob Sitek

On April 12, 2003, Phoenix Police Officer Rob Sitek and his partner attempted to stop a car which was driven by a carjacking suspect. The driver bailed from the car and a foot pursuit and gun fight ensued. Rob was shot four times with two rounds entering his midsection inches below his protective vest. Rob was driven by officers to Maricopa County Hospital which was only a couple miles away. My partner and I were in the parking lot of the hospital when they pulled Rob out and placed him on the rolling stretcher. They cracked his chest open and we watched as a nurse straddled his body and began pumping his heart with her hands inside his chest.

Over the course of the night and into the next morning, we waited. Updates were given, but we were told not to get our hopes up as he had lost a lot of blood and there was ex-

---

[69] Landon J. Napoleon. *Burning Shield: The Jason Schechterle Story* (New York, NY: 7110 True Crime Library, 2013), xi-xiii.

tensive damage, which included a bullet strike to a major artery delivering blood to the lower body. In surgery, his spleen was removed along with parts of his colon and small intestine. He lost the equivalent of five times his blood capacity and according to the United Blood Services website, received one hundred and forty-eight transfusions ranging from red blood cell, plasma, and platelet. I watched and waited as he fought time and time again to survive. And survive he did. Then he rehabbed, came back to work, and still serves on the Phoenix Police Department. He is also a motivational speaker and an advocate for blood donation organizations. He has lectured to new recruits at the academy for years. Rob is also one of those people that you can't help admiring and being inspired by and it is my honor to call him friend.

It is easy to think that these must be outliers and beyond the pale, but they are not. Every day human beings from around the world take their hits and keep pushing forward and unfortunately everyday around the world some of our fellow human beings feel like they can't go on, that there is no hope. I don't have all the answers, but I do know that forewarned is forearmed. Study the brain and you have a shot at understanding performance and recovery from violence and trauma.

I will give one more example of an amazing human being who suffered life threatening violence and her journey right of bang.

Officer Julie Werhnyak

On March 3, 2015, Tempe Arizona Police Officer Julie Werhnyak and several other officers responded to a check welfare call at an apartment complex. An officer at the scene heard what sounded like a woman in distress inside the apartment and they moved closer to the back-patio door to see if they could get a look inside. What they saw was a male subject standing over a bound and gagged female stabbing her with a large hunting knife. Julie and two other officers forced entry into the front of the apartment and Julie lead the charge to rescue the hostage.

In the immediate change of lighting conditions from sunlight to darkened apartment, there was no time to wait for their eyes to adjust. As they moved down the hallway and approached the corner that would lead to the area where the suspect was last seen, the suspect dove over a half-counter to the kitchen and attempted to stab Julie. Julie was able to partially deflect the knife and prevent its downward progress. The sudden attack, with homicidal intensity from the unexpected angle, made this one of the most difficult close-quarter crisis situations you can be faced with. Even with the deflection, and her movement to stop the forward progress of the knife, the large hunting knife entered behind the collarbone and into the side of Julie's neck stopping less than a quarter inch from her carotid artery.

Julie and another officer were able to fire their service weapons and the suspect did not survive the encounter. Their efforts saved the woman's life, who was being held against her will, and at the time of the rescue was critically injured. Julie was able to clear on the radio and explain calmly and under control what had happened and her need for immediate medical assistance for all involved parties. I visited Julie in the hospital that day to see that she was okay and to let her know how proud I was of her and that I was glad she was going to be okay.

The hardest part for me was listening to the media talking about how Julie, a martial arts expert, was ironically stabbed in the line of duty. Ironic? Once again, ignorance of brain science and the emotional system under life-threatening pressure. The fantasy of using their declarative memory systems to define what experts on YouTube and martial arts movie actors can perform so cleanly when there is no pressure and a fake weapon. She, of course, handled the situation with more grace and dignity than I would have when dealing with these comments. But the truth is, the media, police administrators, investigators, and the public at large are not educated on the brain science and the difference between cognitive mental simulations and the actual procedural skills accessible under extreme pressure. Julie and the other officers at that scene's performances were admirable, and her skill set and mental focus kept her in the fight and saved her life. She is now retired and runs her own self-defense seminars and is also a powerful motivational speaker who routinely lectures on performance under stress and recovery from violence. I am also honored and proud to say she is like a sister to me.

I could go on and on with examples, but I hope these three at least partially make my point. Every situation is different; the elements of the situation, the skill set required, and the recovery. But that's not the point. Every one of us, if we still have a heartbeat and conscious thought, can choose to take one more breath, one step forward in faith with one more fraction of an ounce of courage and face it. My heart breaks for anyone who feels like they must take it on alone and doesn't have a shoulder to lean on. If you feel this way or are concerned about what people will think if you ask for help, then know there are resources available for you to remain anonymous and still get help. Forewarned is forearmed.

I am not a big fan of taking medications and this is probably one of the fears of a lot of officers experiencing depression, anxiety, or PTSD issues. But understand that drugs don't have to be the only options. In *Stealing Fire*, the authors Kotler and Wheal discuss alternative methods of treatment.

In 2007, therapist Carly Rogers of the University of California, Los

Angeles blended surfing (a reliable flow trigger) and talk therapy into a treatment for PTSD. It was essentially the same protocol Mithoefer used, with the flow generated by action sports substituted for MDMA [prescription drugs].

Much like in Mithoefer's study, sufferers experienced nearly immediate relief. "After just a few waves, they (the soldiers with PTSD) were laughing in the surf lineup," reported Outside magazine. "Oh my God, our Marines are talking," said the lieutenant who approved the experiment. "They don't talk. Ever."

Since then, the program has been formalized, and more than a thousand soldiers have taken part. Hundreds of veterans and surfers have volunteered their time, including eleven-time world champion Kelly Slater. And their investment paid off. In a 2014 paper published in the *Journal of Occupational Therapy*, Rogers reported that after as little as five weeks in the waves, soldiers had a "clinically meaningful improvement in PTSD symptom severity and in depressive symptoms."[70]

Well, there you have it. I hope you have found the reading educational and not too scientific. I believe this style of brain training is the future, and therefore, the future is looking bright for the current and next generations of law enforcement officers. The answer to most of the current issues plaguing law enforcement from excessive force (whether actual or perceived), implicit bias, PTSD, to de-escalation, can all be positively affected by good brain training and an understanding of the brain under stress. Thanks for checking out the material and I hope you find it useful in your own journey.

---

[70] Steven Kotler and Jamie Wheal. *Stealing Fire: How Silicon Valley, the Navy SEALS, and Maverick Scientists Are Revolutionizing the Way We Live and Work* (New York, NY: HarperCollins Publishers, 2017), 89.

BIBLIOGRAPHY

Bailey, Regina. "Anatomy of the Brain: Structures and Their Function." *Thought Co.*, Updated March 08, 2017 https://www.thoughtco.com/anatomy-of-the-brain-373479

Csikszentmihalyi, Mihaly. *Flow: The Psychology of Optimal Experience.* New York, NY: HarperCollins Publishers, 1991.

Diamond, D. M. Campbell, A. M., Park, C. R., Halonen, J. and Zoladz, P. R. (2007) The temporal dynamics model of emotional memory processing: A synthesis on the neurobiological basis of stress-induced amnesia, flashbulb and traumatic memories, and the Yerkes-Dodson Law. *Neural Plasticity*, vol. 2007, Article ID 60803, doi:10.1155/2007/60803

Eagleman, David. *Incognito: The Secret Lives of the Brain.* New York, NY: Vintage Books, 2012.

Fryer, Roland G., Jr. "An Empirical Analysis of Racial Differences in Police Use of Force." *Journal of Political Economy*, Forthcoming. 2016. https://scholar.harvard.edu/fryer/publications/empirical-analysis-racial-differences-police-use-force

Gonzales, Lawrence. *Deep Survival: Who Lives, Who Dies, and Why.* New York, NY: W.W. Norton & Company, 2017.

Grossman, Lt. Col. Dave and Christensen, Loren W. *On Combat: The Psychology and Physiology of Deadly Conflict in War and in Peace, 3rd Ed.* United States of America: Warrior Science Publications, 2008.

Hall, Dr. Christine. "Excited Delirium: What It Is, What It Isn't and How We Know." Lecture at the Force Science Institute Certification Course: Principles of Force Science. Phoenix, AZ, September 2016.

Johnson, Dr. Richard. "Examining the Prevalence of Deaths

from Police Use of Force." *Force Science*, 2015. www.forcesci-ence.org/forcepresentation.ppt.

Kahneman, Daniel. *Thinking Fast and Slow.* New York, NY: Far-rar, Straus and Giroux, 2011.

Klein Gary. *Sources of Power: How People Make Decisions.* Cambridge, MA: The MIT Press, 1999.

Kotler, Steven. *The Rise of Superman: Decoding the Science of Ultimate Human Performance.* New York, NY: Houghton Mifflin Harcourt Publishing Company, 2014.

Kotler, Steven and Wheal, Jamie. *Stealing Fire: How Silicon Valley, the Navy SEALS, and Maverick Scientists Are Revolutioniz-ing the Way We Live and Work.* New York, NY: HarperCollins Pub-lishers, 2017.

LeDoux, Joseph. *Anxious: Using the Brain to Understand and Treat Fear and Anxiety.* New York, NY: Viking, 2015.

Lieberman, M. D., Eisenberger, N. I., Crockett, M. J., Tom, S., Pfeifer, J. H., Way, B. M. (2007). Putting feelings into words: "Af-fect labeling disrupts amygdala activity to affective stimuli." *Psychological Science*, vol. 18, 421-428.

Morin, Amy. "Why Successful People Don't Crumble Under Pressure." *Forbes*, August 7, 2014. https://www.forbes.com/sites/amymorin/2014/08/07/why-suc-cessful-people-dont-crumble-under-pressure/

Napoleon, Landon J. *Burning Shield: The Jason Schechterle Story.* New York, NY: 7110 True Crime Library, 2013.

Peter, Dr. Laurence J. *Peter's Quotations: Ideas for Our Time.* New York, NY: Quill William Morrow, 1977.

Reynolds, Susan. *Fire Up Your Writing Brain: How to Use Proven Neuroscience to Become a More Creative, Productive, and Success-ful Writer.* Blue Ash, OH: Writer's Digest Books, 2015.

Sajnog, Chris. *Navy SEAL Shooting: Learn How to Shoot from Their Leading Instructor.* San Diego, CA: Center Mass Group, 2015

Salomon, Dustin P. *Building Shooters: Applying Neuroscience Research to Tactical Training System Design and Training Delivery.*

Silver Point, TN: Innovative Services and Solutions LLC, 2016.

Steadman, Andrew, Major, US Army. "What Combat Leaders Need to Know about Neuroscience." *Military Review*, Vol. 91, No. 3, May-June 2011

Thompson, George J., Ph.D. and Jenkins, Jerry B. *Verbal Judo: The Gentle Art of Persuasion.* New York, NY: Harper Collins, 2013.

University of California-San Diego, "War and Peace (of Mind): Mindfulness training for Military could help them deal with stress." *Science Daily*, 16 May 2014.) https://www.science-daily.com/releases/2014/05/140516092519.htm

University of California-Santa Barbara. "Mindfulness improves reading ability, working memory, and task-focus." *Science Daily*, 26 March 2013.) https://www.sciencedaily.com/re-leases/2013/03/130326133339.htm

Van Horne, Patrick and Riley, Jason A., *Left of Bang: How the Marine Corps' Combat Hunter Program Can Save Your Life.* Black Irish Entertainment, 2014.

Vickers, Joan N., PhD. *Perception, Cognition, and Decision Training: The Quiet Eye in Action.* Champaign, IL: Human Kinetics, 2007.

Vickers, Joan N., PhD., Lewinski, William. "Performing Under Pressure: Gaze Control, Decision Making and Shooting Performance of Elite and Rookie Police Officers." *Human Movement Science*, Volume 31, Issue 1, February 2012, Pages 101-117. https://www.ncbi.nlm.nih.gov/pubmed/21807433

Weisinger, Hendrie and Pawliw-Fry, J. P. *Performing Under Pressure: The Science of Doing Your Best When It Matters Most.* New York, NY: Crown Publishing Group, 2015.

CPSIA information can be obtained
at www.ICGtesting.com
Printed in the USA
FSHW010308130321
79443FS